ON
TO THE
YALU

Also by Edwin P. Hoyt:

The Pusan Perimeter

The Glory of the Solomons

Guadalcanal

How They Won the War in the Pacific: Nimitz and His
Admirals

OWN   The Battle of Leyte Gulf

Blue Skies and Blood: The Battle of the Coral Sea

The Lonely Ships: The Life & Death of the U.S. Asiatic
Fleet

To the Marianas

Storm Over the Gilberts: War in the Central Pacific

War in the Deep: Pacific Submarine Action in World
War II

Raider Battalion

Merrill's Marauders

OWN   The Men of the Gambier Bay

U-Boats Offshore: When Hitler Struck America

Sunk by the Bismarck: The Life & Death of the
Battleship HMS Hood

Airborne: The History of American Parachute Forces

Submarines at War: The History of the American Silent
Service

and other naval and military histories

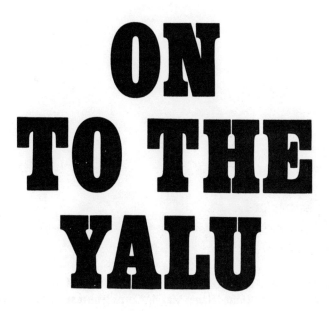

ON TO THE YALU

EDWIN P. HOYT

STEIN AND DAY/*Publishers*/New York

The photographs in this book are reproduced courtesy of the United States Army Signal Corps and the United States Marine Corps. The maps are courtesy of the U.S. Marine Corps and the U.S. Army.

First published in 1984
Copyright © 1984 by Edwin P. Hoyt
All rights reserved, Stein and Day, Incorporated
Designed by Louis A. Ditizio
Printed in the United States of America
STEIN AND DAY/*Publishers*
Scarborough House
Briarcliff Manor, N.Y. 10510

Library of Congress Cataloging in Publication Data

Hoyt, Edwin Palmer.
   On to the Yalu.   3/85

   Bibliography: p.
   Includes index.
   1. Korean War, 1950–1953.   I. Title.
DS918.H659   1984   951.9′042   84-40240
ISBN 0-8128-2977-8

This book is for DPH
and she knows why

CONTENTS

ILLUSTRATIONS

Marines storm ashore at Inchon
Mopping up on Wolmi Island
Waterfront at Inchon blazes
One bulldozer pulling another
Civil government being returned to mayor of Inchon
Colonel Puller studies the terrain
Navy Corpsman treats wounded prisoners
Captured North Korean colonel in jeep
MacArthur at briefing session
U.S. infantry advance up Hill 201
Aiding a wounded soldier while under fire
Heavy trucks cross the Kumho
U.S. tanks move through a roadblock in Seoul
Troops moving to forward positions
Aerial view of Seoul
Street fighting in Seoul
United Nations troops fighting on the outskirts of Seoul
Syngman Rhee at a troop inspection
First Jewish Sabbath service in liberated Seoul
Captured Russian machine gun
Captured Russian weapons
Searching houses in a burning Korean village
The capitol grounds at Seoul
Graves of American prisoners of war shot by North Koreans
The wreckage of the town of Kumchon
South Korean troops marching past the Diamond Mountains
First UN troops past the 38th parallel hold a sign-posting ceremony

MAPS

THE KOREAN THEATER

Nautical miles

(U.S. Navy)

PREFACE

There is a continuing lesson for Americans in the history of the Korean War. It was the nation's first* major military struggle that was not recognized as a war from its beginning. The reason is that the conflict began on one level but did not remain at that level.

When the North Koreans invaded South Korea on June 25, 1950, the United States was totally unprepared. No aspect of American foreign policy provided for such a contingency. Quite the contrary, for two years the Truman administration had been sending signals to the world that indicated that the United States did not regard Korea as within its sphere of influence. In January 1950, Secretary of State Dean Acheson said just that in a speech before the National Press Club in Washington. So, the North Korean People's Republic, a Soviet satellite, acted on the belief that its only opposition would be the puny South Korean army, which it could pulverize in a matter of weeks.

But the Americans proved unpredictable. In two days of meetings, President Truman stiffened what had been an undeniably mushy foreign policy. The North Korean invasion was unacceptable and would be resisted by the force of American arms. The United States was very lucky at that moment;

*The undeclared war with France (1798–1800) was purely naval.

the Soviet delegate to the United Nations Security Council was sulking and refused to attend the meetings. Thus when the other members, equally outraged by the invasion, voted to repel it with UN support, the Soviets weren't there to veto the decision.

For the moment that seemed to be a diplomatic triumph. The United States could then concentrate on the equally serious problem of rebuilding its armed forces, which the administration and congress had allowed to decay so far that they were unable to respond to foreign military initiatives. That dreadful fact became apparent in the first weeks of war, when badly trained and badly equipped American troops were defeated time after time and steadily forced back toward the southern tip of Korea.

There was absolutely nothing surprising in all this. The seeds of this war were sown by the big powers five years earlier, just as were those of the Vietnam War—at the Yalta Conference. Two totally artificial dividing lines were established for the occupation of and influence over Japanese-held territories at the end of the war. One was the old French Indochina colonial federation. The Chinese were given occupation rights above the 16th parallel and the British below. This artificial division had much to do with the development of the Vietnam War. In Korea, the Soviets as a sop to encourage their participation in the war against Japan (which was then wanted) were given occupation rights to Korea as far south as the 38th parallel. That line just happened to coincide with the old territorial ambitions of the Czarist Russian government at the end of the nineteenth century, when Czar Nicholas was seeking warm water ports and timber concessions.

The halcyon outcome of these occupation plans was supposed to be the democratic reunification of the two areas involved under the friendly auspices of the big powers. But who was kidding whom? For years it had been apparent that Soviet, Chinese, and British-American war policies were aimed at different ends. At Yalta the big powers laid the groundwork for two debilitating American wars. Almost immediately after the end of the war against Japan, the first warnings about Soviet ambitions became apparent in Europe, where the Red Army marched in and remained in Poland, Bulgaria, Hungary, and Romania. Under its auspices all four countries were communized in relatively short order. So by the winter of 1945–6 there were very few starry-eyed Americans overseas.

I happened to be the United Press correspondent in Korea in late 1945 and in 1946 and watched the beginning of the deterioration. The U.S. XXIV Corps arrived in South Korea in August 1945, full of vigor after the victorious battle for Okinawa. Almost immediately the corps was decimated by rotation of troops homeward for discharge, and no replacements were supplied. By winter, the 7th Division, in occupation around Seoul, was a shadow of its old self. In response to the inevitable question posed by the string of Very Important Persons who came to the Far East in the next year or so, Lieutenant General John R. Hodge, commander of the corps, liked to say ruefully that he could defend South Korea against Soviet attack "for about twenty minutes" given the terrain and his resources.

As the months rolled by the situation got worse. By the summer of 1946, Washington had recalled more than half the troops, and each month thereafter the number of troops declined further. The military government succeeded the occupation force. In its turn, the military government was supplanted in 1948 by a South Korean elected government, after the Soviet-American Commission for Korea failed miserably in its assigned task of arranging for free elections to unify Korea. The Americans realized that they would never be able to reach agreement with the Soviets on the question of holding "free elections," because the Soviets had no intention of accepting a freely elected government. No free nation has ever voted the Communists into power, and the Soviets knew that very well.

The American troops, then, were totally withdrawn from South Korea by 1949. And what replaced them? There is the rub. The U.S. government couldn't decide what position it wanted to take vis-à-vis South Korea. If, as the Chinese Communists liked to say, President Syngman Rhee of South Korea was a "running dog of the U.S. Imperialists," he was certainly a feisty one. If he was, as the Americans averred, an ally, he was a most uncomfortable one. His eye was ever on the north, and he vowed to unify the country, by force if necessary. For that reason the Truman administration looked, with what turned out to be lamentable reserve, upon President Rhee's constant requests for American aid to build up his army. Even General MacArthur was of two minds. At one point he suggested an army of two hundred thousand men; at another he suggested an army capable only of police action within its own borders. That latter is basically what South Korea got from the Americans. About a hundred thousand troops, mostly infantry, few big guns, few trucks and other transport, no tanks, no antitank warfare training, virtually no navy, and no air force. American officers and enlisted men were sent to Korea to serve as military advisors, which meant to train the South Korean army, but they weren't given much with which to work.

Unfortunately the American intelligence system in North Korea was nonexistent, and President Truman had no inkling that up north the Soviets were building the most powerful military force in Asia aside from their own. The forces of the North Korean People's Republic were modeled on those of the Soviets and were manned by Communists trained in the USSR.

When the North Koreans marched across the 38th parallel, they were led by Soviet-built T-34 tanks with 88 mm guns, and behind them came many more of the same. The South Koreans panicked at the sight of those tanks; they simply didn't know how to deal with them, and if they had known, they had virtually no antitank weapons. Militarily as well as politically, the Soviets and the Americans were playing by different rules. Within forty-eight hours, the North Koreans were in Seoul, and the Rhee government had fled south.

Once the decision to fight in Korea was made in Washington, the whole American military establishment had to be revamped. It took all the available resources of the Pentagon to support the conflict in Korea. First to come were troops of the 24th Infantry Division, who had been fattening in luxury in the fleshpots of occupied Japan. A small unit—Task Force Smith—was sent to stop the North Korean advance north of Taejon. They failed completely; their antitank weapons weren't much better than those of the ROK forces. More Americans arrived from Japan, and more Americans retreated in the sort of rout where soldiers abandon their weapons, their vehicles, and even their shoes.

The second, and even the third, contingent of troops to arrive from Japan were equally incompetent to stem the tide. The defense forces of Americans and South Koreans were pushed back steadily until they occupied the last possible line of defense, the Pusan Perimeter, bounded by the Naktong and Nam rivers. The North Koreans broke through the line and crossed the river, threatening Taegu, the Eighth Army command post. It was only when the 5th Marines were rushed in, arriving in the nick of time from the U.S. mainland, that the tide was stemmed, and the North Korean drive stopped.

To do this, the shrunken U.S. Marine Corps had been forced to strain all its resources. And more marines were wanted in a hurry. What was required was a major change in American defense policy. Once the need was seen, congress responded nobly with money and authorizations. How bad it was can be indicated by one situation. The small bazooka—rocket-firing weapon—of the U.S. forces had proved during World War II to be inadequate to stop German Panther tanks. It was still the basic infantry rocket weapon in 1950, although a new 3.5-inch bazooka had been perfected. But the shortage of money meant that the bazooka rockets never went into production, until the crisis of the Korean War. Precious weeks and lives were wasted before the 3.5-inch rockets began appearing in Korea in August. That was the sort of problem that occurred in virtually every aspect of defense production and delivery.

The buildup began and, as had been the case in the past, the American government, military, industry, and people rose to the crisis. Reserves came into active service. More men enlisted. The factories stepped up production. In three months America gave General MacArthur the capability of launching a second front with the Inchon invasion.

1

Surprise Attack!

Five A.M. September 15, 1950. The marine fighter bombers and the navy fighter planes began taking off from the decks of the five American carriers in the East China Sea. Their mission was to cover the invasion of the port of Inchon, just a few miles from the capital, Seoul, and hundreds of miles behind the extended lines of the North Korean People's Army that still surrounded the perimeter of Pusan, the southernmost port of Korea.

Six A.M. The marine planes slammed down through the clouds to smash the little island of Wolmi-do in the middle of Inchon harbor. (See Map 1.) It was hard going for the pilots through the smoke of fires and shellbursts. For five days marine and navy planes and warships had been striking the island, to try to knock out the guns there that could hamper the invasion of Inchon itself.

Six fifteen A.M. The men of the 3rd Battalion of the 5th Marines were in their landing craft, waiting for the air attacks to end so they could take the next step, the landing at the area called Green Beach. Lieutenant Colonel Robert D. Taplett was in command. His orders were to take Wolmi-do and capture or destroy all its artillery. Rocket ships and destroyers stood off the island, firing until once again the smoke rose high. Seven landing craft suddenly broke loose from the formation offshore and dashed for the beach.

On the bridge of the command ship *Mount McKinley,* General Douglas MacArthur sat watching tensely. Behind him stood Vice Admiral A. D.

17

GREEN BEACH: 3RD BATTALION, 5TH MARINES (INFANTRY)

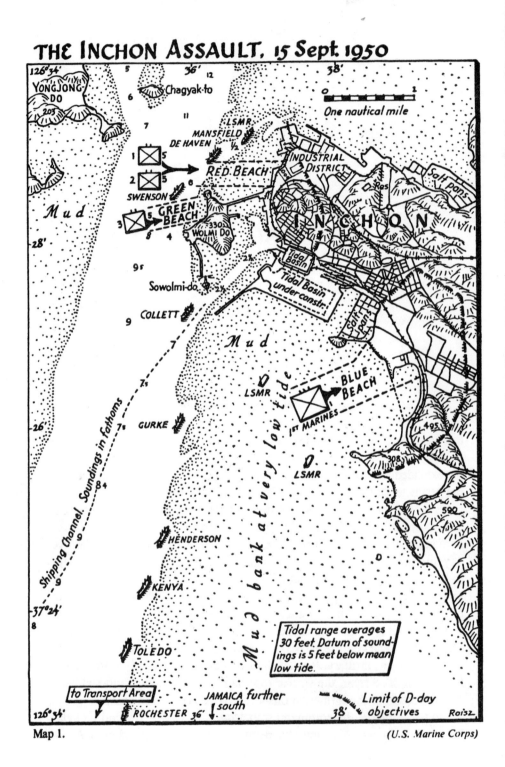

THE INCHON ASSAULT, 15 Sept. 1950

126°34' 36' 12 38'
YONGJONG DO
205
Chagyak-to
One nautical mile
0 1

5
6
7
11
LSMR
MANSFIELD
DE HAVEN ½
1 5
RED BEACH
INDUSTRIAL DISTRICT
2 5
8
SWENSON
GREEN BEACH
3 5
8 4
330
WOLMI DO
INCHON
Ras
Salt pans
Tidal Basin
28'
9
Sowolmi-do 2½
2¼
Tidal Basin under constr!
9 COLLETT
Salt pans
7
Mud
7½
Shipping Channel. Soundings in fathoms
Mud at very low tide
M u d   b a n k   a t   v e r y   l o w   t i d e
LSMR
BLUE BEACH
26' 7½ GURKE
8½
1ST MARINES
9
495
LSMR
308
4½
590
D
HENDERSON
9
37°24' KENYA
8
D
Tidal range averages 30 feet. Datum of soundings is 5 feet below mean low tide.
TOLEDO
to Transport Area
JAMAICA further south
Limit of D-day objectives
126°34' ROCHESTER 36' 38'
Ro'52

Map 1.

(U.S. Marine Corps)

Struble, commander of the naval forces; Brigadier General Edwin Wright, his chief planning officer for this day; and Major General Edward Almond, MacArthur's chief of staff.

General MacArthur raised the powerful field glasses from his lap and watched as the marines swarmed ashore. Rockets and 40 mm shells were still smashing the southern end of the island and the slopes of its highest point, Radio Hill, as the men in green reached the beach.

Six thirty-three A.M. Four platoons of marines from Company G and Company H stormed ashore on Green Beach. So severe had been the preparatory bombardment that only a few scattered shots greeted them. But the severity of the bombardment these last five days had left dozens of wrecked small craft littering the beach. The underwater demolition teams were supposed to have destroyed these obstacles, but they had not. So the marines had a beach fifty yards wide on which to land. Up above, the pilots of the F4Us saw what was coming and pointed their noses down, sped in low, just fifty yards ahead of the assault troops, and spattered the shore and the ground inland with machine gun bullets.

Six thirty-five A.M. The second wave of assault boats beached on the Wolmi-do shore. They carried the rest of the men of both companies. There was a brief pause as the officers organized their men. Then First Lieutenant Robert D. Bohn's Company G turned to the right and headed up the slope of Radio Hill. The effectiveness of the softening-up process showed: they captured many prisoners, and only a few of the North Koreans chose to fight and die.

Six fifty-five A.M. Sergeant Alvin E. Smith of Company G fastened the American flag to a tree on the crest of Radio Hill. Aboard the *Mount McKinley* General MacArthur saw and smiled, and behind him all the others smiled as well. The general got up from his chair.

"That's it," he said. "Let's get a cup of coffee."

MacArthur's brilliant stroke was going well so far. The amphibious counterattack against the North Koreans was on.

Not everyone on the bridge of the command ship that morning had expected it to be so easy. Nothing else about the Korean War had been easy. For weeks the whole American effort had been mired in confusion. Early in July 1950, less than two weeks after the North Koreans had marched across the 38th parallel, General MacArthur began planning an amphibious invasion to strike far behind the North Korean forces. Some in Tokyo thought that it wouldn't be a difficult operation. Their conception of the North Korean People's Army was of a force more or less like the Republic of Korea forces, capable of policing a border and indulging in minor forays against the other side, but not really an army in the big power sense. When the war was fifteen days old, the Americans still believed they were engaged in no more than a "police action" to restore the "border" of South Korea to the 38th parallel. General MacArthur had more in mind—destruction of the North Korean government—but in the confusion no one in Washington was prepared to come to grips with the military and political implications of that particular MacArthur policy.

The counter to the North Korean invasion was termed a "police action," apparently aimed to restore the *status quo ante*, the division of Korea at the 38th parallel. The North Koreans were called on to withdraw behind that line of demarcation.

In Pyongyang, Generalissimo Kim Il Sung, the head of the North Korean state, believed that his drive south could succeed in a matter of days, and the UN would then be faced with a *fait accompli.* The North Koreans paid no attention to the UN demand for withdrawal but continued their rapid drive southward against a collapsing ROK Army. In a matter of hours they had captured Seoul. They expected to capture Pusan before July 15 and then declare the unification of the country under the North Korean People's Republic.

It looked very much as though Kim Il Sung might be able to achieve his goal.

One American division had virtually no effect on the North Koreans. Nor did two, or three. The drive went on with the North Korean forces exerting a pincers movement that threatened to carry all the way to Pusan and force the South Korean army and the Americans into the sea. Only when the Americans had brought in four army divisions, a marine brigade and a British brigade to add to the 90,000 troops of the ROK Army, plus the American Fifth Air Force, augmented by the Australians, and the available air and sea resources of the U.S. and British navies, were they able to stop the North Korean drive a few miles north of Pusan.

The U.S. counterinvasion was scheduled for July 22, but on July 10 the plan was abandoned because the men and materiel were simply not there; the North Koreans were still driving hard against Pusan and the American and South Korean forces were still falling back. Everything MacArthur had or could get had to be thrown into the defense of the Pusan Perimeter, and throughout July the issue was very much in doubt: could the Americans stop the North Koreans at all?

Still, MacArthur had to have a plan for offense, and Brigadier General Edwin K. Wright had the job of making it—or them, as it turned out. He made several plans for invasion of the east coast and the west coast, but each one as it was made became impractical as a result of the continued North Korean drive of July and August.

The major difficulty of that summer of 1950 was the remassing of the American military forces to provide the trained combat troops to send to Korea. This was done by taking a battalion here and a battalion there and by moving artillerymen and other specialists in small units or individually. The result was that the needed divisions were sent to Korea, but by mid-July U.S. military resources were so strained that it was doubtful America could deal with another military crisis if one arose. This was a matter of serious concern in Washington because no one knew what the North Korean invasion really meant, and many feared that it was the forerunner of a general Soviet drive to extend its perimeters of control.

The call to action in Washington showed what can happen when the U.S. government recognizes an emergency. The usual petty bickering in Washington stopped suddenly. President Truman authorized the expansion of the army from 630,000 men to 740,000. Congress, which had been whittling away at defense expenditures for years, gave the president authority to call up reserves and the National Guard. More money was voted to produce and equip the military with the modern weapons that had been withheld in the recent past. World War II warships were moved out of the "mothball fleet" and recommissioned for action.

And, General MacArthur began to get what he wanted to carry out an amphibious operation against the North Koreans: landing craft, engineers, a full division of marines, tanks, and self-propelled guns.

Washington was sending the materiel and the men, but in the desperate days of July MacArthur had to divert the U.S. Army 2nd Division and the Marine 5th Regimental Combat Team directly to Korea to stem the tide of the North Korean advance. Both units had been scheduled for the amphibious assault. It appeared that the amphibious landing scheduled for mid-September would have to be scrapped for lack of resources. The next unit scheduled for Korea was the U.S. Army's 7th Division and it could not be ready for amphibious operations before 1951.

General MacArthur wanted to land at Inchon, because it was close to the capital of Seoul, and the capture of Seoul would have an enormous psychological impact. Almost most of the major north-south roads funneled through this Seoul–Inchon area. Their capture would cut the North Korean army in the south off from its sources of supply and close off most of the escape routes.

But the planners did not like Inchon. It had its problems.

One of the most serious was geographical: Inchon is notable for the enormous surge of its tides, sometimes exceeding thirty feet from high to low. Inchon is also regarded by seamen as the worst major harbor in Korea because of its shallow and tortuous approaches, shifting channels, mudbanks, and the tidal flats which front the harbor. The channels are bracketed by many islands and the main waterway, Flying Fish Channel, is treacherous at best. If the North Koreans managed to mine it, the approach to the harbor might be virtually impossible to navigate. Also, there was the problem of Wolmi-do, which was connected to Inchon proper by a causeway. This 350-foot-high island dominated the harbor and the North Koreans had fortified it with shore guns. The mudflats were so soft that they would not support a soldier. Thus the navy would have to have a tide of between twenty-three and twenty-nine feet to land troops and supplies from LSTs. That meant a landing period of about three hours, and once the troops were ashore there was no getting to them again for twelve hours. The initial landing force would be on its own.

In order to get ashore, the marines would have to go up seawalls fourteen feet high that surrounded the entire harbor. Rear Admiral James H. Doyle, the naval commander, argued against Inchon and for another point slightly south. Major General Oliver P. Smith, the marine 1st Division commander, arrived in Tokyo on August 22, and when he was told about Inchon, he agreed with Admiral Doyle that Inchon presented enormous difficulties to the ships and troops. When he went to call on MacArthur that day he was prepared to argue that Inchon was too hard, and that the date of September 15 was too early. But General MacArthur was obdurate. The landing had to be made on September 15 and it had to be made at Inchon. If there were problems, then that was what staff officers were for: solving problems.

At that moment, General MacArthur was convinced that if he landed at Inchon the war would be over within a month. The North Koreans, he told General Smith, had committed their entire resources to the Pusan drive. There were virtually no defense forces at Inchon.

The discussion was not over, however. Two days later, General Lawton Collins and Admiral Forrest Sherman arrived from Washington, concerned because MacArthur had not been keeping the highest American authorities informed about his plans. In a briefing, they heard the navy and marine objections to Inchon, and they agreed with them. But MacArthur was neither dismayed nor willing to compromise. It had to be Inchon. It had to be September 15.

The general and the admiral returned to Washington and the Joint Chiefs of Staff approved the MacArthur plan, but with a warning. From now on, they said, they wanted to be kept informed of MacArthur's plans and operations. MacArthur shook off the implied slap on the wrist, and on August 30 issued orders for the Inchon landing.

The U.S. Army X Corps would land on September 15 at Inchon and proceed to seize that port city, Kimpo airfield, and Seoul, and to sever all North Korean lines of communication. On D-Day +1 General Walton H. Walker in the south would make a coordinated attack with his Eighth Army to destroy the North Korean army poised on the Pusan Perimeter. This attack would be supported by air and naval operations.

In Washington the admirals and the generals continued to worry. On the day that General MacArthur issued his order for the amphibious landing at Inchon, the North Korean army launched "the Great Naktong Offensive," a do-or-die effort to drive through to Pusan. For the next ten days the fighting all around the Pusan Perimeter was fierce. On September 7 the Joint Chiefs of Staff were so concerned with the outcome that they called to MacArthur's personal attention the fact that he had committed all the Eighth Army's reserves to this battle, and that he could not expect any more reinforcements for some time. All available units had already been sent to him except the 82nd Airborne Division and this was being retained in America just in case some other brush fire started. In brief, the Joint Chiefs were scared and did not have much confidence that the Eighth Army could hold. They called on MacArthur for a "new estimate" of the situation. The implication that they wanted to abandon the Inchon operation was clear.

MacArthur argued that the North Koreans around Pusan had shot their bolt, and there was no chance they could overrun the Eighth Army in the south. The time had come to strike, he said, and even as he sent the message, the troops were embarking for the amphibious operation and the warships were assembling. The Joint Chiefs of Staff were overwhelmed by MacArthur's confident arguments and subsided. On September 8, they gave the general the final approval of the amphibious operation.

As it turned out, MacArthur was almost immediately proved right in half his argument. "The Great Naktong Offensive" collapsed on September 10, and the badly whipped, exhausted North Korean divisions withdrew for rest and reinforcement, admitting that they could not attain their objective of capturing Pusan.

That very day the guns of the warships and the aircraft began their assault against the Inchon area. Five days later the marines began to land.

2

Inchon

By constant pressure, General MacArthur pushed the authorities in Washington into providing what he needed for the Inchon landing, although at nearly every step of the way the generals said it could not be done. On the day of embarkation the U.S. corps consisted of almost 70,000 men: the 1st Marine Division, the army's 7th Division, the 92nd and 96th Field Artillery battalions, the 56th Amphibious Tank and Tractor Battalion, the 19th Engineer Combat Group and the 2nd Engineer Special Brigade.

A good part of these "American" units were made up of Koreans. In August MacArthur ordered General Walker in South Korea to ship over 7,000 able-bodied male Koreans. They were enlisted, given as much training as possible, and assigned to the army's 7th Division. Before the division went into action the Koreans numbered 8,600. The 1st Marine Division strength was 25,000 men, including 2,700 Korean marines. Most of the marines were to board ship at Kobe, Japan, but the 5th Marines were in Pusan, having just come out of battle on the perimeter, and they would leave from that port. The 7th Division would load at Yokohama. Everything seemed topsy-turvy, the planning foreshortened, the units too few and the supporting forces too thin, but General MacArthur indicated that they must strike now. His counterattack was under way.

On September 2, the 1st Marine Division was loading at Kobe when suddenly word came from the meteorologists that a typhoon was on its way and would strike the port the next morning. Everything stopped, as Typhoon Jane swirled in from the east, with winds of 110 miles per hour, sending forty-foot waves crashing up on the beach and covering the piers where the cargo to be loaded still lay. Steel hawsers snapped like kite strings, and seven ships broke their mooring lines. For a while it seemed that the whole Inchon operation would have to be canceled. One report had it that the *Marine Phoenix* had gone to the bottom with all the signal gear of the 1st Marine Division aboard. The *Noonday,* which had lagged behind the other ships bringing the marines over from California, was reported to have sunk. But in a few hours the reports turned out to be exaggerated. Much clothing had been damaged by salt water, and some supplies were lost under the four-foot waves that swept across the loading piers. Nevertheless, by the afternoon of September 3 the typhoon began to lessen its hold on Kobe and by evening was blowing itself out. A quick survey showed that the damage was not serious enough to stop the invasion. A few ships had to go into drydock for minor repairs, but the invasion could go on.

One would expect the North Koreans to know something was coming. The air attacks on Inchon began on September 4 and continued every day thereafter during flying weather. On September 10 the marines began the softening up of Wolmi-do with a series of napalm attacks to burn off the trees that protected the North Korean artillery. Three attacks launched from the carriers left the island burning from one end to the other.

Then came some bad news. Admiral Struble was very much concerned about the danger of mines in these restricted waters. On September 4, the destroyer *McKean* had reported seeing many floating mines off the North Korean port of Chinnampo. British ships operating in those same waters added to the reports in the next few days. That was not too disturbing for Chinnampo was a long way north of Inchon. On September 10, the Republic of Korea patrol boat *PC 703* sank a minelaying sloop off Haeju. Evidently the North Koreans were doing what Admiral Struble had feared. The constricted and muddy water around Inchon was admirable for mining, and if the enemy could mine Flying Fish Channel thoroughly, the sinkings would tie traffic in the approaches into a gigantic knot. Two days later *PC 703* sank three more minelayers.

The prospects were more than a little disturbing.

By September 10, the day before the deadline, the ships at Kobe were loaded. On that day and the day after, sixty-six cargo and passenger ships sailed, just ahead of reports of a new typhoon heading toward the islands of Japan. The big flying boats used as patrol planes had to be moved back to

Okinawa for safety, and Admiral Struble lost the "eyes" of his fleet for the moment. Still the timetable had to be met, even if the weather was so bad that the carrier task force offshore could not conduct air operations. The 7th Division sailed from Yokohama, and the 5th Marines sailed from Pusan. Vice Admiral Struble's flagship, the cruiser *Rochester,* sailed on September 12, and the next day General MacArthur's party came down from Tokyo to board the *Mount McKinley.*

On September 13 the new typhoon, named Kezia, hit part of the fleet off Kyushu.

As the ships steamed north toward Inchon, Major General Almond and General MacArthur conferred aboard the *Mount McKinley* about last minute details. Almond, the commanding general said, was to be in charge of X Corps, which meant he was to command the ground forces in the north, as General Walker commanded those in the south.

They expected far less trouble than Washington had anticipated. The intelligence estimates indicated that the North Korean force at Inchon numbered only about twenty-five hundred men, and that at Seoul only five thousand, with another five hundred soldiers stationed at Kimpo airfield. They did not anticipate any air opposition for, as far as intelligence knew, the North Koreans had only nineteen planes left, and these were all obsolete, suitable only for training. The fighter planes that had appeared during the early weeks of the Korean War had all been shot down or destroyed on the ground by the United Nations air forces—American, British, and Australian. As for naval opposition, all the North Koreans could now muster were small craft of the patrol boat type.

So MacArthur was convinced that the North Koreans would be unable to respond with reinforcements to the Seoul–Inchon area. If they brought troops up from the south, so much the better, for General Walker's troops on the Pusan Perimeter could then swing up and attack them from the rear.

As for Wolmi-do, no one was quite sure what existed there. Preliminary reports had said that the island was lightly defended by guns, but an intelligence mission conducted by navy Lieutenant Eugene F. Clark reported the contrary. Clark had been landed on September 1 on the island of Yonghung-do, fifteen miles below Inchon, and he had employed a number of Koreans to gather intelligence about the Inchon area. They had reported that Wolmi-do was bristling with artillery. And now, after the air strikes, was it still bristling? Those officers who had memories of the guns of Iwo Jima and Okinawa in World War II wondered if the North Koreans had lifted a page or two from the Japanese camouflage and concealment manuals. Admiral Struble decided to give Wolmi-do a day of naval bombardment and maybe two.

At 7 A.M. on September 13 a long column of gray ships headed up Flying Fish Channel toward the Inchon area. The destroyer *Mansfield* led and behind her came the *DeHaven, Swenson, Collett, Gurke,* and *Henderson.* They were followed in by the American cruisers *Rochester* and *Toledo,* and the British cruisers *Jamaica* and *Kenya.*

Shortly after ten o'clock the ships were in the approaches to Inchon harbor. At 11:45 a string of mines was sighted off to port of the column. What the naval force needed were minesweepers, but the minesweepers were in mothballs back on the Pacific Coast. They would be recommissioned, but it would be weeks before they could arrive in Korean waters. Only seven minesweepers were available in Far Eastern waters, and these were back with the transports to protect the thousands of invasion troops.

There was nothing to be done but quit or forge on, and quitting was out of the question. The destroyer *Henderson* was detached to move around and sink mines by gunfire. The rest of the column proceeded on the fire mission.

Just before one o'clock that afternoon the destroyers opened fire on Wolmi-do. Admiral Struble had planned this mission for the daylight hours because he wanted to draw enemy fire from the island and the Inchon shore and thus see what the opposition really was. They were not long in finding out that the air strikes had certainly not disabled the shore guns. Within a few minutes enemy shells began to find the ships.

The *Collett* was hit by nine 75 mm shells, one of which destroyed her fire control computer. Three shells hit the *Gurke.* A near miss killed an officer aboard the *Swenson.* But in return the destroyers fired a thousand 5-inch shells toward the defenses, and when they had finished, the cruisers came up and continued the firing for the next three hours.

If there had been doubts in the North Korean high command about the ability of the UN forces to launch an amphibious invasion so soon after the deadly fighting in the south, they were now erased. The air waves were full of messages from North Korean commands warning of an invasion of Inchon. Nor were the enemy guns silenced. As the ships left the harbor, the guns of Wolmi-do were still firing.

This sent waves of pessimism through the marine and naval officers aboard the *Mount McKinley.* They had never liked the idea of Inchon, they had lost the element of surprise, and they feared the guns of Wolmi-do might turn out to be devastating.

General MacArthur was unperturbed. There was no doubt in his mind about the outcome of the Inchon landings. But that night Admiral Struble decided on another day of bombardment, and the destroyers moved back up the channel off Wolmi-do.

On September 14 the destroyers and cruisers bombarded the island again and planes from the carrier task force bombed and strafed. By the end of the day the firing from the shore guns was erratic and slight, and no ships had been hit. It seemed certain that the strength of the artillery had been blasted away.

Shortly after midnight, on the morning of September 15, the attack group of ships followed the destroyers, entered Flying Fish Channel, and the marines got ready to make the landings on Wolmi-do. The air strike came in on schedule.

With Wolmi-do's guns silenced, the invasion fleet moved into the Inchon inner harbor for the next step. By six o'clock the ships were in position, the marines were in their landing craft and the landing craft were circling, waiting for the signal to speed into the shore at Wolmi-do. Overhead, the planes of the task force were softening up the enemy, screaming down in dives to bomb and rocket, and strafing the streets and buildings beyond the port. There were three points of landing. Wolmi-do's Green Beach was first. Then would come Red Beach, which lay on the edge of the Inchon industrial district, and last, Blue Beach below the town on the edge of the salt pans. At 6:15 three rocket craft moved in, toward Wolmi-do, each prepared to fire a thousand 5-inch rockets. They began firing on the beach areas. At 6:28 the first wave of landing craft crossed the line of departure and headed in for the shore. The destroyers and cruisers ceased fire and let the marine Corsairs overhead strafe the beaches.

At 6:33 the first wave of troops hit the shore, in a welter of dust, smoke, and explosion. The resistance was hardly discernible at this point, in the noise. Thirteen minutes later the first supply ships brought in their cargoes to support the assault force. Thirty minutes after that the American flag was up, General MacArthur had gone below on the *Mount McKinley* for his cup of coffee, and the assault on Inchon proper was about to begin.

However, there was still more fighting to be done on Wolmi-do. The marines held the top of Radio Hill, but the area facing Inchon had to be subdued. Captain Patrick E. Wildman attacked across the island with most of Company H. At 6:46 the third wave of marines came in to Green Beach and the tanks landed. One carried a flamethrower, and one, a bulldozer blade. These were weapons that had proved invaluable in the island fighting in the Pacific in World War II, and the marines had them along, just in case.

Company I of the 3rd Battalion had been held in reserve, and it landed just before seven o'clock that morning. Captain Robert A. McMullen led the men across the land that had supposedly been cleared by Company H, but all of a sudden the marines were hit by a flurry of hand grenades and they scattered for cover. It did not take them long to find the source of trouble, a line of defensive positions along the shore facing Inchon, which had been missed by the fast-moving Company H. A platoon of North Koreans were in those holes. They would jump up, throw grenades, and then jump back into the holes. Captain McMullen shouted for his interpreter and he came up. The interpreter crawled up to the bluff above the defenses and told the North Koreans their position was hopeless. The answer was a shower of grenades. McMullen then called up Lieutenant Granville Sweet's tanks, and they came along. McMullen selected the 'dozer tank to do the job. The others covered, while the tank moved slowly up to the defenses and systematically sealed up all the holes into which the North Koreans had crawled. End of difficulty.

Company I forged on ahead toward the Inchon causeway. They passed a number of caves and checked them out. They were empty. But from one came a few noises, and the marines stopped. Riflemen covered the entrance, and a tank rumbled up and fired two rounds into the opening. The resulting series of explosions must have blown the inside of the island apart. It had to be an ammunition dump. First came noise, and then came smoke and fire, and then out of the entrance came thirty enemy troops with their hands in the air.

Thereafter things went well, and soon Colonel Taplett could send a message to the *Mount McKinley*:

"Captured 45 prisoners. Meeting light resistance."

The North Koreans seemed to recognize their defeat, and most of them surrendered without a fight.

Colonel Taplett kept the command ship informed with a series of messages, and by eight o'clock it was all over but the mopping up on Wolmi-do. When that report reached MacArthur, he went into his cabin and penned a message in his usual florid style:

"The Navy and the Marines have never shone more brightly than this morning."

General MacArthur had reason to be grateful to the marines. They had proved him right once again. All those faint hearts aboard the command ship had been wrong.

That signal was sent by the coffee-drinking MacArthur to Admiral Struble, who received it aboard the *Rochester* just as he was about to go into a small boat to have a look around. Struble then dropped by the *Mount McKinley* and picked up MacArthur and took him along for a look. Their carefree appearance so close to the firing line so early in the game was a sure sign of the nature of the battle. They went over to Wolmi-do and found everything under control. So far, it was a nice little invasion with only seventeen marines wounded; the four hundred men of the North Korean garrison had been killed or captured for the most part. Washington really did not seem to have much to worry about this morning.

As the marines moved around the island, they saw that Lieutenant Clark had not been as badly informed as they had begun to believe. Radio Hill was ringed by mutually supporting trenches. On one side of the ridge were parked two 76 mm antitank guns which could have played hob with the boats and tanks coming ashore. But the North Koreans had not manned them; later the marines learned that the enemy troops had been demoralized by the ship and plane attacks on the beach. More antitank guns were scattered around the causeway that led to Inchon. These, too, had been left unmanned.

In midmorning all seemed secure on Wolmi-do, but there was one more point that had to be taken, the tiny islet of Sowolmi-do, connected to Wolmi-do by another causeway. It did not seem much of a job. Colonel Taplett ordered Company G to do it. Lieutenant Robert Bohn of Company G ordered Lieutenant John D. Counselman's 3rd Platoon to do it. Counselman took an infantry squad reinforced by extra machine guns and a section of tanks. After all, it was a very small islet.

To reach it the marines must traverse that nine-hundred-yard causeway that looked ten miles long to each marine who gazed across to the little hill at the end. But there was nothing to be done but move on, and they did. As they had half expected, when they stepped up to the entrance to the causeway, they were greeted by a hail of machine gun and rifle fire. Here was a handful of North Koreans who were not planning to give up. Colonel Taplett was told what was going on. He ordered up a strike from marine air. A few minutes later a handful of Corsairs appeared over Wolmi-do and flew down the causeway, dropping napalm on the islet at the end. Then the 81 mm mortars were turned on the islet, and under their cover, the tanks began to move on the seaward edge of the causeway. The mortar platoon fired lustily as the tanks ground along, the enemy's heads were forced down, and the tanks and the infantry behind them reached the end of the causeway. The infantry fanned out at the end and began to engage the defenders. The tanks covered them. In an hour it was all over. With machine guns, rifles, grenades, and a flame-thrower the marines settled the issue. But they were still another hour sealing up all the caves just to make sure. Even then they did not quite eliminate the enemy. Eight North Koreans somehow managed to hide out all day, and that night they were seen escaping across the tidal flat to the mainland.

By noon all was silent in Inchon harbor. The Americans were in position, but they could not land until the tide changed, and that meant evening. Just now Inchon harbor was one big mudflat, with Wolmi-do perched high above the mud.

That afternoon intelligence offices sorted out what could be learned from the survivors of the garrison at Wolmi-do. That garrison was part of the two-thousand-man defense force assigned to Inchon. The failure of the defenders to fight a delaying action was ascribed to their lack of training; these were green troops, freshly conscripted.

All afternoon the marines on Wolmi-do looked across the mud flat at Inchon through their field glasses, trying to make out defense points and call down fire on them. They found only one. Meanwhile, the artillerymen came ashore on Wolmi-do and prepared to bring their howitzers in on the evening tide.

The seven minesweepers had come up with the transports, and they were busily checking all the anchorages. Planes circled lazily in the air, their motion belying their mission: observers were keeping a careful watch on the shore defenses.

Every ninety minutes a dozen fighter-bombers swept in from the carriers to drop bombs and napalm on suspected defense points on the mainland. Around the air space of the city, fighters patroled unceasingly, to make sure that there was no surprise from the north.

As the waters of the tidal basin rose again in midafternoon, the activity aboard the ships increased. At one o'clock the troop transports and LSTs were able to begin moving in toward the shore. By midafternoon the landing troops were getting into their boats. At 4:15 that afternoon the guns began to fire again and by five o'clock the bombardment was in full force, with five hundred landing craft milling about in the water. The scene was much the same as that of the morning: bombardment, air strikes, the rocket ships, and then the infantry moving toward shore in their little craft. The amphibious envelopment of the North Korean armies buried deep in the heart of South Korea was about to begin.

3

The Landings

The idea, said orders from the high command, was to soften up Inchon without destroying the port facilities, which would be needed in the next few weeks. So at about two thirty on the afternoon of September 15 the Allied warships in the harbor began firing on the shore in what they hoped were selective patterns. The targets were the defensive areas around Red Beach on the northeastern outskirts of Inchon and Blue Beach on the southern edge.

The U.S. cruisers *Toledo* and *Rochester* fired 8-inch shells at the targets marked out for them. They were responsible for the Red Beach bombardment. The Royal Navy's *Kenya* and *Jamaica* covered the approaches to Blue Beach. And they were supported by destroyers, firing their 5-inch guns.

Soon fires began rising from the old Asahi brewery, the railroad yards, and factories on the outskirts. A great flashing explosion announced that a shell or two had struck an oil tank. Black greasy smoke rose high above the town.

Rear Admiral James H. Doyle, commander of the amphibious group, announced that H-Hour, the time of landing, would be five thirty that afternoon. The landing craft were in the water, the men aboard and waiting.

Soon bombers and fighters from the carrier force joined the bombardment with their air attacks. Rockets screamed down on the targets. A butane gas tank exploded. Another factory went up. Within an hour the whole shore was obscured from the men on the ships by smoke and dust.

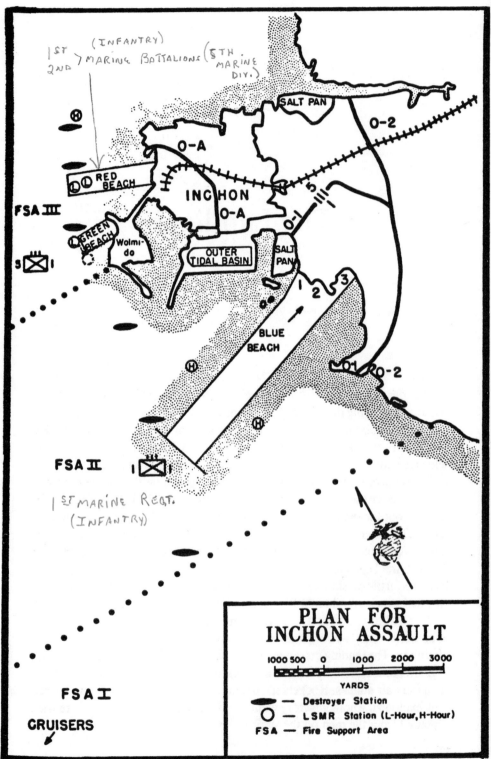

PLAN FOR
INCHON ASSAULT

1000 500   0   1000   2000   3000

YARDS

⬛ — Destroyer Station
◯ — LSMR Station (L-Hour, H-Hour)
FSA — Fire Support Area

Map 2.

Lieutenant Colonel Raymond L. Murray's 5th Marines would lead the assault. (See Map 2.) The 1st and 2nd battalions would land abreast on Red Beach, actually a 650-foot-wide stone and concrete quay, guarded from the ravages of the tides by a stone seawall. And from where the marines sat, nothing about Red Beach looked as though it was going to be easy. North of Red Beach a finger pier stuck out into the harbor. If the North Koreans had machine guns there. . . . The veterans of Tarawa could remember only too well how the finger pier on tiny Betio Island had given the Japanese a position of enfilading fire that had proved enormously costly to the marines. From the transports there was no way of telling what might lie concealed there on the finger pier. The latest set of aerial photographs, passed around by intelligence that day, showed a number of bunkers and interconnecting trenches on the left, where the railroad line runs by Cemetery Hill, the red cliff that faced the sea and sloped down in the back. The whole beach area was broken by pillboxes and trenches.

Colonel Murray's mission was to seize an area three thousand yards long and a thousand yards deep, extending from Cemetery Hill at the top down to the Inner Tidal Basin at the bottom and including the promontory in the middle called Observatory Hill. (See Map 3.) The observatory tower commanded the town and the port. To take it meant moving in open ground and also through a maze of streets and alleys. Lieutenant Colonel George R. Newton's 1st Battalion would be on the left, against Cemetery Hill and the northern half of Observatory Hill. Lieutenant Colonel Harold S. Roise's 2nd Battalion would take the southern half of Observatory Hill, the British Consulate, on a little hill of its own, and the Inner Tidal Basin.

Three miles to the southeast, the 1st Marine Regiment would be landing on Blue Beach, which was divided into two sectors. Blue Beach One was on the left, five hundred yards wide, flanked on the north by the rock wall of a salt evaporator that jutted out into the water. The south boundary was a wide drainage ditch. A dirt road led from the beach up to the town, and behind it was a steep hill.

Blue Beach Two lay south of the drainage ditch and extended another five hundred yards. On its right was a narrow ramp, and behind the ramp was a cove. All these places could give trouble to the 2nd and 3rd battalions, and to Company A of the 56th Amphibian Tractor Battalion. The 2nd Battalion would move against Blue One, and the 3rd Battalion against Blue Two and the amtracks would move where they could.

Thus, the two regiments would form a pincers around Inchon, and presumably would force the North Koreans to retreat from the port areas. That was precisely what General MacArthur wanted, for it was essential that the port be

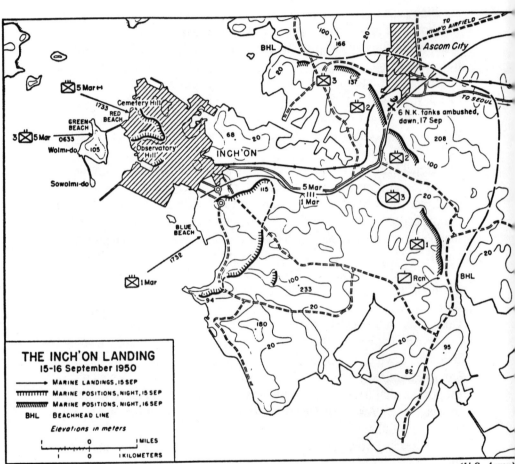

THE INCH'ON LANDING
15-16 September 1950

→ MARINE LANDINGS, 15 SEP
⊥⊥⊥⊥⊥ MARINE POSITIONS, NIGHT, 15 SEP
⊤⊤⊤⊤⊤ MARINE POSITIONS, NIGHT, 16 SEP
BHL   BEACHHEAD LINE

Elevations in meters

1 MILES
1 KILOMETERS

Map 3.

(U.S. Army)

retained in working order if his plan of cutting off the North Koreans by driving across the middle of the peninsula was to succeed. The four assault battalions of these two regiments would have just about two hours of daylight to get ashore and establish themselves before dark.

In midafternoon, Colonel Taplett on Wolmi-do suggested that he move a force across the causeway to Red Beach. If the movement was relatively unopposed, the troops would stay. Otherwise it could be called a reconnaissance and might give some valuable information for the other battalions. But his commander, Brigadier General Edward A. Craig, said no. The high command really had little concept of the sort of defense they were going to encounter, and Colonel Taplett's plan seemed much too risky.

So the afternoon wore on, with the officers in the boats looking anxiously at their watches.

Shortly after the bombardment picked up, storm clouds clustered over Inchon harbor, and rain began to blow along in squalls. The heavy overcast melded with the smoke and dust of the bombardment and made the visibility even worse, particularly on Blue Beach. The assault craft seemed to do nothing but mill about, but actually they were kept under control by the central control ship, the transport *Diachenko.* Lieutenant Commander Ralph H. Schneeloch's Red Beach control vessel motored toward the line of departure, trailing behind it a column of assault craft like a duck with her ducklings. Lieutenant Theodore B. Clark did the same with the assault craft destined for Blue Beach. At four forty-five the first wave of marines headed in for Blue Beach. They would arrive in forty-five minutes. Over the heads of the marines the shells from the bombarding ships whistled inland. Shortly after five o'clock the shells were joined by the screech of rockets from the rocket ships. Once again, General MacArthur was seated in the swivel chair on the command bridge of the *Mount McKinley,* his staff and commanders around him to watch the show. From the ship's bridge the "talker" was giving them over the "squawk box" a blow by blow description of the developments as reported by the aerial observers over Inchon.

This was indeed the hour of decision. The American commanders had learned the hard way not to underestimate the North Korean enemy in the first two months of war when the UN forces had been driven back, back, back. The comparison with Tarawa was not far from many marine minds— Tarawa, where the Japanese enemy had been lying, waiting, and had blasted the first waves of marine invaders with a hail of fire that seemed to cover every inch of the landing beach. Would the marines now face the same sort of bloody battle? No one knew, nor did they know how it would go in the crooked streets of the old Korean town, where every byway might conceal a machine gun.

When the leading assault boats were halfway in to the beach, the naval bombardment stopped. For the next five minutes marine and navy planes strafed the landing areas. The officers in the assault craft called out targets as they spotted them, and the planes came down to strike, so close overhead that their 20 mm shell casings dropped into some of the boats.

In this twilight the sky was even more murky and the wind whipped rain and spray into the faces of the troops. The flashes of the guns and rockets stood out brightly in the gathering gloom. From the air the scene below was like a water pageant, with the assault craft forging ahead, trailing the tails of their wakes. Then, the force heading for Blue Beach slipped under the pall of smoke and could be seen no more from the air.

On Red Beach, the murk was farther back. The men in the assault craft could see their objective, but not too much beyond it. Blue Beach was virtually obscured from the view of the 1st Marines as they came in.

The first eight LCVP assault craft headed in toward Red Beach. It was eight minutes before H-Hour, and the first wave of the 5th Marines was nearly ashore. Four of the boats carried marines of Company A of the 1st Battalion, who would move against Cemetery Hill. In the other four boats were men of Company E of the 2nd Battalion, whose destinations were the right flank of the beach and the British Consulate.

As the boats neared Red Beach, they got additional support from Colonel Taplett's marines on Wolmi-do, who fired machine guns and mortars, and from the tanks that fired their guns to cover the landing. Engineers from Wolmi-do moved forward to clear the causeway so that the tanks might proceed just as soon as the landings had been completed. The marine aircraft above the beach came down for their final passes and were joined by navy planes. They were still firing on the shore when the landing craft were thirty yards off the seawall.

As the landing craft struck the wall, the men could see that although the tide was rising rapidly, still the seawall projected about four feet above their level. They were ready with scaling ladders, and at one minute after H-hour they were at the wall. Marines hurled grenades over the wall, and the scaling ladders went up. One by one the marines scrambled up and over. In a few moments every man of Company E's 1st Platoon was on the beach. There had not yet been a casualty.

On the landward side of the seawall, the marines moved inland. A few stray shots were heard but no one was hit. They prepared to cover the landings of the second and third waves, which would bring the rest of Company E ashore.

Further to the north, the men of Company A hit the seawall two minutes later. The engine of one boat failed just offshore, but the other three came in. Boat No. 2 was unlucky enough to arrive directly in front of a North Korean bunker on the other side of the wall, and as the marines scrambled over they were met by heavy fire from submachine guns, the favorite weapons of the North Korean infantry. Several marines were hit, and the rest from Boat No. 2 were stopped right there.

Boat No. 3 hit the wall directly under the muzzle of a machine gun that protruded from a pillbox. For some reason the gun did not fire. Lieutenant Francis W. Muetzel led his men over, and they were followed by others from Boat No. 4, including a bazooka team. They jumped down into a long trench that ran parallel to the seawall. It was empty. They saw the pillbox ahead, and two marines threw grenades inside. The explosions drove out six North Korean soldiers, who were captured and left in the trench under marine guard.

Lieutenant Muetzel's immediate objective was the Asahi brewery, which the marines dearly wanted to take intact. He led his men across the beach past smoking buildings and flaming wreckage. In a few minutes they had passed south of Cemetery Hill and were in the streets of the town, heading for the brewery.

The 1st Platoon was having trouble with that North Korean bunker. Technical Sergeant Orval F. McMullen finally got ashore with the second half of the platoon after the landing craft's pesky engine was started. At about that same time Lieutenant Baldomero Lopez' 3rd Platoon also scrambled up over the seawall, but both groups found themselves under heavy fire from the bunker. Lieutenant Lopez snatched a grenade from his web belt and armed it to throw. Just then he was wounded in the right arm and he dropped the grenade. Painfully he crawled forward and smothered it with his chest and took the full impact to protect his men. He died there on the seawall.

Two marines with flamethrowers came up to attack the bunker but they were both shot down and the flamethrowers put out of action. There was plenty of trouble there on the left, and when Captain John Stevens came up two minutes later he saw how serious was the crisis. Lopez was dead, and in the confusion Stevens could not find Sergeant McMullen. He ordered the company executive officer, Lieutenant Fred Eubanks, Jr., to take over the left and get the men moving inland. It was important that they take Cemetery Hill, which loomed up high above the seawall, before the enemy could get any better organized than they were, for men atop the red cliff could control the beach here, and hundreds more marines would be landing in the next few hours.

Lieutenant Muetzel saw that the 1st Platoon would be some time in getting going, and he had contingency orders to help take their objective, Cemetery Hill. He observed that the route to the top was a gentle slope from the south, and he decided to take the chance. His marines moved swiftly up the incline, and in the process they came across a handful of North Korean soldiers. As on Wolmi-do, most of the North Koreans surrendered without firing a shot. Muetzel's men reached the summit, and there on the top of Cemetery Hill they encountered a whole mortar company, which immediately surrendered. The North Koreans were marched down the hill under guard. The capture of Cemetery Hill had taken about ten minutes and the marines had not suffered a single casualty. Lieutenant Muetzel could now consider the problem of the 1st Platoon down below and he was ready to send help. But it was not necessary. Lieutenant Eubanks had spent the intervening time hurling grenades into the enemy bunker and then had sent a flamethrower to burn it out. The bunker fell silent and the 1st and 3rd Platoons broke through and made contact with the 2nd Platoon. Just before six P.M. Captain Stevens fired an amber flare: Cemetery Hill was secured. What had appeared to be one of the most dangerous points was not a problem.

Meanwhile, farther south on Red Beach Company E landed and pushed forward. Captain Samuel Jaskilka came ashore ten minutes after H-Hour and organized his men near the Nippon Flour Company warehouse. One platoon moved down the railroad tracks and captured the British Consulate. Another platoon took the lower slope of Observatory Hill. This much was accomplished before seven P.M., but the enemy still held Observatory Hill and had to be dislodged. That task was given to Company C and Company D. Then, for the first time the marines ran into trouble.

The trouble began with a mixup in landing, so that parts of both companies landed on the wrong beaches. Captain Paul F. Pederson of Company C was delayed when the commander of his assault boat decided to stop and tow a stalled LCVP. All this delay gave the enemy on Observatory Hill a chance to pull themselves together after the bombardment and air bombings.

Eight LSTs were waiting out in the channel for the clearing of the beaches, and at six thirty they began moving. Twenty minutes later they were under fire from mortars and machine guns on Observatory Hill. They fired back, not only at Observatory Hill but at Cemetery Hill, and that fire chased Lieutenant Muetzel's men into running for cover. Colonel Roises's 2nd Battalion headquarters and weapons companies were also fired on by the LSTs and one marine was killed and twenty-three were wounded before they could get into the shelter of the Nippon Flour Company.

When the firing began on Observatory Hill, Lieutenant Byron Magness took the 2nd Platoon of Company C up the hill. They took a part of it and Company B came ashore to attack the hill as well. The hill was two-peaked, with a saddle between. Magness' men held the saddle, and Captain Francis Fenton, Jr.'s B Company attacked the north peak, in a two-column movement, although darkness had already fallen. Once again, compared to the fighting in the Naktong Bulge, the going was easy. Six marines were wounded but by eight o'clock that night Fenton's men held the crest of the hill and he was in contact with Magness's platoon down below in the saddle.

Responsibility for the southern peak of Observatory Hill rested with the 2nd Battalion of the 5th Marines. The unit assigned the capture was Lieutenant H. D. Smith's Company D. The troops marched up the hill and soon had part of it. But as they advanced to the top, they ran into some determined North Korean troops with a machine gun. The North Koreans opened fire, the marines tumbled off the left side of the road, and the fighting began. It was fierce enough, with one marine killed and three others wounded. Lieutenant Michael J. Dunbar was wounded, too, before the marines drove the enemy troops into retreat. Men of Company F also came up and soon the whole of Observatory Hill was held by the marines. So, as night closed in they held all parts of their first objective but the Inner Tidal Basin.

The 1st Marines landing on Blue Beach had no idea of what they were moving into because by H-Hour the smoke and rain had completely obscured the shore. This would have been trouble enough for any unit; the 1st Marines suffered from the problem that had bedevilled the Americans from the beginning of the Korean War: lack of experience. The regiment had been operating on the cutback basis for a long time and only in recent weeks had it been brought up to three-battalion strength. The regiment as now constituted had never even conducted a training operation. It did, however, have the good luck to get back its old World War II commander, Colonel Lewis Burwell Puller, commonly known as "Chesty," a very tough gentleman with the face of an unfortunate boxer, who held four Navy Crosses. If anybody could whip a regiment into fighting trim in a hurry, Puller was the man.

The mission of his 1st Marines in this landing was to take the beachhead that covered the city of Inchon proper, and the road to Yongdungpo and Seoul. Lieutenant Colonel Allan Sutter's 2nd Battalion would land on the left at Blue Beach One (see Map 4) and Lieutenant Colonel Thomas L. Ridge's 3rd Battalion would land on Blue Beach Two. Informally, a little cove around the corner south of Blue Beach Two was called Blue Beach Three, but it had no official part in the plan and no one knew what would be found there. As in the south around Pusan, the troops fighting in Korea soon discovered that the Americans had paid so little attention to South Korea during the three years of occupation that they had virtually failed to map the country or chart the waters. Consequently they were forced back upon the old Japanese maps and charts, and since the Japanese had never conceived that they might lose this part of their empire most of the land maps were inadequate. Besides, in the postwar period the Koreans had changed all the Japanese place names to Korean ones.

The 1st Marines' landings on Blue Beach were hardly a model for the future. The blame lay largely on the shoulders of the navy, which suffered from a lack of control vessels (not much more than ten percent of the indicated number). The first three waves of the regiment came in right on schedule, but the following waves were thrown into complete confusion.

Amphibious tractors of Lieutenant Colonel Allan Sutter's 2nd Battalion were first to make the shore. Nine landing craft deposited the first wave on Blue Beach One at exactly H-Hour. The marines met no opposition and started along the road below the salt evaporator. (See Map 4.) The naval bombardment had dislodged a huge mass of earth from the high ground above the beach, and it blocked the road. The amtracs ground to a halt. The second wave came up behind. The third wave grounded in the mud about a quarter of a mile offshore and the marines had to wade in through the muck. They lost some radio equipment when marines fell into potholes on the way. Enemy resistance was very light. A few mortar rounds came in, most of them creating mud geysers beside the amtracs. One machine gun somewhere up ahead could be heard rattling. Soon six hundred marines and thirty vehicles had made the beach, and it was getting crowded in front of that mass of dirt that blocked the road exit.

The infantry would have to move forward without the vehicles, which could not move until the amtrac crews cleared a lane through the mess. It was getting dark, the reserves and much of the equipment were still offshore, waiting for room, and the troops had to move out. Company D and Company F moved.

The amphibious tractors of Company G headed into the drainage ditch since it seemed to offer an easy route to the shore. That was illusory: the lead tractor in Company G's column bogged down in the mud of the ditch, blocking the other five vehicles behind it. The troops got out and walked. Lieutenant Colonel Thomas L. Ridge, commander of the 1st Battalion, was riding in another amtrac, and it made the beach without difficulty in the little cove to the right of the ditch. This cove proved to be an excellent landing place and its use mitigated the difficulties encountered in the landing areas to the north.

Thirty minutes after H-Hour, all three battalions had their assault troops ashore, and the situation could be said to be in hand, although Colonel Puller was anything but satisfied with the confusion that continued at sea.

By nightfall, the 1st, 2nd and 3rd battalions of the 1st Marine Division had all made reasonable progress against their objectives. The 1st Platoon of Company H made a night attack against a company of North Koreans on Hill 94. The North Koreans were entrenched there, but after very little resistance they abandoned their positions, leaving about thirty dead and wounded.

So on that night of September 15, the marines had come ashore and established themselves in and around Inchon. (See Map 3.) In spite of all the complaints made by the admirals the navy had done its job pretty well, considering the haste in which the operation had been mounted, and the state of its amphibious training. Admiral Doyle had landed thirteen thousand troops and their equipment at Inchon. That included the assault waves, the followup infantry, and two battalions of 105 mm artillery of the 11th Marines. Casualties had been extremely light, 21 men killed, 1 missing, and 174 men wounded. They had taken about three hundred prisoners and had killed a large number of North Koreans, but no count was kept by either side. Many of the North Korean casualties must have been from the "softening-up" process, carried out in the spirit of those bombardments against the Japanese of World War II. The marines had attained their primary objectives, and they settled down within their unit perimeters to sleep a little and wait for morning when the real battle might begin. Colonel Puller was ashore checking up. At one thirty in the morning of September 16 he reported to General Smith that the situation was satisfactory, and then he crawled under a poncho to snatch a few hours of rest. General Smith, writing in his log of the day, noted matter-of-factly that the landings had "gone about as planned." Perhaps. But a few weeks earlier many of the officers involved had said Inchon was impossible, a few days earlier, many had said the operation could not be mounted in time, and a few hours earlier on that morning of September 15, there were a good many officers on the bridges of those ships who were wondering what they would meet and were half-prepared for a bloodbath. Instead, the navy and the marines had achieved a most successful landing against minimal opposition. It looked as though General MacArthur was prescient when he said that the war should be over in a month.

Since there was so little opposition to the landings of the marines at the north and south ends of Inchon, Admiral Struble decided to take a long

chance that could pay off nicely in speeding up the assault. After dark, eight
LSTs came in on the flood tide and grounded on Red Beach. This decision
was made to make sure the troops ashore had the supplies they would need to
push off in the morning. Each LST carried fifty tons of ammunition, fifteen
tons of water, thirty tons of rations and five tons of diesel oil or gasoline. If the
LSTs had not come in then, they could not get in again across the mud flats for
twelve hours, and that would have left the thirteen thousand marines ashore
high and dry in case of any enemy countermoves.

All this was done under fire. The LSTs came in shooting their guns and
caused those casualties up on Cemetery Hill, before the marines could get
down to the water's edge and stop them. The enemy continued to shoot. To be
sure, the fire from the North Korean defenders was not intensive, but it
existed. One mortar shell hit *LST 973*'s cargo of gasoline drums, and started
several of them leaking. Gasoline dripped down into the crew's compartment
and the danger of fire was imminent. The skipper ordered all electric motors
cut off, and the mess was cleaned up. There was no fire.

LST 857 also took some hits from mortar and machine gun fire which
caused gasoline drums to leak, and one shell killed a sailor and injured
another, and another sailor aboard *LST 859* was wounded by mortar fragments. But when one can count the casualties on the fingers of one hand, the
opposition can't be called very serious. The landing was really almost like a
training exercise, but unfortunately some marines were lulled into thinking it
was just a training exercise. Two of them wandered off the perimeter that
night in the Cemetery Hill area and were cut down by a burst of fire out of the
blackness. Their fellow marines tried to get to them, but were driven back
repeatedly by enemy fire. The North Koreans were located in a cave on the
side of the hill. An interpreter came up and warned the North Koreans that if
they did not surrender tanks and flamethrowers would be brought in. The
cave would be seared and then bulldozed shut forever. The North Koreans
considered that prospect and decided to surrender. Troops of Company A
rushed in to find their comrades. One marine was dead and the other dying of
his wounds.

That night of September 15–16 while the marines up front got a little sleep,
the beach area was humming like a beehive. The engineers brought in
floodlights and set them up on the seawalls. The ramps opened and the
vehicles began coming off. Then the cargo was unloaded. By the time of the
morning tide the LSTs were empty. They backed off and gave place to a new
batch of LSTs.

As dawn came, the marines had jeeps and trucks and artillery and plenty of
ammunition ashore. The tanks landed on Wolmi-do had come across the

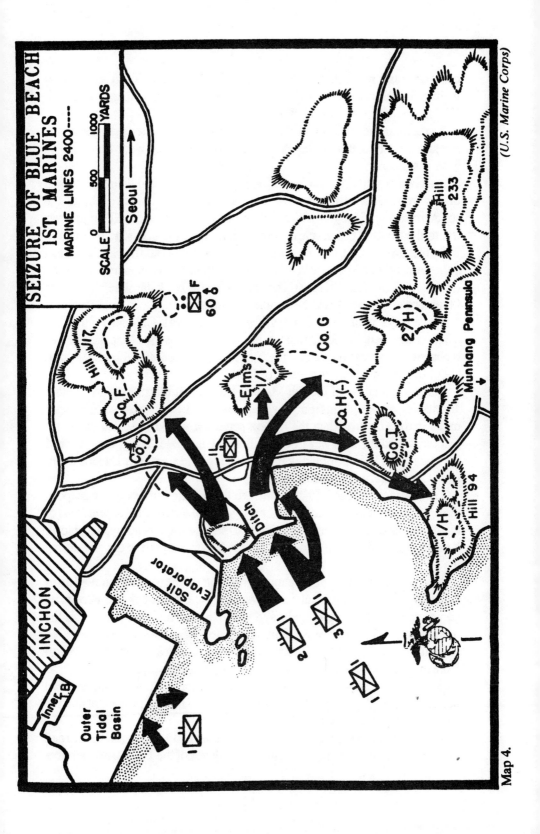

SEIZURE OF BLUE BEACH
1ST MARINES
MARINE LINES 2400----

SCALE
0   500   1000
YARDS

Seoul

INCHON

Outer Tidal Basin

Inner T.B.

Salt Evaporator

Ditch

Co. D

Co. F

Hill 117

Elms 1/1

Co. G

CoH(-)

Co. 1

2/H

Hill 94

1/H

Munhang Peninsula

Hill 233

(U.S. Marine Corps)

Map 4.

causeway, and more tanks were landed on the island to do the same. That night of September 15, the 3rd Battalion of the 5th Marines crossed over from Wolmi-do to join the regiment at Inchon.

By morning the engineers and shore parties had constructed prisoner of war stockades on Red Beach and Blue Beach. Already they were beginning to have customers.

As dawn neared, Colonel Murray and Colonel Puller had their operational orders from General Smith. The 5th Marines would march through the southern sector of Inchon without attempting to clear the city. That job was left to the South Korean marines who had joined the division. This action freed the Americans from the difficult job of weeding out the North Korean adherents. Three months earlier the North Koreans had been merciless in their treatment of the ROK sympathizers and officials. Now the shoe was on the other foot and there would be another bloodbath.

Three miles inland the 5th Marines came up with Colonel Puller's 1st Marines who had moved up that far the evening before. (See Map 4.) The two regiments began moving along the Inchon–Seoul road and reached a point about five miles inland at the end of the day.

The 2nd Battalion of the 5th Marines led off that morning, with Captain Jaskilka's Company E in front. Two hills lay ahead, and if these were brought under marine control, then the Inchon peninsula would be sealed off.

Jaskilka led the men out from the British Consulate. When they reached the Inner Tidal Basin, Company F fell in behind, and Company D came down from Observatory Hill and followed.

The marines marched quickly through the deserted streets of the seaport; the only movement they saw was the wriggling of curtains in the windows of the houses as civilians peeked out shyly to see the soldiers go by. The North Korean army units slated to defend Inchon had moved out of the city during the night.

Just outside the city the companies turned left off the road and moved up to attack the two hills that would command the area. No attack was necessary, they simply marched up the hills and took possession. At nine thirty on the morning of D+1 Inchon was secure and sealed off.

That information was obviously unknown to at least part of the North Korean defense force further east. When the news of ships in the harbor at Inchon reached Seoul, elements of the North Korean 22nd Regiment had been sent down the road, but when they learned of the bombardment and the landings in force, they turned back.

When the marines got on top of their hills they had a good view of the road toward Seoul, past Ascom City, the supply depot of the U.S. Army Services

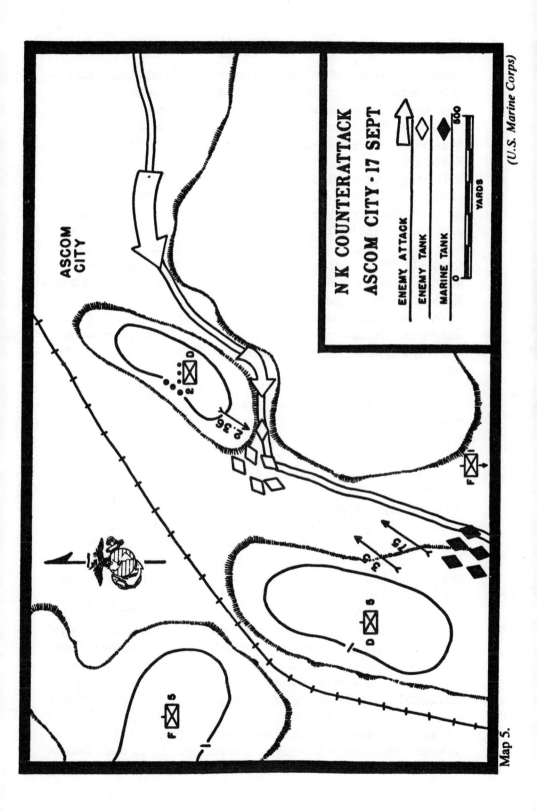

ASCOM
CITY

N K COUNTERATTACK
ASCOM CITY · 17 SEPT

ENEMY ATTACK
ENEMY TANK ◇
MARINE TANK ◆
0   500
YARDS

(U.S. Marine Corps)

D 2

2:36

F 1

D 5

F 5

3:35

:15

Map 5.

Command in the days of the American occupation. Up that road on the way to Inchon came six North Korean T-34 tanks hurrying along the highway. (See Map 5.) They were quite alone, without infantry support, and when they reached the village of Kansong-ni, just west of Ascom City, they were spotted by a strike force of eight Corsairs of marine squadron VMF-214 led by Major Robert Floeck.

The fighter planes nosed over and came in, guns spitting. Major Robert Floeck hit the lead tank with a container of napalm, and the tank burst into flames. Another pilot loosed rockets that knocked the tread off the second tank. Another tank was hit and disabled, but it did not burn. The tanks fired back with their machine guns, and bullets knocked out the oil system of Captain William F. Simpson's plane. His plane did not respond when he tried to pull out of his screaming dive, and he plowed it into the ground next to the highway with an enormous explosion.

The planes of the first strike then flew away to seek other targets, not realizing that they had not knocked out all the tanks. The second strike came in shortly afterwards, and those planes saw the tanks on the road. They then proceeded to destroy the two tanks that had already been knocked out. The crewmen ran for shelter into the huts of the village, and the planes dropped napalm that set fire to the huts and burned them out. The other four tanks, lying doggo, escaped attack, although several other vehicles were caught in the open and attacked.

On the ground, the marines of Company D moved along the Seoul highway with a platoon of Company A tanks. They were followed by two companies of the 1st Marines. At eleven o'clock that morning they reached the village of Sogam-ni, not far from Kansong-ni.

South of the highway, the 3rd Battalion of the 1st Marines attacked in the Munhang Peninsula. That afternoon, the marines held the Inchon and Munhang peninsulas. The Inchon beachhead could now be considered a safe and established port facility for future operations. There was no way the North Koreans could outflank the marines on land.

The next move was to add to this holding the Namdong Peninsula to the south and move along the Seoul road past Ascom City. This would pave the way for an attack on Kimpo airfield, the largest and most important in Korea.

At one thirty in the afternoon the 5th Marines attacked north of the highway, meeting some resistance from North Koreans, particularly snipers. Having had a good deal of experience with the North Koreans in the Naktong line, the men of the 5th Marines moved carefully. At Kansong-ni they came to a sharp bend in the road which moved around a hill, concealing the far side. The tanks were in the lead. Lieutenant Joseph Sleger, Jr., the commander of the tank platoon, stopped on his side of the hill and sent two tanks up a dirt track to the top to take a look. These tanks were the new Marine Pershing M-26 type with the 90 mm guns and hydraulic turrets. They moved up to the top of the knoll. There below the tankers saw three of those T-34 tanks, sitting snugly in column along the road, ready for action, with their 85 mm guns pointed directly at the road bend. The North Korean tank crews saw the marine tanks and began traversing their guns to fire, but the North Korean T-34 85 mm guns were equipped with manual turrets which had to be cranked by hand, and before they could get their guns aimed, the M-26s had sent off twenty rounds of 90 mm armor-piercing ammunition. In a few minutes all three enemy tanks were burning hulks. The marine attack rolled by those three wrecks and the two others knocked out in the morning by marine aircraft. One tank had escaped back along the road, probably because it had been damaged in the morning attack.

The marines then moved along the road through Ascom City and stopped to dig in for the night on the high ground on both sides of the highway at Hill 132.

Except for the action with the tanks, there had been remarkably little fighting that day. A large amount of enemy supply and materiel was captured, including two 76 mm antitank guns, some Soviet 120 mm mortars, four coastal guns, many rifles and machine guns, and a whole dump of small arms ammunition. A number of prisoners were taken. Early in the day there was almost no resistance; by later afternoon light resistance had developed, but it had not seriously slowed the marines down. By day's end the marines had lost four men killed and twenty-one wounded. They had killed or wounded about a hundred and twenty North Koreans and captured thirty prisoners.

That afternoon of September 16, General Smith conferred with General MacArthur and said he was ready to take command. The operation was moving from the amphibious phase, and the navy would now go into support of the land operations. MacArthur urged General Smith to seize Kimpo airfield as soon as he could and then they parted and Smith went ashore to establish his command post at Inchon.

4

Breakout

Back in the south, Lieutenant General Walton H. Walker's U.S. Eighth Army had orders to launch a general attack along the Pusan Perimeter in coordination with the Inchon landing. General MacArthur reasoned that this attack would prevent the North Koreans from moving troops in the main North Korean army force up north to defend Seoul. If General Walker could break through he was to drive north the 180 miles to join up with the X Corps outside Seoul.

In preparation for this new phase of the war, the U.S. Eighth Army was reorganized. General Walker remained in command overall, but his divisions were now to be separated into two corps, I Corps and IX Corps. At nine o'clock on the morning of September 16, the troops were to move. The main effort would be made in the center of the perimeter by I Corps, to which were assigned the 5th Regimental Combat Team, the 1st Cavalry, the 24th Division, and the British 27th Infantry Brigade. The ROK Army's best division—the 1st Division—was also attached to this I Corps. The 5th Regimental Combat Team and the 1st Cavalry would attack across the Naktong River near Waegwan. The 24th Division would then cross through the assault force and attack toward Taejon, and the 1st Cavalry Division would follow and serve as rear guard. This main attack was to be made by the troops General Walker considered to be most reliable. The ROK 1st Division was to try to cross the river above Waegwan. This would be difficult because, as usual, Walker was short of equipment and did not have enough engineers and bridges to make many crossings simultaneously.

Because of the shortage of communications equipment IX Corps was not to become operative for another week. For the first week of the offensive the troops who would become IX Corps would operate directly under General Walker. He didn't really expect a lot from them. They were the men of the U.S. 2nd Division and of the 25th Division on the southwest, who would engage the enemy, stall them, and perhaps have a chance to break out. Walker wasn't counting on it. Over on the east coast, the ROK I and II corps were to engage the enemy on the eastern side of the peninsula. If they managed to keep the North Koreans there occupied, General Walker would be satisfied. A single ROK regiment, the 17th, was to move to Pusan and take ship for Inchon so that the Republic of Korea would be represented in the drive on Seoul.

From General MacArthur's standpoint it was a simple and sound plan. But the staff officers of the battered Eighth Army gloomily doubted if it could be done with the forces at hand. They believed that the North Korean force around the Pusan Perimeter totalled more than a 100,000 men. The total UN force was 157,000 men. Why, then, was there any cause for worry?

It was partly because the Eighth Army staff had little confidence in some of the American units and even less in the Republic of Korea's 73,000-man army. That lack of confidence was based on performance during the first two and a half months of the war. The American divisions had entered the war understrength, undertrained, and underarmed. Facing a highly skilled and determined enemy they had lost battle after battle and been forced back to within thirty miles of Pusan. They had suffered nineteen thousand casualties and the South Korean casualties had been at least twice that high. The Eighth Army staff knew that the effective rifle strength of the fighting companies was down to about 25 percent. And, the dispirited staff totally overestimated the numerical strength, weapons, and morale of the North Korean enemy just as badly as they had underestimated these factors three months earlier. The fact was that the North Koreans had taken a tremendous mauling in trying to achieve the breakthrough into Pusan by September 1 that had been ordered by North Korean President Kim Il Sung. The cost had been extremely high. Eighth Army intelligence estimated the NK 15th Division strength at 7,000 men. Actually it numbered about 500 at this point. The NK 13th Division was estimated at 8,000. Actually it numbered 2,300 men. And all the other units of the North Korean People's Army on the Pusan Perimeter were far weaker in men and weapons than the Americans suspected. One enemy battalion, for example, actually counted noses and equipment. The whole battalion consisted of 6 officers and 34 noncommissioned officers, and 111 privates. They had three pistols, nine carbines, fifty-seven rifles, thirteen automatic rifles, six light machine guns, and ninety-two grenades. In other words, this battalion was the equivalent of an understrength and underarmed company.

This battalion was in worse shape than most, but the whole North Korean Army in the south was in bad shape. Of the ninety thousand men who had invaded the south, more than sixty thousand had been casualties. The casualties had been replaced mostly with raw recruits, and most of these were from South Korea. Few of the South Koreans were eager to fight for North Korea, and they were kept in line only because they had seen enough incidents to know that their officers would shoot to kill if they tried to escape or if they failed to move forward when ordered. Morale of the North Korean People's Army was at its lowest ebb.

In effect, the UN forces were far stronger than the North Koreans. They had more men, more equipment, and their preponderance of guns and tanks was at least five to one. It seems remarkable that the American intelligence officers had so little understanding of the true situation. Part of this was a linguistic problem; even after years of occupation of South Korea few American military men spoke the language. But more important, they simply did not get proper briefing and intelligence from the ROK forces, either through negligence, incompetence, or the unwillingness of the local population to assist the ROK Army.

Because of this misconception the morale of the UN troops was not a great deal better than that of the North Koreans. Too many defeats, too many casualties, too much concern over the strength of the enemy had sapped them. General Walker realized the extent of the problem, and that is why he delayed the "jump-off" of the troops for twenty-four hours after the Inchon landings. He wanted his men to have the lift they would get from knowing the X Corps had landed behind the enemy and was driving on Seoul.

Just after dawn on September 16, eighty-two B-29 bombers crossed the coastline of South Korea from their bases on Okinawa and Japan and headed for the Pusan Perimeter around Waegwan. They were to deliver a saturation bombing that was to stun the North Korean troops and make it easy for the U.S. 38th Regiment to cross the Naktong River. However, the morning of September 16 dawned with a heavy overcast and heavy rain. Typhoon Kezia may have blown out over Japan, but she was hanging on over

BREAKING THE CORDON
16-22 September 1950

FORWARD POSITIONS, EVENING, 15 SEP
FORWARD POSITIONS, EVENING, 22 SEP

Elevations in meters

10   0   10 MILES
10   0   10 KILOMETERS

Map 6.

(U.S. Army)

Korea, and the air commander found it impossible to bomb so close to his own troops. So the B-29s went on up the peninsula to strike secondary targets at Pyongyang and Wonsan. The raid may have been valuable in the great scheme of the war, but it didn't do the Eighth Army a bit of good in its hour of need.

So the troops waiting for the bombing attack would have to move without it. And while they were waiting for their H-Hour of 9 A.M., the North Koreans were attacking at several points along the perimeter. As far as the enemy troops were concerned they were still committed to drive on to Pusan. Nobody had told them about the Inchon landings and nobody would tell them for a week.

Without the expected air support, the big drive up the center bogged down completely. That first day the only significant gains made by the UN forces were by the ROK 1st Division (they never expected much in the way of either air or artillery support), which drove through the enemy line near the old Walled City north of Taegu. Surprisingly, in the south, the U.S. 2nd Division broke through five miles to the hills above the Naktong.

But what happened that day in the 2nd Division area is indicative of the state of the fighting:

The division was scheduled to launch a three-regiment attack. On the right (see Map 6) the 38th Infantry would move out. In the center so would the 23rd Infantry. On the left the 9th Infantry would attack Hill 201.

The 9th Infantry came up against the North Korean 4th Infantry and failed to take Hill 201. The North Korean 9th Division did not wait for nine o'clock, but launched one of its night attacks before dawn, which penetrated the 23rd Infantry lines and caused twenty-five casualties, including all the officers of Company C, which was in the line of attack.

But the 3rd Battalion of the 23rd Infantry attacked at 10 A.M., supported by tanks. The battle seesawed until midafternoon, when the North Koreans began to give ground. Soon they vacated their dug-in positions and retreated back toward the Naktong. American artillery and tanks cut them off and from high ground poured heavy weapons fire into the enemy as they tried to move down the bank of the Naktong. As the skies cleared in late afternoon, F-80 jets and F-51 fighters came down through the holes in the overcast and strafed. The North Korean 9th Division was not in good shape before this action. At the end of it, the division scarcely remained as a unit.

On the right of the American line, the 38th Infantry regiment also moved ahead, helped immeasurably by air strikes from the P-51s using napalm and rockets. The fighters panicked some of the enemy and then strafed the retreating groups as they headed for the river. The NK 2nd Division withdrew totally and moved its command post across the river.

Thus, although the drive north did not get anywhere on that first day, the UN forces had gone on the offensive.

In the south, Major General William B. Kean faced a serious problem in trying to get his 25th Division on the left flank of the line moving. Once again the problem involved the 24th Infantry Regiment, which had performed so badly in the fighting of the summer months that Kean had asked that it be dissolved and the troops reassigned. That request had been turned down for political reasons by higher authority (the 24th Infantry was a black regiment). But the order to use the 24th Infantry did not mean that the unit would perform any better than it had before. General Kean was supposed to advance along the roads to Chinju. Those roads were located on both sides of a mountainous area held by the North Koreans against the 24th Infantry, which had failed completely to dislodge the enemy. The 35th Infantry on one side and the 27th Infantry on the other could not move ahead, leaving a large number of enemy troops in the center. So until the mountain areas called Battle Mountain and Sobuk-san could be cleared, there could be no advance.

To solve the problem, General Kean organized a battalion task force under Major Robert L. Woolfolk to drive through the Battle Mountain area.

On September 17, in the northwest area of the line the picture seemed a little brighter. The sky was still heavily overcast in the morning with many rain squalls, and no B-29 missions could be scheduled. But the planes stood by, waiting for a call. And as soon as the weather cleared over the Naktong, the fighter planes came in to attack the retreating North Korean soldiers. In the 38th Regiment's area, three enemy regiments were trying to cross. They were harried constantly by the P-51s, and the retreat became a rout with the abandonment of large quantities of equipment. The pilots returned to tell air intelligence officers their stories, and they added up to 1,200 North Koreans killed trying to cross the river. West of Changyong the American infantry captured nineteen artillery pieces and eighteen antitank guns and many mortars and machine guns.

But in the north, the fighting was not going well. The 1st Cavalry Division was held up by a strong North Korean defense at the walled city of Tabu-dong. Fighter bombers dropped many tanks of napalm there that day. They also bombed and strafed many North Korean groups around Pohang.

In the south, Major Woolfolk's battalion attacked the heights of the mountain area, but were driven back.

At Eighth Army headquarters, General Walker was eager to get his main offensive off the ground, but that offensive depended on air power to stun the North Koreans so that the American infantry could cross the river. The news was bad these first two days but late on September 17 Walker had a glimmer of hope from the meteorologists. It should begin clearing the next day, they said. So Walker ordered up air strikes for September 18: B-29 Superfortress attacks on two target areas, each 250,000 yards square, which lay on the sides of the Naktong at Waegwan, where the rail and road bridges crossed.

As dawn came up over the Naktong, forty-two B-29s of the 92nd and 98th Bombardment groups laid sixteen hundred 500-pound bombs in those two areas.

As the offensive began, over on the east side of the peninsula the ROK II Corps faced the enemy 8th and 15th divisions. Both of these units had been exhausted by the fighting in early September, but for that matter the ROK troops were nearly exhausted themselves. The ROK high command decided to try a commando-type operation. Ships of the American task force carried a special guerrilla battalion, supposedly highly trained, to land at Changsa-dong, ten miles north of Pohang-dong. The idea was to harry the rear of the North Korean 5th Division, while the ROK 3rd Division attacked from the south toward Pohang-dong.

The tonic news of the landings at Inchon did marvels for South Korean morale, and on September 16 the ROK 6th Division began to move. The move was supported by Rear Admiral Charles C. Hartman's Task Group, which included the big battleship *Missouri,* now out of mothballs. The one-ton shells of the battleship's 16-inch guns did a great deal to help when it appeared off Pohang-dong.

As the American counterattack began, perhaps the hardest fighting was in the arc just above Taegu, where the U.S. 1st Cavalry Division and the ROK 1st Division faced elements of the North Koreans' 1st, 3rd, and 13th divisions. Sixty percent of the casualties in the first two days of fighting occurred in this sector. The 1st Cavalry's major mission was to hold these troops and allow the 5th Regimental Combat Team to move across the Naktong and head westward.

On September 17 the 24th Division was ordered to cross the Naktong. First it had to cross a big tributary, the Kumho, which arches around Taegu. Then it was to cross the Naktong near the Hasan-dong ferry west of Taegu. The crossing would first be made by the 21st Infantry in assault boats. The regiment would then attack north along the west bank of the river to a point opposite Waegwan at the highway to Kumchon. Other elements, including the 19th Infantry, would cross farther south and block the road to Songju which was an enemy strong point. But on the morning of September 18, when the 21st Infantry reached the Kumho, they discovered that the engineers had failed in their task of bridging that river. So there was delay while the engineers repaired an underwater bridge (just below the surface) so that the troops and vehicles could cross. Jeeps had to be ferried across. As night approached, a line of vehicles five miles long backed up at the Kumho. It was obvious that the 21st Infantry would never reach the Naktong that day.

Over on the east coast, the guerrilla battalion behind the North Korean lines had gotten into difficulty. The North Koreans here showed a flash of their old spark and the ROK troops showed a flash of their old confusion. The North Koreans sent a battalion into the hills where the guerillas had gone and completely routed them. They fled to the coast. On September 18 the American naval forces operating off the east coast came inshore and picked the ROK survivors off the beach.

On September 18 patrols of the U.S. 38th Infantry crossed the Naktong River near Changyong and found the high ground west of the river clear of enemy. Colonel George Peploe, the regimental commander, ordered the 2nd Battalion to secure a bridgehead across the Naktong. By rubber boat about three hundred troops of the battalion made it across the twelve-foot-deep river. During the day's light fighting they captured about a hundred and thirty prisoners and discovered several caches of ammunition and supplies, including a number of new rifles still in their packing. That indicated the rear echelons of the North Korean People's Army were still sending down supplies as of mid-September, for in the battling of the first part of the month the North Koreans had been very short of rifles. The Americans captured Hill 308, which dominated the Changyong–Chogye road. (See Map 6) This was the first breakout of any unit of the Eighth Army. But the 38th Infantry's line still was ragged. In the south, the NK 9th Division still held the height called Hill 201, which had been the scene of so much action in the last few weeks. To the north, troops of the NK 10th Division held Hill 409. These would have to be cleared before the regiment could make a general advance. So would a large number of small bands of enemy troops, cut off from their own lines, who were moving around behind the 2nd Division front.

That day the 38th Infantry's advance was unique. The 23rd Infantry sent a large patrol to cross the Naktong but it was driven back by heavy enemy fire from the west shore. The Fifth Air Force provided heavy air support for the 1st Cavalry Division in the center of the line, along the Tabu-dong–Sangju road and this included P-51 strafing and napalm attacks in close support of the troops, sometimes only fifty yards ahead of the U.S. positions. Even so, the

North Koreans in this sector held firm, and the 1st Cavalry Division was unable to break out.

The 5th Regimental Combat Team was moving slowly north along the Naktong River road toward Waegwan. Weeks of fighting had left this unit badly depleted. Instead of the usual eight hundred-plus men of each battalion, the three battalions could each muster about six hundred. But the news of Inchon had boosted their morale and they were moving.

In the south, General Kean's 25th Division was still stalled, the 27th and 35th regiments on left and right ready to move up the Chinju roads, but the 24th Infantry bogged down behind Battle Mountain. Major Woolfolk's special battalion attacked again on September 18, supported by two field artillery battalions and a number of air strikes from the Fifth Air Force. Again it was driven back down the heights with heavy casualties. The whole effort seemed a failure, so that night the special battalion was dissolved.

On the east coast on September 18 the *Missouri* came inshore again to assist the ROK 3rd Division, which was engaged in a desperate battle to cross the river at Pohang-dong. The enemy on the dikes on the other side had been ordered not to let them pass, and the machine gunners were ordered to die in their positions. Following the shelling by the *Missouri,* elements of the ROK 3rd Division tried to cross and lost about two hundred men, without making it. Later in the day thirty-one ROK troops volunteered to die if necessary to make that crossing, and they started over. Nineteen Korean soldiers fell, but eleven made the other side and gained control of the crossing. The North Korean machine gunners did indeed die at their guns.

All night long on September 18–19 the engineers tried to hurry the 21st Infantry's crossing of the Kumho and get the men up to the Naktong. But it was five thirty on the morning of the 19th before the first assault boats pushed off into the Naktong River six miles below Waegwan. Across the river lay the height called Hill 174 and a long finger of high ground that dominated the crossing site. The boats moved out into midstream, and the first wave launched. Almost at that moment the enemy began firing from both flanks and caught the infantrymen in a vicious crossfire. Enemy mortars and artillery then began shooting on both sides of the river and at the vessels in midstream. The 1st Battalion suffered 120 casualties in the crossing and for a time it seemed that the whole move would have to be abandoned. But the air force came to the rescue and sent in fighter planes with napalm, which quieted down the guns on Hill 174. The 1st Battalion reorganized on the west shore of the river and by noon had captured Hill 174. That relieved the pressure and the 2nd and 3rd battalions were able to cross during that night.

That same day, Hill 201 in the 9th Infantry sector still caused problems.

The 1st and 2nd battalions of the 23rd Infantry came up to help. A platoon of tanks ran up the hill to the summit and paved the way for the infantry to capture the last part of that stronghold. So, the way was clear for the entire 2nd Division to cross the Naktong.

That same day, farther south, the 19th Infantry began the Naktong crossing at four o'clock in the afternoon. Enemy fire was strong as long as the Americans were on the east bank, and crossing, and the regiment suffered about fifty casualties. But once they hit the west bank, the North Koreans retreated, and the Americans moved toward the high ground along the Songju road.

On September 19, the 38th Infantry's 3rd Battalion crossed the Naktong and was followed by artillery and tanks. The 3rd Battalion would take over Hill 308, enabling the 2nd Battalion to advance. But if the advance was to succeed it would depend on a steady line of supply and more heavy equipment, so the engineers began construction of a pontoon bridge to replace the Changyong–Chogye highway bridge, which had been destroyed in the earlier fighting.

On September 19, the 38th Infantry moved in the south central area, and the 5th RCT began to attack Hill 268, southeast of Waegwan, which was the key to the North Korean line and the control of Waegwan.

This hill was held by troops of the NK 3rd Division. They had artillery and tanks, and their morale seemed strong for they fought hard. The 5th RCT's 3rd Battalion won part of the hill before nightfall, but the North Koreans still had the northeast slope. About two hundred troops were holding the position in log-covered bunkers with interconnecting trenches. Still, the Americans were now able to move around the hill. The 1st Battalion headed northwest and the 2nd Battalion captured Hill 121, which was just a mile south of Waegwan. Except for those stout defenders of Hill 268, the troops of the NK 3rd Division began to lose heart and their unit control unraveled as swiftly as had that of the Americans and South Koreans in the opening phases of the war. Air strikes were an important factor in destroying North Korean morale. It was unsettling for the North Korean soldiers to see planes flying overhead all day long, searching out the troop concentrations, and to know that they had to be UN planes because the North Korean air force had been so badly decimated in the last two months.

The combined attack along the line finally broke the NK 3rd Division. That morning of September 19 what must have been two battalions panicked and rushed to the bank of the Naktong just north of Waegwan to cross over to the safety of the western side. At about 9 A.M. they were caught by F-80 jet fighters and B-26 bombers in the open, and the planes came in to slaughter.

By midmorning, hundreds of troops in Waegwan, a major command post, began fleeing along the roads out of that city, abandoning artillery, machine guns, and even their small arms. The flight continued all day long.

On the east coast, the ROK 3rd Division managed to get patrols into the now ruined fishing village of Pohang-dong by evening of September 19. The next day they captured the place.

On September 19 in the southwest area, patrols on Battle Mountain discovered that Major Woolfolk's attacks had not been in vain as believed. The North Koreans had abandoned the crest of the mountain during the night. The 1st Battalion of the 24th Infantry moved up to the top and occupied it. On the right the 35th Infantry could now get moving. The movement went swiftly until the 1st Battalion reached the Chungam-ni area. There the North Koreans concealed in holes in the ground let them pass, and then they fired on them from the rear. This stopped the advance until the area could be cleared of enemy troops. Meanwhile, on the left, the 27th Infantry was stalled by the strong defensive action of the North Koreans of the NK 6th Infantry Division.

On September 20 the men of the 5th RCT's 3rd Battalion renewed their assault on the bunkers of Hill 268. At midday a number of F-51 fighters came in to drop napalm on the bunkers and they set the logs afire. The American soldiers pushed hard, and the North Koreans slowly gave ground and finally retreated from the hill, leaving about two hundred dead, including a regimental commander.

Meanwhile the men of the 1st and 2nd battalions of the 5th RCT were pushing forward on both sides of the hill and chasing North Korean soldiers toward the river. On the afternoon of September 20, the two battalions met inside Waegwan, and by midafternoon, the 2nd Battalion had passed through the town, surprising a group of North Korean engineers who were just then trying to lay a minefield along the road. For, as Major General Hobart Gay, commander of the 1st Cavalry Division, said with some relish, with the capture of Waegwan, and the breakout from the Naktong line, Inchon and Seoul lay ahead with no natural defenses of any importance between. "From now on," the general said, "it's a tank battle." What the North Koreans had done to the UN forces at the beginning of the war, General Gay now proposed to do to the People's Army.

That evening, the 1st Battalion of the 5th RCT began crossing to the west bank of the Naktong a mile above the old Waegwan railroad bridge and moved a mile to the west. The 2nd Battalion crossed over that night as well. This move rolled up the entire north end and part of the center of the line held by the North Korean 3rd Division, and meant the rest of the division to the south would have to withdraw or be surrounded.

Over to the east coast, the ROK 3rd Division began to gather momentum, driving toward Yongdok, with support from American warships and UN fighters.

In the south, the 27th Infantry was still held up on the lower road to Chinju by the NK 6th Division. But on the upper road, the 35th Infantry captured Chungam-ni. On September 21 the regiment captured The Notch, which had been the scene of so much bloody fighting in August, and then began to roll on, without opposition. To the south, the 24th Infantry and the 27th Infantry moved up, slowed only by the terrain, because the North Koreans had retreated ahead of them. There were still casualties, because some stragglers had been left behind, and they invaded the bivouac areas of the 24th Infantry, which was not keeping its perimeter guard properly, and killed a number of officers and men.

The North Korean 6th and 7th divisions were withdrawing northwest as swiftly as they could. The only major fighting came on September 22, when the North Koreans held Chinju Pass all day long against the 35th Infantry, to protect their line of retreat. On September 23 aerial observation showed that the North Koreans were in retreat all around the Pusan Perimeter. Indeed, there was no such thing as a perimeter any more. The Eighth Army in the south was now in position to pursue the North Koreans. As General MacArthur had predicted, the Inchon landing had already turned the war around.

5

Kimpo

Just after dawn the quiet of Inchon harbor was broken by the sound of aircraft engines. Aboard the cruiser *Rochester,* anchored off Wolmi-do, a sentry on the fantail saw two planes coming in low. They were a Yak-3 and a Stormovik Il-10, and their intentions were obviously unfriendly. The sentry began firing his rifle. The planes bored in and dropped bombs. One 100-pound bomb glanced off the cruiser's aircraft retrieval crane, but did not explode. The others blew up in the water nearby, causing no damage.

Three miles away the British cruiser *Jamaica* was anchored and she was the next target. The two planes came in, with machine guns and cannon spitting. The fire killed one sailor and wounded two. But unlike the crew of the *Rochester,* the men of the *Jamaica* were on their toes this morning, and their antiaircraft guns began to bark. The Stormovik crashed into the sea, although the Yak-3 got away.

On the night of September 16, when the 5th Marines were bivouacked astride the road to Seoul in the Ascom City area, a lone North Korean truck drove into the American lines and was captured. The officer and four men inside the truck had no idea that the Americans were so far advanced, for the commander of the NKPA 18th Division at Seoul seemed to have lost touch. That incident was followed the next morning by an unwitting counterattack by the North Koreans which proved the point.

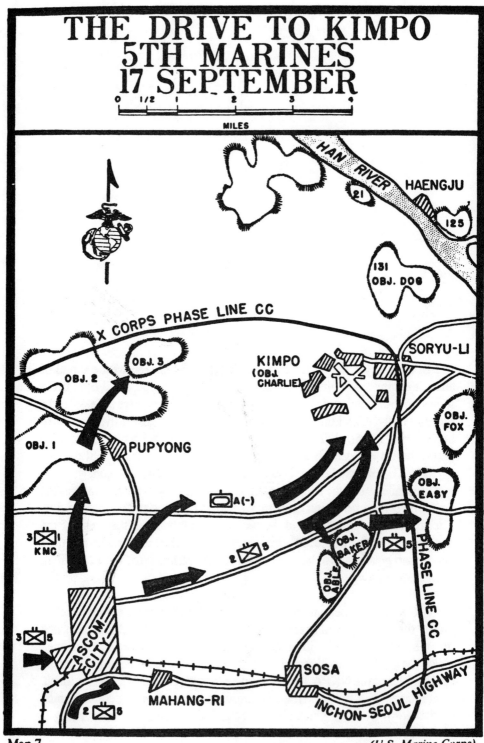

THE DRIVE TO KIMPO
5TH MARINES
17 SEPTEMBER

0 1/2 1   2   3   4

MILES

HAN RIVER

HAENGJU

21

125

131
OBJ. DOG

X CORPS PHASE LINE CC

SORYU-LI

OBJ. 3

OBJ. 2

KIMPO
(OBJ. CHARLIE)

OBJ. 1

PUPYONG

OBJ. FOX

OBJ. EASY

A(-)

3 ⊠ 1
KMC

2 ⊠ 5

OBJ. BAKER

1 ⊠ 5

PHASE LINE CC

OBJ. ABLE

3 ⊠ 5

ASCOM CITY

SOSA

MAHANG-RI

INCHON-SEOUL HIGHWAY

2 ⊠ 5

Map 7.

(U.S. Marine Corps)

The 5th Marines position near Ascom City controlled the three hills above the railroad and the road. (See Map 7.) M-26 tanks were along and across the highway. Atop the hills the marines had placed machine guns, bazookas, and 75 mm recoilless rifles. They were ready for trouble. It came in the form of a North Korean column that moved down the road from Seoul at dawn into the Ascom City area, led by six T-34 tanks, with infantry riding on top. The column was spotted first by Lieutenant Lee R. Howard of Company D, from his vantage point on the leading knoll at the edge of Ascom City. He reported back that six tanks were coming up, but Colonel Roise was skeptical. Lieutenant Howard was a second lieutenant without much experience and Colonel Roise knew that unblooded second lieutenants were prone to illusion. It seemed unbelievable that half a dozen tanks would come grinding into the maw of the enemy without a scouting force.

But Lieutenant Howard was not seeing things or exaggerating in the slightest. He saw that the North Koreans on the tanks were anything but tense. They were laughing and relaxed, and he did not believe they suspected there were Americans near. His next move was hardly that of a tyro. He let the lead of the column slip by below, and then when the leaders had moved into the trap between his hill and the next where the antitank guns were clustered, and the platoon of M-26 tanks across the road, Lieutenant Howard ordered his machine gunners, BAR men, and riflemen to open fire on the infantry. They did, and shot a number of them off the tanks, and shot others as they moved along the road. Corporal Okey J. Douglas moved down the knoll with his 2.36-inch bazooka until he was about seventy-five yards from the lead tank. He fired several rockets and destroyed this tank. He then fired more and damaged the second tank.

The four other tanks and the damaged tank slewed around the bend in the road below Lieutenant Howard's knoll, trying to get off the road into the rice paddy where they would have room to maneuver. But they had run into a real hornet's nest. The platoon of M-26 tanks across the road opened fire on them with their 90 mm guns. The antitank company's 75 mm recoilless rifles began firing. The 2nd Battalion's assault platoon added to the fire with its 3.5 mm bazookas. In five minutes all the T-34 tanks were wrecked and burning and two hundred North Korean infantrymen lay dead along and around the roadway. The marines suffered one casualty, a rifleman slightly wounded.

The smoke from the brief battle had not yet cleared when up the road from Inchon came a caravan of jeeps. General MacArthur was coming to visit the front, with his whole entourage: Admiral Struble, Commanding General Almond of the X Corps, five other generals, and a larger assortment of colonels and lieutenant colonels. Right behind them were more jeeps loaded with press photographers and reporters. They all stopped at the scene of the carnage and MacArthur got out. The press got out and flash bulbs began popping and cameras whizzing.

"... A good sight for my old eyes," the general said, as he observed the carnage. He might have remarked, if someone had explained what had just occurred to him, that the T-34 tanks that in the beginning of the war the army infantry had said they could not stop with the 2.36-inch bazooka had not held up very well this time. The fact was that Corporal Douglas knew what had to be done: he had opened the tank battle from seventy yards, which was the killing distance for his weapon.

In a few moments, MacArthur and his entourage were gone. They had come up searching for Colonel Puller of the 1st Marines and had found him up front as usual. The general had announced that he was giving Puller a Silver Star medal, and then he had awarded others to General Craig and Lieutenant Colonel Murray, and two more to ROK officers in the interest of Allied amity, and he had finally arrived at the 5th Marines' position, where he and his entourage really ought not to have been at all. Shortly after their departure the marines routed seven armed North Korean soldiers out of the culvert on which MacArthur's jeep had been parked. If MacArthur's luck had not been with him that day, President Truman would have been looking for a new commander.

On September 17, the 5th Marines were to lead the attack on Kimpo airfield. MacArthur was extremely urgent in his request for early capture of this field for it was the largest air base in all of Korea, a mile long and three-quarters of a mile wide. Once it was secured, the Fifth Air Force could bring fighters and bombers up from Japan to operate more easily against North Korea. The 3rd Korean Marine Battalion was attached to the 5th Marines for this operation and its task was first to clear the western end of Ascom City and then advance to high ground on the left (objectives 1, 2, 3 on Map 7). The 2nd Battalion of the 5th Marines would advance in the center against several points, including Kimpo airfield. The 1st Battalion would veer off to the right to take the high ground there.

The Korean marines moved out at 7 A.M. The 5th Marines were delayed by the North Korean tank fight, but they were in motion by nine o'clock, with Company E in the lead. This whole area around Ascom City was ideal for defense by small units, because it had been built up by the Americans during the occupation as a service center. It consisted of many roads and streets, buildings, houses, and warehouses. Captain Samuel Jaskilka's Company E had to stop repeatedly to deal with small pockets of resistance. The process took up the entire morning, and neither they nor the Korean marines found all the enemy in the area.

Meanwhile, Company F marched through Ascom City proper, and the 3rd Battalion of the regiment moved north to help the Korean marines clear their area, because they were running into heavy resistance, and the tank platoon threaded its way toward Kimpo to participate in the assault. A broken bridge across a small stream held them up for a while. As it was being repaired by the engineers and Korean villagers, another platoon of tanks came up.

Back at Ascom City, Lieutenant Colonel Murray moved his command post to a point north of the railroad station, and his staff fanned out on their duties. Warrant Officer Bill E. Parrish had to find a site for the regimental ordnance dump. With a patrol he crossed the railroad tracks and climbed a little hill to take a look around. When he reached the top he looked over at an orchard and rice paddy beyond. Suddenly small arms began to crackle. Warrant Officer Parrish fell dead, and two of his men were wounded. Down there in the orchard were North Korean infantrymen.

The fusillade was heard at the command post and Lieutenant Nicholas A. Canzona brought a platoon of Company A engineers to the knoll, and they engaged the North Koreans. They killed ten soldiers, and South Korean police flushed out another seven prisoners.

At about the same time, Major James D. Jordan came up to find a site for Battery A of the 11th Field Artillery and his group also came under small arms fire. Technical Sergeant Kenneth C. Boston and Technical Sergeant Donald Comiskey went forward and killed four more North Korean soldiers.

And there was still one more incident that day near the command post and another marine was killed. So, although the marines were gaining ground rapidly, it was obvious that they were leaving pockets of the enemy behind, a matter that would have to be dealt with, and one that meant a course of caution was in order.

The attack on Kimpo airfield was carried out by Colonel Roise's 2nd Battalion. The men started out cautiously but soon learned that the North Koreans had abandoned positions on the hills around the airfield and speeded up their movement. They ran into no resistance on the hills called Objective Able and Objective Baker and the ground ahead seemed clear. Colonel Roise's battalion moved ahead, bothered only by a little sniper fire. The tanks came up on the left and encountered some enemy infantry. These were troops of the 877th Air Force Defense Unit. Tanks and infantrymen soon disposed of this resistance, killing the 877th's commander in the process.

By six o'clock that evening the main runway of the airfield was in sight. By dark, the southern portion of the runway was in the hands of the marines. It was too late to go further. Colonel Roise ordered his company commanders to create their own perimeters. Before this could be done, however, Lieutenant Edwin A. Deptula's platoon had raced north to occupy the village of Soryu-li, ahead of the company line. Company E dug in on the east side of the long main runway, with Deptula's platoon isolated out front. Company D dug in on the west, and the tanks joined it there. Company F put down on the south side, with a roadblock across the road to Ascom City.

Lieutenant Colonel Newton's 1st Battalion had come up on the right, to points about a mile southeast of the 2nd Battalion with Company A taking the southern part of Objective Easy. (See Map 7.) Company B took the northern part. Company C bivouacked on a hill to the west. The 3rd Battalion was in reserve, about two miles behind across the road to Ascom City.

That night there was more trouble back at the regimental command post. A North Korean officer came through the perimeter and wounded Lieutenant Lawrence Hetrick of the engineers, then escaped back across the line.

That night at Kimpo, the North Koreans were organizing their defense of the airfield. The unexpectedness of the Inchon landing had caught the North Koreans without adequate defenses in this area. Kimpo was under the command of Brigadier General Wan Yong. His troops were a conglomeration of half-trained fighting men and service forces. One of his two infantry regiment commanders had already fled across the Han River toward Seoul to escape the fight. The general was supposed to stop a marine division with tanks on flat land backed up by the wide river. The position was almost as bad as the morale of the men who, by the second day of the invasion, realized that they were not going to get any help from the North Korean officials in Seoul. The problem was underlined when white coats, trousers, and rubber shoes were issued to the men, so that they could don them and slip away among the white-clad civilian population as the fight was lost.

The general decided that a night attack was the best countermove he could make. This tactic was borrowed from the Chinese Communist armies (in which he had been trained) and had been used successfully against the Americans in the early part of the war. But a successful night attack presupposed a highly disciplined body of troops, and here General Wan had a problem: the combination of poorly trained infantry, engineers, air maintenance crews, finance units, and quartermaster troops could hardly be called commando material.

The first North Korean assault came against the weakest point of the American line—Lieutenant Deptula's platoon stuck out in front of the Company E perimeter. At 3 A.M. the North Koreans made their move,

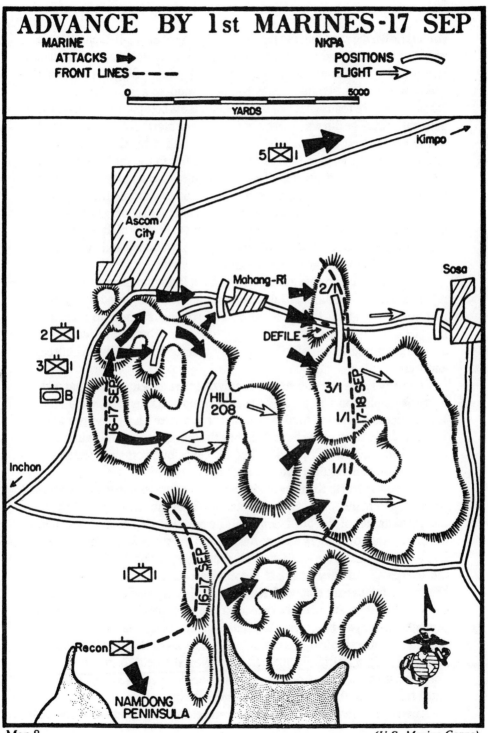

ADVANCE BY 1st MARINES · 17 SEP

MARINE
ATTACKS ➡
FRONT LINES – – –

NKPA
POSITIONS
FLIGHT ⇒

0   5000
YARDS

5🔲1   Kimpo

Ascom
City

Mahang-Ri   2/1   Sosa

DEFILE

2🔲1

3🔲1   3/1

▢B   1/1   17-18 SEP

16-17 SEP   HILL
             208

Inchon   1/1

16-17 SEP

1🔲1

Recon🔲

NAMDONG
PENINSULA

Map 8.   (U.S. Marine Corps)

coming down the road that ran through the village of Soryu-li. Deptula's men were dug in on both sides of that road at a junction. Deptula held fire until the enemy had marched into the village, and then up jumped Sergeant Richard L. Marston, shouting "United States Marines," and spraying shots from his carbine along the road. That was the signal for the whole platoon to open with automatic fire. The din was enormous and a dozen North Korean soldiers fell. The others turned and ran. Soon they were rallied by their officers and attacked again, but again the marines opened fire in the same manner and again the North Koreans fled. Two more times, the commander brought them back (the marines recognized his voice) and two more times they were driven back. Finally a T-34 tank came up to lend them courage and power, and Lieutenant Deptula rallied his men to retreat to the line of the company in the south. They made it back, with only one man wounded and one killed in the four contacts with the North Koreans.

The next attack came against Company E not long after Deptula's men had rejoined. At first Captain Jaskilka believed he was being fired on by other marines of Company D. He stood up and shouted at them to stop. This unusual action must have surprised the North Koreans because he was not hit. Just as he realized his mistake the company came under attack from both east and west.

Company F was also engaged by enemy counterattacking forces that night. The assault platoon was holding the area around an overpass, and a North Korean demolition team tried to blow the bridge. (See Map 8.) Sergeant Ray D. Kearl drove them off by himself, killing the officer leading the unit and two of the men. There were other scattered incidents, but, perhaps because they were so disorganized, they came to nothing.

At dawn, the North Koreans made their last attempt to stop the Americans, coming up from the south against the marines. They moved across the front of the 1st Battalion of the 5th Marines and were sighted. The marines called down a barrage of artillery and mortar fire and the attack was blunted before it reached the line of the 2nd Battalion. Only one platoon managed to reach the overpass, and they attacked the engineer unit. The engineers fought briskly, Staff Sergeant Robert J. Kifka was killed as was Sergeant David R. De Armond, but the marines drove off the attackers, and they retreated through the rice paddies toward the Han River. By midmorning they were all gone, and Kimpo airfield was securely in the hands of the marines. The first Allied aircraft, a marine helicopter, landed on the field, bringing General Shepherd up for a look. Colonel Roise's troops held Hill 131, which dominated the bank of the Han north of the airfield.

General Shepherd found that Kimpo airfield was in excellent shape; the enemy had not had time to do any major demolition. In fact, several enemy planes were still on the field, intact. A number of others had been destroyed by the North Koreans. So Kimpo now could become the center of Allied land-based air operations for the drive north. The progressive use of helicopters for air evacuation of wounded, for reconnaissance, and to attack, would be one of the hallmarks of the Korean War.

The capture of Kimpo also meant the fighter planes could come up and two days after the marines drove onto the field, Marine Air Group 33 fighter planes launched their first missions from the field, striking enemy troop concentrations and the rail lines. The 5th Marines now waited at Kimpo for the 1st Marines to accomplish their objectives and come up along the Inchon–Seoul highway to the south, to capture Sosa, and drive on Yongdungpo.

Comparatively speaking, the 5th Marines had found the going easy. Colonel Puller's 1st Marines encountered much more stringent opposition on the drive along the Seoul highway, starting that morning of September 17.

As that column of T-34 tanks and infantry had moved up against the 5th Marines that morning, farther south a column of North Korean infantry had moved along the hills south of the Inchon–Seoul road, apparently in an attempt to outflank the Americans as they had done so often in the south. But it was apparent that the North Korean intelligence in this sector of Korea was not nearly so successful as it had been in the south; the North Koreans were unaware of the strength and disposition of the marine forces, because their "flanking" force consisted of only about a company of men. This force was dispersed that morning by Company F of the 2nd Battalion. Instead of fleeing, however, these troops moved up onto a hill southeast of Ascom City and set up a defense. They controlled the highway at Mahang-ri, a village half a mile from Ascom City, and had to be ousted. Hill 208, as it was called, was not easy to take. It sprawled southward and was large enough to command the attention of the entire 2nd Battalion. Advancing along the road, the 2nd Platoon of Company E was pinned down by fire from two hills and a roadblock in front. It was reinforced by Lieutenant Johnny L. Carter, and bazookas and 75 mm fire were brought against a group of huts where North Koreans were holed up. These were destroyed. The platoon then advanced to a hill to the right of the roadblock and the two other platoons came up. But it was noon before Hill 208 were secured, and Mahang-ri was still in enemy hands, blocking the road.

The 3rd Battalion's Company G came up to Mahang-ri, led by a platoon of tanks. Someone spotted the snout of an 85 mm gun sticking out of a hut, and an M-26 tank turned its attention there. Two 90 mm armor-piercing shells later the T-34 tank that had been concealed in the hut blew up. Shelling of other huts brought an enormous explosion from one; obviously it had been an ammunition dump. But as the marine infantrymen tried to advance along the road, they were engaged sharply by a number of North Korean soldiers and the fighting began, the North Koreans firing and retreating, then firing again. It was four o'clock in the afternoon before the marines took Mahang-ri. They moved on.

The North Koreans had retreated about a mile further along the road to a defile—half the way to Sosa. (See Map 8.) Here they had mounted another delaying defense, which included antitank guns.

The marines first encountered this defense when Lieutenant Bryan Cummings' M-26 tank moved into the pass with an infantry detachment, several of the men riding on top. The tank was hit immediately by a heavy concentration of small arms, machine gun, and antitank gun fire. The tank's engine stopped. Lieutenant Cummings opened the hatch, looked around for riflemen, found one, yanked him inside and slammed the hatch as a spatter of bullets and grenades bounced off the tank. A grenade bounced in through the pistol port, exploded, and wounded Cummings and several others. North Koreans swarmed over the tank, but as they did, Sergeant Marion Altaire's M-26 moved up and swept the top of the tank with machine gun fire. North Koreans fell like sprayed flies and as the survivors ran back, down came a flight of marine fighters, which splashed the area with machine gun fire.

Staff Sergeant Arthur MacDonald led another section of the tank platoon into the defile. Those tanks engaged in a firefight with the antitank guns. MacDonald's tank lost a track and two others were damaged, but before the fight was over they had destroyed six antitank guns. On the south, Company G reached high ground above the pass, and that helped the men of the rest of the 2nd Battalion to take the ground on the left. On top they fired after the retreating North Koreans, but since darkness was on them, they established their perimeter and stopped at the defile for the night. Meanwhile the 3rd Battalion of the regiment had come up on the south, without much action. That night was quiet, except for the hammering fire of HMS *Kenya,* the British cruiser back in Inchon harbor, which was called on for fire on the Sosa area to keep the defenders quiet.

That night the North Koreans evacuated Sosa and moved back to high ground beyond. On the morning of September 18, the marines moved ahead with very little opposition and captured Sosa. (See Map 9.) Once again the southern units kept pace against even less opposition. On the night of September 18 they dug in along a north-south line at the eastern outskirts of Sosa on Hill 123. They had now come up even with the 5th Marines at

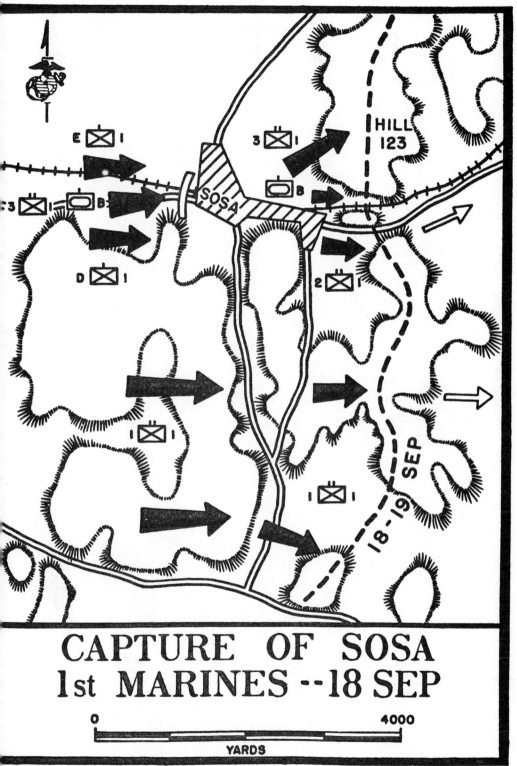

HILL 123

SOSA

18-19 SEP

E ⊠ 1
3 ⊠ 1
3 ⊠ 1
B
B
D ⊠ 1
2 ⊠ 1
1 ⊠ 1
1 ⊠ 1

CAPTURE OF SOSA
1st MARINES -- 18 SEP

0   4000

YARDS

Map 9.

Kimpo, and General Smith was prepared to drive to Yongdungpo and across the Han River.

6

The Road to Yongdungpo

The Inchon landing took the North Korean People's Army completely by surprise. Aware of the extreme difficulty under which the Americans had been operating in the south, they did not dream that General MacArthur would be able to launch a full-scale invasion of the north. It took the North Korean People's Army two days to realize that the invasion was real and not a feint. By that time Inchon was secured and the vital airfield at Kimpo was falling to the marines.

The initial press reports in Pyongyang and Peking indicated that an attempt had been made to land at Inchon but that it had been repelled. But as the marines continued to move toward Seoul the tenor of comment had to change. So did the activity of the North Korean military force. As noted, General Walker's Eighth Army was supposed to kick off on a drive to the north to compress the North Korean forces in an anvil movement. The drive was slow in getting started because the North Koreans were still thinking in terms of assaulting Pusan, and their orders were to hold and fight in the south. But on September 18 all this changed. One would expect that, in the south, General Walker would feel the change with the sudden softening of the ring around Pusan. The reason should have been that the North Korean I and II corps recognized the danger of being cut off from their lines of supply and their home territory, and would begin to move north to fight for the lines of communication that ran through the Seoul corridor.

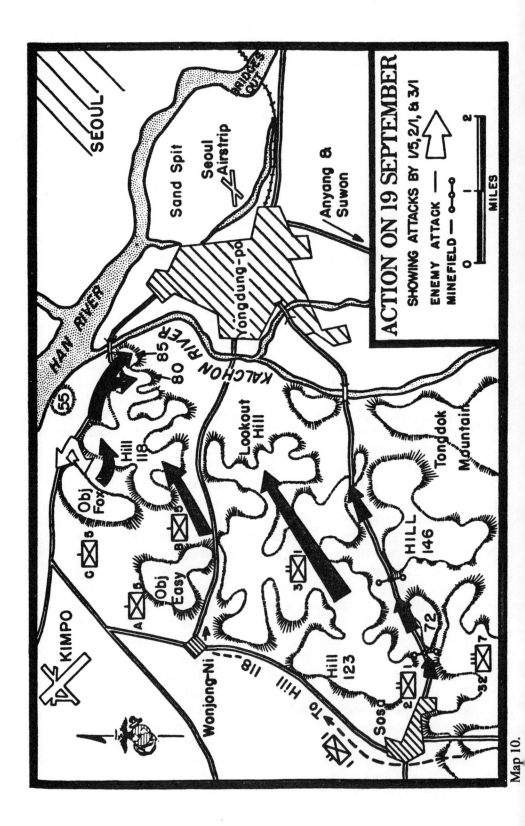

ACTION ON 19 SEPTEMBER

SHOWING ATTACKS BY 1/5, 2/1, & 3/1

ENEMY ATTACK ———
MINEFIELD — o-o-o

0   1   2
MILES

SEOUL

HAN RIVER

Sand Spit

Seoul Airstrip

BRIDGES OUT

Yongdung-po

Anyang & Suwon

KALCHON RIVER

55

80 85

Hill 118

Obj Fox

c 5

Lookout Hill

Tongdok Mountain

A 5

Obj Easy

3/1

HILL 146

KIMPO

Wonjong-Ni

To Hill 118

Hill 123

72

2/5

3/5

7

Soso

Map 10.

The Seoul area was then defended by the NK 18th Rifle Division—about 10,000 men, the Seoul City Regiment—about 3,500, an antiaircraft artillery regiment—1,200, about 3,500 special troops, such as security forces, plus the remnants of the Inchon and Kimpo defense forces that had been able to retreat. The plan, as of early September, was to divert the 18th Rifle Division to the south for the drive on Pusan, while other forces were on their way from North Korean territory. On the day after the landing Pusan had to be put aside in order to counter the new threat, the extent of which was not known. The movement of the 18th Division was stopped cold, and its commander was ordered to recapture Inchon—certainly an indication of the confusion in the North Korean ranks. In the deep south, the 105th Armored Division, newly arrived, was turned about toward the north. From Suwon, the 70th Regiment, in reserve from the southern fighting, was ordered back to defend the Seoul corridor and began moving. On September 18 marine aircraft operating along the Seoul–Pusan corridor spotted elements of armor and infantry going north. The planes reported buildup of supplies in the Yongdungpo area. (See Map 10.) Other information indicated that the North Koreans were mining the Sosa–Yongdungpo road in the face of the 1st Marine advance. Troops of the NK 9th Division appeared at Yongdungpo, and to the northwest, the North Koreans were digging in along the hills that protected Seoul. In the north, new units were headed down from Pyongyang and Kaesong and Chorwon. The ease with which MacArthur's new force had moved as far as Kimpo was illusory. The North Koreans were getting over their shock and preparing to fight off this threat to their lifeline to the south. But they were not panicking; the troops in the south still knew virtually nothing about the Inchon landings and General Walker's force was still bogged down. Only the senior officers knew that a new threat had appeared.

On the evening of September 18 the American line lay just east of the Kimpo-Sosa axis. About a thousand enemy troops in the Kumpo Peninsula (See Map 10.) were still caught between the marines and the Korean marines back in the Inchon–Ascom City area. The ROK 17th Army Regiment landed to help clear up that large space behind the marine lines.

The UN drive east now depended on capturing Yongdungpo, the industrial area which adjoins Seoul, and crossing the Han River. The 5th Marines on the north would have to cross the Han, and in connection with the 1st Marines would have to seize the high ground west of the Han's tributary, the Kalchon River, which acted as a defensive moat for Yongdungpo. The key to the advance in the middle was a high point called Hill 118 by the marines, but Paeksok by the Koreans. (See Map 10.)

As of the end of September 18, the 1st Battalion of the 5th Marines had taken the high ground just east of Kimpo airfield. The next day's work for Lieutenant Colonel Newton's troops would be Hill 118. At dawn they were to move.

But at dawn on September 19, the North Koreans moved first. A hail of machine gun and mortar fire rained down on Company C on "Objective Fox." (See Map 10.) Then perhaps two companies of enemy troops began to move toward the height. Another two companies headed along the Seoul–Kimpo highway, bent on recapturing the airfield. Company C stood and fought, and its mortars punched huge gaps in the enemy line. Meanwhile Company B moved up from the south and captured Hill 118 at 11 A.M. without suffering a single casualty. The North Koreans on the low ground were trapped between marines on the two hills, and they suffered. Finally they broke up into small bands and retreated toward the Han, having lost about three hundred men killed and a hundred captured. Marine casualties in the engagement were two killed and six wounded.

The next important points before the marines in this sector were Hills 80 and Hill 85, which overlooked the Kalchon on the northwest end of Yong-dungpo. The North Koreans were congregating here. As the marines advanced and the marine aircraft attacked from overhead, the North Koreans moved toward the Kalchon River bridge. The marine infantry called for artillery support, and the howizters at the rear began to fire. They did great damage in the enemy ranks, and they also knocked out the Kalchon River bridge by mistake. But by two o'clock that afternoon Company C was moving toward Hill 80 and Hill 85, covered by tanks. Before five o'clock that evening they took both heights. A combination of artillery fire and air strikes had taken the stuffing out of the North Koreans and there was almost no opposition.

That afternoon, the 1st Battalion of the 1st Marines got into trucks south of Sosa. These marines were to relieve the 1st Battalion of the 5th Marines on those heights, hills 118, 80, and 85. They were taken by road as far as the village of Wongjong-ni, but then they had to get down and march the rest of the eleven miles to their new positions. The road was too poor for truck traffic. It was late afternoon when Company A took over on Hill 118. Lieutenant Colonel Jack Hawkins, commander of the battalion, had a real problem. Companies B and C were supposed to take over Hill 80 and Hill 85, but darkness was falling and they still had not been brought up by truck to the marching point. What to do? Hawkins saw how difficult it would be to take over unknown ground in the dark, so he and Lieutenant Colonel Newton of the 5th Marines agreed that the 1st Marines would not try that night.

Newton's troops evacuated hills 80 and 85, and they became a no-man's-land. When Companies B and C came up, they dug in on or just below Hill 118.

During the twilight hours, Captain Robert H. Barrow of Company A did some looking around the battalion's position. He saw that Hill 80 and Hill 85 were enormously important, overlooking the river and Yongdungpo as they did, and he radioed battalion headquarters for permission to occupy those hills since Companies B and C would not be able to make it before dark. Permission was refused, because Lieutenant Colonel Hawkins had decided against spreading out too thin before dark.

While all this was happening in the north on September 19, the remainder of Colonel Puller's 1st Marines were moving just to the south. Their objective was a height known as Lookout Hill. (See Map 10.) They were slow getting started because they had to wait for the army's 31st Infantry to come up and occupy their positions before they could advance. The army regiment was green and slow, but that was not the real reason for the delay. The army unit commander did not know that he was supposed to be there on the morning of the 19th. His orders said to advance to the position and be prepared to move out on attack on the morning of the 20th. So the marines fidgeted while they waited. Finally at ten thirty in the morning Colonel Puller sent two battalions forward, leaving the reserves (1st Battalion) to hold the position until the army arrived. They did, and that is why they were so late in coming up to relieve Colonel Newton's 5th Marines on hills 80 and 85. Thus a failure in communications between army and marines created the situation in which two important points, once taken, were abandoned.

Late on the afternoon of September 19, the 3rd Battalion of the 1st Marines captured Lookout Hill and looked down upon Yongdungpo on the far side of the Kalchon.

The 2nd Battalion's task was to move along the Kimpo–Seoul highway, and they set out, led by tanks. They had moved forward only a quarter of a mile when they ran into a minefield, announced by an enormous explosion that blew a track off the leading M-26 tank. It had run over a Soviet-type wooden box mine. At the same time the troops came under fire from Hill 72 on their right.

The following tanks tried to pass around the shoulders of the road, but discovered that the North Korean engineers had done a good job with their minefield. They were stuck. They tried to blow up the mines with their machine guns, but that did not work. They were bogged down until the engineers came up and exploded the mines with small charges. Then the main roadway was cleared and the tanks moved on. (The shoulders were ignored and later accounted for several casualties to jeeps and other vehicles.)

The infantry did not wait for the bogged-down tanks. They moved on, under cover of artillery and air strikes. They were stopped by enemy troops on Hill 146. The North Koreans were dug in well. The road below the hill had been blocked by trees, sandbags, and broken machinery. The roadblock was effective and the enemy position on the height was dangerous. Actually this hill was in the zone of activity given over to the army 31st Infantry, but the 31st Infantry had not yet appeared, and the marines could not go past a flanking position as strong as this. The enemy had fieldpieces and machine guns up there. The marines had to stop and take the height. While they slogged away on the slope, aided by artillery and marine aircraft overhead, the roadblock back at the minefield was cleared away and the tanks began to move up. It was one thirty in the afternoon.

The tanks moved up the road to Hill 146. Again they were stopped by the roadblock. A tank with a bulldozer came up to clear the mess. It smashed through the line of trees, and then came an explosion. It had run into another minefield.

Again the tanks were stopped and the infantry went ahead. At five thirty in the afternoon the marines took the hill and the road beyond. The enemy had fled precipitately, abandoning equipment, including a whole truckload of box mines. The marines dug in. They had advanced three miles, and had suffered only twenty-two casualties in fighting that had lasted for seven hours. They were less than three miles from Yongdungpo, but still had a river to cross.

On September 19, the marines had yet another barrier to overcome, the Han River. In the Haengju area of the northeast bank of the Han River in the 5th Marines' sector, the enemy was digging in, and in the 1st Marines' area to the south, North Korean troops were already in place to defend Yongdungpo. Once the Han was crossed successfully, and Yongdungpo taken, the way was clear into Seoul. But the Han could be as great a barrier for the Americans as the Naktong had been for the North Koreans in the first phases of the war.

In the north, in spite of the apparent confusion of the enemy, the marines had already experienced their first indication of serious opposition to the Allied drive east. It came on the afternoon of September 18, in the 5th Marines' position on Hill 123. (See Map 10.) The North Koreans opened up with a mortar barrage which lasted over an hour and caused thirty marine casualties. Later in the day, other gunfire announced that the North Koreans were prepared to defend all along the line. September 19 promised to be a different sort of day. The marines were to cross the Han River and prepare to seize Yongdungpo.

That day the plans were made by General Smith at division headquarters. The crossing would be made opposite Kimpo airfield at the village of Haengju. There were not enough pontoons to bridge the Han, but the marines had their amphibious tractors (LVT) and the engineers could build rafts to carry over tanks and artillery. Within a matter of hours they hoped to be able to fabricate some sort of bridge.

So the 5th Marines were on the north for this landing, and the 1st Marines were on the south, to move against Yongdungpo. The Army 32nd Infantry Regiment of the 7th Division had come ashore at Inchon and was to move up on the far south, to protect the flank of the 1st Marines. The rest of the 7th Division, the 17th and 31st Infantry regiments, were to come up to join the advance troops of the X Corps, but as noted, the army's way is not the marine way, and by marine standards the army was very slow.

It would have been helpful if on September 19 the Eighth Army in the south had been driving north, pushing the North Koreans ahead of it, to create the anvil effect that General MacArthur wanted. But General Walker's troops had only begun to penetrate on the Naktong River line. General MacArthur did not have much faith in General Walker's ability to break out, a fact he had telegraphed to Walker by his appointment of General Almond to run the northern campaign, while Walker, who might have expected to be put in overall charge, was simply given an equal assignment in the south. On the afternoon of September 19, MacArthur mused over the situation reports on the command bridge of the *Mount McKinley*. That night he called a meeting of his staff: Admiral Struble, the navy commander, General Shepherd, the marine commander; General Almond, the X Corps commander, and several other generals and admirals. MacArthur expressed his dissatisfaction with the performance of the Eighth Army. He had hoped that Walker would break out on September 16, but here on the 19th Walker had not yet breached the Naktong River line in any force and was still nearly two hundred miles away. MacArthur did not say so, but he had really given up on the idea that Walker could produce the anvil effect. He suggested that another landing be made about halfway up the coast from Pusan to Inchon. He suggested Kunsan. (See map page 10.) The operation was to be carried out within the week.

Having given the orders, the general retired for the night to wait what the next day would bring on the X Corps front.

As the afternoon of September 19 became evening, the 5th Marines were

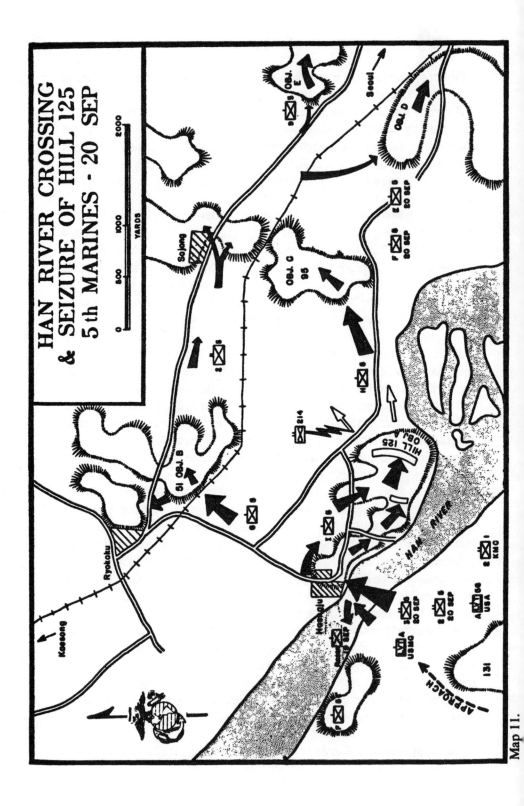

HAN RIVER CROSSING & SEIZURE OF HILL 125 5th MARINES · 20 SEP

YARDS

Map 11.

still not sure what they would find when they crossed the Han. One intelligence report told of some mining of the roads in the Haengju area. Another indicated an important enemy buildup on the north bank of the Han opposite the crossing place. But it was all very inconclusive, and there was only one way to find out what the situation actually would be. The way to find out was to send men across.

The men chosen were a swimming team of the regiment's reconnaissance company, under the command of Captain Kenneth J. Houghton. The swimmers would cross just after dark, and if no enemy were about, they would signal for the rest of the company to follow in LVTs. They would seize a bridgehead around three hills. (See Map 11.) They would hold this ground until Colonel Taplett's 3rd Battalion crossed over just before dawn. The other two battalions of the 5th Marines would cross over later in the day.

As darkness began to lower, Captain Houghton got his swimmers ready. He would lead. Lieutenant Dana M. Cashion and ten enlisted men would be with him, and so would two navy officers; one of them, Lieutenant Horace Underwood of an old Korea missionary family, would be interpreter.

Night came down dark, without a moon. The swimming team approached the bank of the Han, carrying two small rubber boats for equipment and their weapons. It was eight o'clock that night when they moved through the paddy field to the edge of the river, stripped to their underwear, and entered the water. They swam slowly across, making as little ripple as possible.

Life became complicated when someone put a shell into a Korean thatched hut on the far side and it began to burn, lighting up the water with a reddish glow. But the swimmers did not lose heart, and they were not seen. Forty minutes after they started out, they moved ashore. Immediately they encountered a pair of Koreans in civilian white, whom they captured. Lieutenant Underwood spoke to them, and the Koreans said they were civilians, escaping from the North Koreans at Seoul.

Captain Houghton sent Lieutenant Cashion and several men to reconnoiter Hill 125. (See Map 11.) He remained on the beach with the prisoners and dispatched other men around the area to check for enemy activity.

"The Marines have landed and the situation is well in hand," Houghton radioed back to the rest of his company on the other side.

Still, he had to make sure. The patrols continued to spread out.

They discovered nothing, and Houghton concluded that the enemy were not here. He gave the signal, and on the far shore of the Han, the rest of the company was waiting. Lieutenant Ralph B. Crossman had brought them to the water's edge with their amtracs at eight o'clock when Houghton had announced that he was beginning the crossing. Now that Lieutenant

Cashion's patrol had reported that they had found nothing on Hill 125 he was ready to make his move.

Nine amtracs clattered up to the shore of the Han, making so much noise that Houghton could hear it clearly on the far side of the river. So did the enemy. As the amtracs moved into the water Hill 125 suddenly erupted. Bullets and antitank gun shells began to lace the water around the amtracs. Other guns from the hill worked over the beach line, and one of Houghton's men disappeared.

The worst complication began when four of the amtracs grounded in the mud. When Captain Houghton learned this bad news he decided to swim out with his men to rescue the amtracs and lead them to the north side. But the enemy fire grew stronger. The two prisoners tried to escape and had to be shot. Obviously they were not what they had said.

Houghton then decided to abandon the position and lead the swimmers back to the marine shore. They hid the boats and jettisoned some weapons to prevent capture. They began to swim and were immediately beset by fire from both sides, mortar fire from the marine side and machine gun and rifle fire from the North Koreans on the north bank. Several of the swimmers, including Houghton, were wounded during the swim, and he came out on one of the amtracs; most of the others made the far bank.

In about an hour all were back, except Houghton and some of his men, who had reached the stranded amtracs, which were stuck in the mud like giant turtles. Two of them were extricated from the mud, but two were abandoned. Dawn found the wounded on the way to the field hospital at Kimpo. The attempt to cross the river had failed, and the reconnaissance company had lost its commanding officer to wounds. Before he left for the hospital, Houghton estimated the enemy on the far side as a battalion—about a thousand men.

But the 5th Marines were determined to get across the Han that morning. The plan had miscarried, so the plan was revised. The artillery would bombard the far shore for fifteen minutes, beginning at 6:15, and the LVTs would cross at 6:30.

The barrage was laid down on schedule by two battalions of the 11th Marines artillery, but the guns were not on target and many of the shells fell into the river and on the beach. Where they should have been falling was on Hill 125, for this was the center of enemy resistance, and when the amtracs began to cross the river antitank guns and machine guns opened on them once again. Fortunately the LVTs were armor-plated and the infantrymen were protected. But when the marines landed, the gunfire was even more intense and the casualties began to fall.

The first wave of amtracs stopped and their .50 caliber machine guns began spitting back at the enemy. Then in the growing light along came four Marine fighter planes to strafe Hill 125. Under that cover several of the amtracs waddled eastward to a position where they could fire properly on Hill 125.

Company I led the advance, the 2nd Platoon on the left of Hill 125 and the 3rd Platoon on the right, with the 1st Platoon in reserve. They moved up doggedly in spite of many difficulties, including amtracs that stalled. On the right the advance bogged down on a plateau, and enemy machine guns caused many casualties among the men of the mortar section. The 3rd Platoon fell back. Captain Robert McMullen ordered the 1st Platoon to come up, and move through the 3rd. The latter unit was reorganized under Lieutenant Wallace Williamson, when platoon commander Lieutenant William Sparks was wounded. It went around to the left to outflank the enemy.

This time the marines enveloped the plateau before Hill 125, and they kept going, although they had taken many casualties. Even Captain McMullen was wounded, though he stayed in the fight. The North Koreans began to move back to the flat ground north of the hill. They were found by marine fighters, which pursued and strafed. By the time the marines reached the top of the hill, the enemy had given up hope of holding. Many North Korean soldiers were shot down as they changed into white civilian clothes to try to escape into the countryside.

Hill 125 turned out to be the key to the defense. Once it had fallen, Hill 51 and Hill 95 were taken with little pain. The marines had their first objective of the day. They had suffered forty-three casualties, most of them from Company I, but the Han River barrier had been breached, and Seoul lay ahead.

With the securing of these objectives, the marines had time to clean up and take stock. They recovered the two grounded LVTs in the river. They recovered the boats and the weapons Captain Houghton had hidden the night before. The marine who had been declared missing in action showed up. He had inadvertently been left behind by Houghton but had taken cover and saved himself during the long night. He had a good deal of information for the intelligence section about the North Korean activity and dispositions.

By 10 A.M. on September 20, more marines were ferrying the river in the amtracs. The 2d Battalion of the 5th Marines was to pass through the 3rd Battalion and attack along the Kaesong–Seoul railroad line. Tanks and men moved across the river in a long stream, most of the infantry ferried by amtracs. Vehicle ferries were improvised and the process of moving an army across the river continued. There was little hope of using any of the old bridges; the North Koreans had effectively destroyed the highway and railroad bridges between Yongdungpo and Seoul. But the marines were making out well enough with the resources at hand. They had redeemed all General

MacArthur's promises to a skeptical Washington, and to show his gratitude the general awarded General Smith a Silver Star medal for gallantry before he headed back that day to Tokyo.

As of the end of September 20, then, the 1st Marine Division lay along both banks of the great river. The plan now called for the 5th Marines to open up the north bank so that the 1st Marines could land in the Yongdungpo area. The 1st Marines would then move toward Seoul and capture South Mountain, then move north and east, while the Korean marines (for political purposes) attacked Seoul itself. The 7th Marines would march north guarding the flank, and the 5th Marines would go into divisional reserve. But it was not going to be as easy as it had been, that much became apparent on September 20. The North Koreans were catching their balance and moving first-class fighting troops up to the Seoul area. The evidence came in the early hours of September 20, when the commander of the Yongdungpo forces sent an attack against hills 80 and 85, which he had seen occupied by the marines. The North Koreans were pleasantly surprised to see that the Americans for unknown reasons had deserted these important positions and they were soon on top, taking over the foxholes left by the 5th Marines.

The campaign assumed a new aspect on September 21, when General Almond came ashore at Inchon and took command of the X Corps. The general was in an enormous hurry to capture Seoul by September 25, a date that at that moment seemed important: it would be the ninety-day "anniversary" of the North Korean assault across the 38th parallel.

The 7th Division was ordered up on the right flank of Colonel Puller's 1st Marines. Colonel Puller was waiting impatiently for them so that he could move against Yongdungpo.

Since the capture of Hill 80 and Hill 85 had proved so simple, the North Korean commander got cocky, and decided it would be equally simple to take Hill 118. The infantry moved, but the marines threw them back easily, assisted by planes of VMF-323.

At the same time, the Yongdungpo commander sent forth another body, about a battalion strong, along the Seoul–Inchon highway, against the position held by the 2nd Battalion of the 1st Marines. This force was led by five T-34 tanks and in front of all for some strange reason moved a truck full of ammunition. (See Map 12.) Company D and Company F were dug in on high ground south of the road. Company E was west of them, and its line extended north of the road. The first sign the marines had of an enemy movement came with the noise of tank engines and clanking tracks before 4 A.M. Half an hour later the marines on the hill south of the road saw the lead truck and the tanks pass by, moving toward Company E's lines. The road had

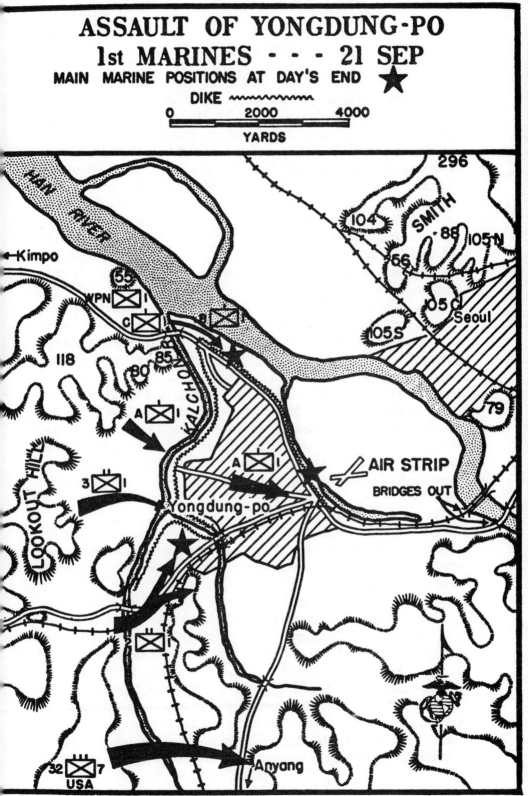

ASSAULT OF YONGDUNG-PO
1st MARINES - - - 21 SEP
MAIN MARINE POSITIONS AT DAY'S END ★

DIKE ~~~~~~~~~~~

0   2000   4000

YARDS

296

HAN RIVER

104

SMITH

88   105 N

Kimpo

55

56

WPN

105 C

Seoul

C

105 S

118

85

80

KALCHON

79

A

A

AIR STRIP

BRIDGES OUT

3

Yongdung-po

LOOKOUT HILL

Anyang

32   7

USA

Map 12.

been mined by the engineers. Private Oliver O'Neil, Jr., apparently in the belief that the units below were marines, got up and shouted out a challenge. He was killed by a burst of automatic fire. No other marines asked any question, but began firing everything they had at the vehicles on the road. The column stopped. The ammunition truck and two of the tanks had reached a point almost at Company E's front when the firing began. One of the Company D marines got up and threw a grenade at the leading vehicle, the truck. The results were all a marine could ask for: the ammunition truck blew up. The tanks' turrets whirled wildly as the gunners tried to find their enemies. Interspersed among the tanks and behind them were the infantry and more vehicles. The marine fire was devastating, and the infantry men began scrabbling up the slopes of the hills—into the guns of Company D and Company F.

In the Company F sector, Private First Class Walter C. Monegan, Jr., ran raggedly across the hill with his 3.5-inch bazooka. Three hundred yards away was the point he had selected for his attack on the tanks. He was followed by Corporal Bill Cheek, leader of the bazooka team, carrying three rockets. It was easy enough to see in the flames from the blazing ammunition truck. They reached a little knoll which offered cover. Monegan fired his first rocket. It missed by ten yards. They had to get closer, Monegan said. Down below he saw a water tank. They sped for the water tank, and behind them came Private First Class Robert Perkins, the second member of Monegan's bazooka team. Cheek loaded and Monegan sighted on the third tank in line in the light from the blazing ammunition truck. Monegan was only fifty yards from the T-34.

"I've got it," he said.

"Fire," shouted Cheek.

Monegan let go with a rocket. The tank burst into flames. The other tanks spun their turrets, firing their machine guns. Bullets sprayed around the water tank.

Meanwhile Monegan's teammate, Private Perkins, had reloaded the bazooka with another rocket. Monegan picked up the weapon and moved up against another tank. He scored another hit, and the second tank went up in flames. A third tank began backing to turn around. Monegan shouted to Perkins to hurry with the reload. He sighted the bazooka. But just then an enemy machine gunner spotted the bazooka and shot Monegan down. Someone else fired the shot that exploded the third tank. Perkins scrabbled up the hill shouting for a medic. Corpsman Sterling Lee Bruce scrambled down the hill behind Perkins. They reached the shelter of the water tank, and Bruce opened Monegan's shirt. There was no need to unsnap the first aid kit.

Monegan was dead. They pulled his body beneath the water tank and hid it from the North Koreans, then they went back up the slope.

The effectiveness of the North Korean attack had been smashed, but the enemy troops continued to fight until dawn. There was no way back for them; around them were the marines, and the artillery closed off the road to Yongdungpo with a barrage of fire. One of the T-34s was finally captured intact, with its crew. But as for the rest, as the light grew bright the marines could see the road and roadside littered with the remains of tanks, trucks, and the bodies of three hundred North Korean infantrymen.

After the North Korean attacks were repelled, Colonel Puller ordered his 1st Marines to move onto the offensive. The 1st Battalion would retake Hill 80 and Hill 85. The 3rd Battalion would hold on Lookout Hill. The 2nd Battalion would advance to the highway bridges that crossed Kalchon Creek, opposite Yongdungpo. The Army 32nd Infantry was to capture Tongdok Mountain, two miles from Yongdungpo.

At about the time Monegan was wrecking his first tank, Lieutenant Colonel Hawkins was moving his observation post to Hill 118. He sent Company C to take hills 80 and 85.

The company commander, Captain Robert P. Wray, decided to approach from the south. The 2nd Platoon was sent to clear a village across the road to Hill 80. That meant a rush across a quarter of a mile of open ground. The platoon set out and made it, but as the men approached the village, they came under fire from a little knoll at the back. The platoon stalled. Captain Wray sent his other two platoons around the flanks, and the North Koreans retreated to the slopes of Hill 80. From Hill 118 the mortars and machine guns of the company's weapons platoon covered Company C's advance very ably, and on the hill the North Koreans kept their heads down.

Late in the afternoon Captain Wray launched an assault on the hill. Lieutenant Henry A. Commiskey took the 3rd Platoon to the right, and Lieutenant William A. Craven took the 1st Platoon to the left. They met resistance from North Koreans holed up in huts along the way, but a few rounds of 3.5-inch rockets put an end to that bother. Before evening the marines held Hill 80 once again.

The remaining North Koreans had all clustered atop Hill 85, and the North Korean commander had stuck out flank troops to prevent encirclement. Captain Wray's platoons tried another envelopment, but it was not so easy. This time Lieutenant Craven's platoon covered the assault from Hill 80, along with the company's machine guns. The 2nd Platoon moved on the left, and Commiskey's 3rd Platoon took the right. The lieutenant bounded forward ahead of his platoon, hit the top and jumped over to find himself in an enemy

machine gun position. He killed four of the men in there and was assaulting
the fifth when his men caught up with him. The lieutenant rushed forward to
another gun position and began clearing that out single-handed. The fury of
his attack unnerved the survivors, who fled down the hill's eastern slope
toward the Kalchon River.

Lieutenant Guild's 2nd Platoon did not fare so well. Guild was badly
wounded as he neared the top of the hill on his side. But he urged his men on,
and they went. He stayed on his feet and turned back to tell Captain Wray that
his men were moving. He fell at Wray's feet and then refused the help of a
corpsman. Let Wray send the corpsmen ahead to help his fighters, Guild said.
And then he died.

There was a good deal of confusion later in the day. Many of those escaping
North Koreans hid in the brush along the river's edge. They ambushed two
parties of engineers, communications and service units, coming up to string
wire and bring supplies, in the belief that since the high ground around
Yongdungpo was held by the marines, all was safe. Several marines were
killed and more were captured, virtually under the eyes of the combat units on
the hills, who could not get down to the flat to rescue their fellows.

During the day the marines consolidated positions in front of Yongdungpo,
taking Hill 55 and several villages on the southeast bank of the Han River.

At 10 A.M. General Almond arrived from Inchon to look over the situation
and confer with Colonel Puller. The result of the conference was an order for
the artillery to soften up Yongdungpo. From the rear, the 4th Battalion of the
11th Marines—the artillery—kept up a continuous fire on the enemy positions in Yongdungpo. Marine aircraft bombed and strafed the town, too.
From the top of Lookout Hill the marines of the 3rd Battalion of the 1st
Marines had a fine view of Yongdungpo, except that for the most part a pall of
smoke and dust hung over the area. The 11th Marines fired more than three
thousand rounds of 105 and 155 mm shells into the enemy positions and into
concentrations as asked by the infantry commanders. Under the umbrella of
the artillery, the 2nd Battalion moved out just before 7 A.M. to drive along the
Seoul–Inchon highway toward the bridges across the Kalchon. They reached
the bridge across the western branch shortly after noon. The engineers came
up to inspect the bridge and announced that it was in shape to carry tanks in
the assault on Yongdungpo scheduled for September 21. The battalion dug in
on the west side of the creek, to wait for morning.

To the south, on the UN force's right flank, the Army 32nd Infantry moved
up against Tongdok Mountain, using the Seoul–Inchon highway as its route.
The North Koreans had planted a field of box mines along the road, and the
32nd lost three tanks in moving through. Colonel Charles E. Beauchamp

narrowly escaped death when his jeep ran across a mine. The driver was killed and the colonel's radio operator was wounded, two of the forty-three casualties the 32nd suffered in their first day of fighting. The marines, who had already learned about box mines the hard way, might have helped out here, but communications were still anything but superior between marines and army. Lieutenant Colonel Alan Sutter, commander of the 2nd Battalion of the 1st Marines, from his new position on the west bank of Kalchon Creek looked over the terrain ahead. A little more than a mile past the first bridge was the second, which spanned the eastern branch of Kalchon Creek. A high ridge on the right hand side of the highway was swarming with North Koreans. He wanted to call on the artillery to hit this concentration, but the rub was that the hill was in army territory. Sutter got in touch with Lieutenant Colonel Charles M. Mount, commander of the 32nd's 2nd Battalion. They agreed that the hill should be shelled. But to do so Mount had to put his request through 7th Division headquarters. From there it went to X Corps headquarters. From there it went to 1st Marine Division headquarters. From there it went to the 11th Marines who would do the shooting. By the time the approval reached the 11th Marines, it was dark and they did not know quite what they were shooting at. Among other things, they blew up the Kalchon Creek bridge on the east, an act the engineers did not appreciate.

7

The Fight for Yongdungpo

On the night of September 20, the marines and the army troops held the heights above Kalchon Creek and the Seoul–Inchon highway. Beyond was the creek which branched opposite the town. From the North Korean commander's point of view, the defensive position was most inadequate: there was too much rice paddy between hills, too little high ground on the east of the Kalchon. (See Map 13.) He had his men build earthworks to block the northwest approach, where the 1st Battalion of the 1st Marines were dug in on hills 80 and 85, waiting for dawn. In the southwest, the North Koreans concentrated a large force of infantrymen of the NK 87th Regiment between the two branches of the Kalchon. But they left the western approach unguarded in the view that the UN forces were most unlikely to come that way since it involved a long march across open rice paddy. So the North Korean defense was split. It was a powerful defense, including field guns, heavy mortars and tanks, and all the ammunition the soldiers could use.

All through the night of September 20 and the early hours of September 21, the artillery bombarded Yongdungpo, and the town burned. As dawn approached, the marines prepared to move out, all along the line. They would have to cross the Kalchon, then the dike that protected the town from the river's flooding, the defense lines, and then fight in the narrow streets of the town.

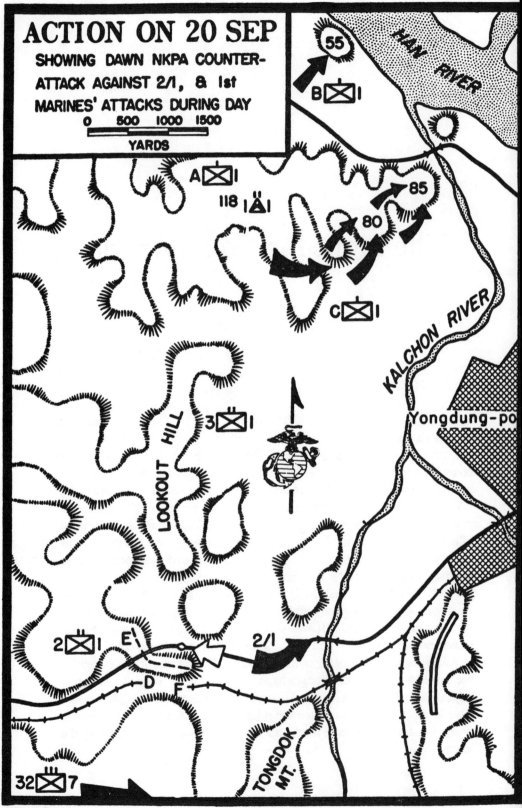

ACTION ON 20 SEP

SHOWING DAWN NKPA COUNTER-
ATTACK AGAINST 2/1, & 1st
MARINES' ATTACKS DURING DAY

0   500   1000   1500
YARDS

Map 13.

Company B led off across the wreckage of the Kalchon bridge. The men were covered by machine guns, mortars, and tanks on Hill 85. They crossed the creek and captured an undefended knoll on the other side. But beyond lay the dikes, which met in a V north of the town. One dike ran along the western end of the town to the top. There it met the dike that protected the town from the flooding of the Han River. Here was the center of the North Koreans' northern defense force. The North Koreans had established fields of crossfire and a concentration of weapons.

Captain Richard Bland decided to move down the territory along the northern or Han side. The going was anything but easy; these men of the NK 87th Infantry were trained and tough. If the marines had enjoyed some easy going until now, it ended here. Supported by the artillery and several air strikes, Bland managed to advance a mile along the dike, rolling up the North Korean defenders on this side, squad by squad. Casualties were heavy; by early afternoon two of his platoon leaders were wounded and out of action, and so many men of the 1st and 3rd platoons had been hit that he consolidated the combat-effectives into one unit. Staff Sergeant Frank Quadros became the leader of the provisional platoon. With this force, Captain Bland then turned toward the Kalchon levee. He called for artillery support, but the artillerymen assumed that he used the wrong coordinates. They thought he had attacked through the Kalchon levee, and that the area was already in marine hands. Several times Bland called for fire, and each time it was withheld because the marine gunners did not want to risk shooting down their own men. The confusion went on during most of the afternoon, making Bland's task much harder. Only very late in the day did he get what he wanted.

Meanwhile, Colonel Sutter's 2nd Battalion set out at dawn to cross the Kalchon on the highway bridge. Company D and Company E led the assault. They made it fairly easily across the first bridge, but when they moved toward the second, the North Koreans on that ridge to the right of the highway suddenly awoke and brought down concentrated fire on the marines. Once again Colonel Sutter asked for help from the army artillery, and once again it was delayed—apparently interminably—by the red tape of transmission of orders between marine and army commands. Impatient, Sutter used his own 4.2-inch mortars to prepare the way for the attack on the hill that had been so imperfectly shelled the day before.

Companies E and F then turned toward the hill and fought upward on the slopes. The battle lasted all day. The marines did reach part of the crest by the end of the day.

Company D moved forward on the left side of the highway against the dike along the Kalchon. This, too, was a hard and slow fight. Colonel Puller saw how slowly it was going, and in midafternoon committed his reserve, the 3rd Battalion, to the relief of the 2nd Battalion. They fought hard and managed to reach the dike, move along it, and then make the bridge into the city. As evening came, the marines of Company E and Company F still did not hold enough of the ridge to make their position tenable for the night. Colonel Sutter ordered them to come down and dig in with Company D. Their retreat down the hill was covered by planes of VMF-214, which delivered rockets and napalm to keep the North Koreans off balance, and strafed within a few yards of the marine line. As darkness fell, the 2nd and 3rd battalions of the 1st Marines were dug in along the left side of the Inchon-Seoul highway.

In the south the army was having a better day. The 1st Battalion of the army 32nd Infantry seized the high ground at Anyang, cutting the railroad and the road from Suwon, that road along which the North Koreans had brought up reinforcements. But the army forces were far to the south, and the gap between them and the marines was so great that it hardly seemed they were fighting the same engagement.

The most successful move of the day was that of Company A of the 1st Battalion. Lieutenant Colonel Hawkins had taken the calculated risk that the North Koreans did not believe he would move across the open land. He had sent troops through the unprotected flat of the rice paddies to make a frontal assault on Yongdungpo. Captain R. H. Barrow of Company A put the 3rd Platoon on the left, the 2nd Platoon on the right, and the 1st Platoon with the mortars and machine guns in the middle, behind. Thus they marched through ripening rice that was as high as a man's head, and perhaps because of that, although they could hear gunfire on both sides, they marched all the way to the Kalchon without incident. Suddenly the rice paddy ended, and they were completely exposed as they stepped into the waters of the little stream. Surprisingly, not a shot was fired at them. They moved across and onto the dike. Still no shots. A hundred yards east of the levee were the first buildings. In a few minutes they were in Yongdungpo. They marched along the main east-west street through a town that seemed completely dead. They could still hear the sounds of fighting on both sides, to the rear, but they saw no enemy. Barrow could tell from the sounds that they were ahead of all others, and he radioed battalion for instructions. Sutter told him to keep on going, so he did.

Barrow's field map showed that just east of Yongdungpo the Seoul–Inchon highway intersected the street on which he was moving. He ordered the 1st Platoon up on the right; the noise of fighting was greatest in that direction.

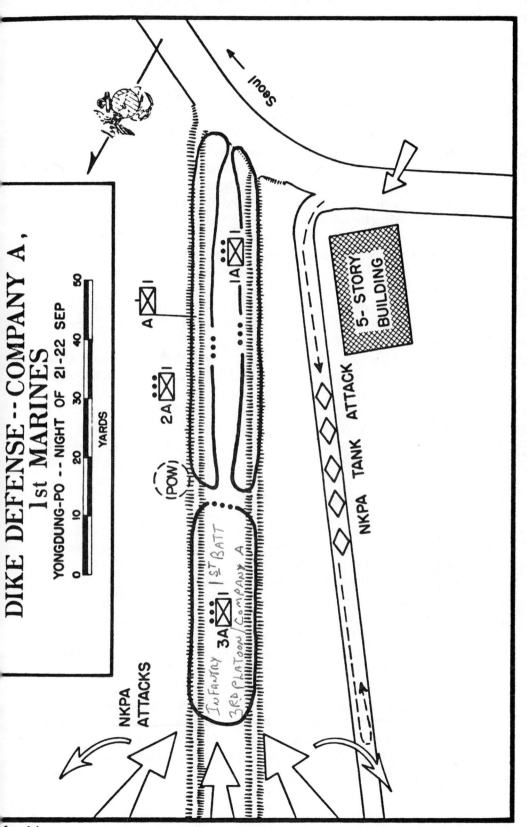

DIKE DEFENSE--COMPANY A, 1st MARINES

YONGDUNG-PO -- NIGHT OF 21-22 SEP

YARDS

0   10   20   30   40   50

Seoul

5-STORY BUILDING

NKPA TANK ATTACK

(POW)

A I

1A I

2A I

3A I

INFANTRY 1st BATT

3RD PLATOON Company A

NKPA ATTACKS

Map 14.

Hardly had the platoon come up when the action began. The first indication was the sound of chanting. A flanker lifted his rifle, signaling that the enemy was in sight. It was a column of North Korean infantry, swinging along the main Inchon–Seoul highway from the east. The riflemen sought cover, in doorways and behind corners of buildings. Silently they waited and listened as the unwitting enemy came singing along, bound for the fight against the 2nd Battalion. Lieutenant William McClelland, the platoon leader, waited and watched. When the enemy was in view, he made the chopping motion with his right hand that signaled the platoon to open fire. The popping of rifles and the rattle of Browning Automatic Rifles suddenly cut off the sound of singing. North Koreans dropped in their tracks, some began to crawl toward the side streets.

The 3rd Platoon crossed the Inchon–Seoul road with its streetcar track, reached the eastern end of the town, and established a defense atop the eastern dike. It was twenty-five feet high and thirty feet wide. (See Map 14.) Company A's position offered a splendid view of the future. Beyond, to the east was a sand spit two miles long, which held a dusty airstrip. Beyond the airstrip was the Han River, and beyond the Han was Seoul. Barrow chose a strip of the dike about a hundred yards long and organized his three platoons: one covering the north end, and the other two back to back on the sides of the levee. They pulled out their entrenching tools and began to dig. For once it was soft dirt, easy going, easy, easy, easy. Even the weapons pits were no real trouble. Still, the sun was dropping fast in the west when the marines were dug in for the night, surrounded by their enemies.

All afternoon, Captain Barrow had been in frequent touch with battalion headquarters, and Lieutenant Colonel Hawkins was well aware of his break-through. But for some reason, Hawkins did not exploit this opportunity to cement the gap Barrow had driven through the Yongdungpo defenses. Company A was on its own for the night. And for some reason Colonel Puller at regimental headquarters knew nothing of this move. Nor did General Smith at division headquarters or General Almond at X Corps headquarters.

On the north end of the defense position Lieutenant John J. Swords saw a column of North Koreans moving into the sand spit and the machine gunners opened fire, inflicting heavy casualties on the enemy.

As daylight faded, the North Koreans around the marines began moving. A patrol—about a squad—came up to the intersection of the east-west road with the Inchon–Seoul highway. The marines watched. The enemy troops seemed to be looking for something behind a huge pile of something. One marine said it was coal. Another said it was supplies. The marines opened fire. One marine fired a rifle grenade. It fell short, on top of the pile. The "coal pile" erupted in an enormous explosion that shook the marines to their boots; it was the enemy's main ammunition dump. The smoke and flame rose in a column that could be seen back to Inchon.

Captain Barrow was on the radio just then, explaining to battalion headquarters where he was. Battalion seemed unusually dense, unable to understand that its single company had penetrated into the heart of the enemy.

"Did you see that explosion?" the captain said.

"Yup," said battalion.

"Well, that's where we are," said Barrow.

And then the radio quit.

After the debris settled, the marines took a look around. They had taken control of more than just the ammunition dump—buildings around the area were filled with American equipment and medical supplies captured by the North Koreans during the early days of the summer. East of the warehouse was the Yongdungpo city hall. On the south was a school. On the north was a factory.

Late in the day, the North Koreans made several attempts to dislodge the marines from this position, but Barrow's men fought off every attack. As darkness neared and the men opened their C rations, Captain Barrow checked his perimeter. The men were in their foxholes. Some foxholes were up high on the slope. Some were low. Machine guns and BARs were put up on the shoulders of the dike on top so that automatic fire could move in any direction. The wounded were dug in and as comfortable as the medics could make them. Eighteen prisoners were crowded into an improvised stockade on the west side of the dike. The marines of Company A settled in for the night, surrounded by their enemies.

The enemies were not long in making themselves felt. For the second time that day the first intimation of trouble came by ear. The marines heard the clanking of metal on metal, the rattling and growling of tanks coming up the Inchon–Seoul highway from the southwest. Then five T-34 tanks appeared on the road. (See Map 14.) They turned just before the crossroads and clanked up the street parallel to the dike. The turrets swiveled to point the guns at the dike, and the five tanks loosed a hail of machine gun and 85 mm gunfire from a range of thirty yards. The marines ducked deep into their foxholes.

Corporal Francis Devine popped out of his hole, aimed his 3.5-inch bazooka at a tank, and let fly a rocket. The whole turret of the lead tank blew off, throwing the gunner into the road, and the tanks lurched off into a side street behind the city hall and disappeared.

The other four tanks ground up the road toward the factory, turned around and came back, again firing as they came. There were no hits this time as they moved on the road to the schoolyard, where they turned around for another run. This time the bazookamen were ready, and they damaged two of the tanks, which disappeared in the shadows of the side streets. The other two made one more run and then they, too, gave up.

With the end of the attack Barrow counted noses, fearful that the ferocious barrage of fire had cost him dear. But he had only one casualty. The 85 mm shells had either gone deep into the dike and blown up harmlessly, or passed over; the machine guns had either fired overhead or their rounds had also gone into the dirt. The single casualty came from concussion from one 85 mm shell that exploded near a foxhole.

The real problem was ammunition. Every shot had to count from now on.

An hour after the tank attack, noises began to emerge from the supply warehouse. The marines waited. Finally a party appeared, apparently North Korean soldiers looking for ammunition. The 1st Platoon held fire until the foragers were exposed, and then opened up with a brief burst. The North Koreans fled.

At about 9 P.M. Lieutenant Swords' platoon on the north end of the position heard shouts and footsteps. The lieutenant cautioned the men to hold their fire and save their ammunition until the enemy was up close. The marines waited.

A green flare went up. From experience the marines knew this was the North Koreans' infantry signal for attack. Shouting "Mansei, Mansei" (the Korean equivalent of the Japanese Banzai), the North Koreans came charging. Still Swords waited. When they were only fifteen yards away he gave the signal and the marine guns burst fire. The North Koreans retreated.

Ten minutes passed. The marines heard talk, an officer rallying his men. Again the North Koreans attacked. Again they were driven back.

A third time they came, and this time one of the American captives, an officer, managed to escape the position, and ran into the darkness shouting "Don't attack, don't attack, the Americans are too strong."

The North Korean infantry officer was a determined man. Once more he exhorted his men to attack and this time they came into the American position before they were stopped and driven back.

Then the streets were silent.

Corporal Billy Webb told his fire teammates that he was going out for a look and would be coming back. Then he darted down the bank of the dike and into a side street, clutching his M-1. He heard a voice around the corner. He crept up to the corner of the building and looked around. An officer was standing in the street, talking loudly and seriously to some soldiers. He switched the rifle to manual, drew a bead on the officer, and fired a single round. The officer dropped. Corporal Webb hightailed it back to the dike and his foxhole.

Even with the officer down, the North Koreans made one more attack against Swords' men. But it lacked the fervor of the other four, and Swords' men had no trouble in driving it off.

Quiet descended on Company A, a silence punctuated only by the sounds of movement some distance away, particularly in the south. In the early morning light, the marines on the dike began to move around cautiously. Just outside the perimeter they counted 275 dead enemy troops, fifty automatic weapons, and four abandoned T-34 tanks. They found no live North Koreans. The marines were grateful. Some of the men had the last clip in the rifle. But they were better off than the North Koreans, who had counted on the contents of that ammunition dump by the highway to replenish their ammunition. That became apparent at 8 A.M. when the 1st and 3rd battalions of the 1st Marines kicked off the morning attack ordered by Colonel Puller. There was no attack because there was no enemy; the North Koreans had pulled out of Yongdungpo during the night, leaving behind hundreds of their dead, and tons of abandoned guns, trucks, supplies, machine guns, and small arms.

The 1st and 3rd battalions marched into Yongdungpo unmolested, and at the dike were greeted by their benefactors, the men of Company A—fewer than 150 of them—who had penetrated deep into the heart of the enemy's defense, beaten him in battle, destroyed his defense, and forced him to retreat, all without "the brass" knowing a thing about it.

8

On to Seoul

Through the courtesy of Company A of the 1st Marines, the American advance on Seoul was speeded by several days. On September 22 when the rest of the regiment caught up with the company on the eastern edge of Yongdungpo, the advance was easy. Colonel Puller took advantage of the absence of the enemy to spend much of the day reorganizing the battalions and patroling.

Further south, the army's 7th Division moved easily on a broad front in the hills south of Seoul, cutting off the Suwon–Anyang road at Toksan-ni, three miles south of Yongdungpo. But in spite of specific orders that the division maintain constant contact with the marines on their left, Major General David G. Barr failed to do this, and thus the marines had no idea where the army was or what it was up to. More important, the army moved forward, but left a wedge of North Korean troops buried between its left flank and Colonel Puller's right, a most unhealthy situation. During the fight for Yongdungpo the marines complained bitterly that they were receiving heavy fire from an area the army claimed to control. The army denied it. The issue was never resolved for the marines captured Yongdungpo in spite of it, but the major difficulty was that the incident destroyed whatever confidence the marines had in the 7th Division and its commander.

On the afternoon of September 21, the 7th Division's reconnaissance

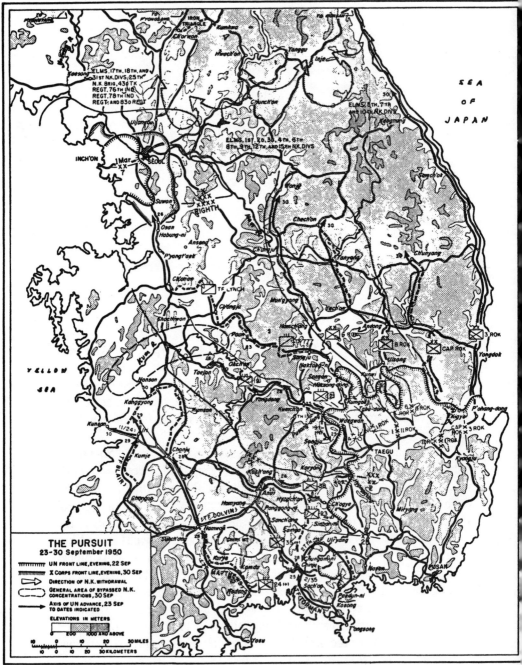

THE PURSUIT
23-30 September 1950

UN FRONT LINE, EVENING, 22 SEP
X CORPS FRONT LINE, EVENING, 30 SEP
DIRECTION OF N.K. WITHDRAWAL
GENERAL AREA OF BYPASSED N.K.
CONCENTRATIONS, 30 SEP
AXIS OF UN ADVANCE, 23 SEP
TO DATES INDICATED

ELEVATIONS IN METERS
200   1000 AND ABOVE

Map 15.

company was ordered south of Suwon to take the airfield there. (See Map 15.) At four o'clock that afternoon the troops moved out, led by a platoon of tanks under Lieutenant Jesse F. Van Sant. Just before the Americans reached the walled town a naval air strike knocked a wooden building off the East Gate, and this blocked the gateway. The column had to move around to find another entrance to the town.

Several groups of soldiers arrived on the scene, including the division assistant intelligence officer, Major Irwin A. Edwards, and the operations officer, Lieutenant Colonel Henry Hampton. Inside the town they came across a pair of North Korean officers trying to run out in an American jeep. They shot one and captured another. The latter turned out to be a battalion commander of the NK 105th Armored Division, a nice find for intelligence.

The Americans in Suwon fought their way through the town against only minor opposition. They went out and south, but because no one had brought a map they missed the airfield and ended up a mile south of it, along the road. It was growing dark, so they established their defense perimeter there.

At nine o'clock that night Major General Barr began to worry about his reconnaissance company. He sent a number of tanks and troops south to Suwon to find it, along with Lieutenant Colonel John W. Paddock, the division intelligence officer. They called the impromptu unit Task Force Hannum, after the commander of the 73rd Tank Battalion.

The task force moved south. Colonel Paddock made radio contact with Major Edwards and asked him for instructions about reaching the perimeter south of town.

The column reached Suwon at about midnight and came up against that blocked East Gate. They moved around to find another entrance. As they came in, a concealed T-34 tank opened fire with its 85 mm gun and knocked out the leading American tank, killing Captain Harold R. Beavers, commander of the tank company. Other U.S. tanks destroyed the T-34 but another T-34 escaped. The soldiers gave chase but the tank got away at the edge of the town. Not knowing the terrain, Colonel Paddock decided to wait where they were until morning, and he established a perimeter.

Down in the perimeter the men heard tanks rumbling around to the north. Lieutenant Van Sant suggested that they sounded like T-34s. He was ignored by Colonel Hampton and Major Edwards, who assured him they had to be the tanks of Task Force Hannum. So these men started north in four jeeps. About a mile north they saw four tanks coming down the road. Major Edwards flicked the lights of his jeep in a recognition signal. The tanks immediately opened fire. The men spilled out of the jeeps and scrambled across the shoulders of the road for the ditches—all except Colonel Hampton.

The colonel was so certain that these were American tanks and that it was all a mistake that he walked toward them, waving his arms. He was killed by the machine gunner of the lead tank, and the tank moved forward and crunched Edwards' jeep and the two behind it.

The tanks moved south toward the perimeter. So did one jeep, which had turned around and escaped ahead of them. The jeep driver gave the alarm, just in time. The four T-34s entered the perimeter, but Lieutenant Van Sant was ready for them. The American M-26 tanks destroyed the first two T-34s at a range of forty yards. The other two T-34s turned around and headed back north.

Major Edwards made his way back overland on foot and rejoined the reconnaissance company. At dawn he led the whole group to the airfield.

At daylight, Task Force Hannum began moving south. They passed the three squashed jeeps and saw the bodies lying in the road. They saw the airfield and the reconnaissance company and joined up. So now the UN forces held two major airfields in central Korea.

Later in the day two battalions of the 31st Infantry arrived to take over control of the airfield, and the reconnaissance company moved south to see what was happening at Osan. Task Force Hannum went back to division headquarters at Anyang. Both units had been blooded and in future would be more careful in their operations. There had been other sacrificial lambs like Colonel Hampton, and there would be more until the American units toughened. That was the way of the war, another indication of the spotty state of readiness of the American military three months after the Korean War began.

On September 22, seven miles northeast of Anyang, troops of the 1st Battalion of the 32nd Infantry ran into a North Korean ambush and Company B, which was affected, fled back along the road. The other companies of the 1st Battalion drove the North Koreans off. The 2nd Battalion that day captured the hills south of the railroad and highway bridges across the Han below Seoul. The 32nd Infantry had some hard fighting, an indication of the renewed determination of the North Korean high command to persevere in the face of this sudden adversity.

In the 5th Marines' sector, there was also indication that the easy days of the Inchon invasion had ended. The reason was the appearance in the Seoul area of two first-class fighting units of the North Korean People's Army, the 78th Independent Regiment and the 25th Brigade, about seven thousand troops in all.

The 5th Marines became aware of the change on the night of September 21.

The command post of the regiment was located in a thatched house near Sojong, two miles northeast of the point where Captain Houghton had first crossed the Han. On the night of September 21 a lucky shot from a North Korean artillery piece landed squarely in the middle of the house and severely wounded Lieutenant Colonel Lawrence C. Hays, Jr., the regimental executive officer. Colonel Murray, the commanding officer, was in the house at the time but he escaped with a minor wound. That night he moved the regimental command post to a cave nearby.

On the morning of September 22 the 5th Marines were prepared to advance again, but this time against heavier opposition in hilly terrain that was admirably suited for defensive operations. The regiment was reinforced by the 1st Korean Marines, who had been placed in the center of the line, with the 3rd Battalion of the 5th Marines on the left and the 1st Battalion on the right. At 7 A.M. they began moving toward the ridge line opposite the sandspit across the Han from Yongdungpo. (See Map 16.)

The North Koreans were dug in here along a series of hills that gave them an enormous geographical advantage. Hill spurs stuck out onto the plain, with narrow draws or defiles on either side, giving command of the lowland. Interlocking fields of fire enabled one hilltop defense group to protect the flank of the next.

The first move was made that morning by the Korean marines against Hill 104 in the middle of the mass. They were stopped almost immediately by heavy artillery and mortar fire from the hills. The advance bogged down while American artillery began searching out the enemy strong points and marine air strikes were called down.

On the left the 3rd Battalion of the 5th Marines' objective was Hill 296, a half mile from the starting point on Hill 216. At first the going was very easy. By 9:45 A.M. Company H announced that it had captured the summit. This was true, but between the summit and Seoul were six other hills, all heavily fortified, which would have to be taken. Here the North Koreans had established their main line of resistance in the battle for Seoul. Before noon the fighting had intensified. Several North Korean counterattacks were stopped by marine riflemen supported by tanks.

On the right of the UN front the 1st Battalion's objective was Hill 105-S. (There were three hills called 105.) It was about a mile and a quarter southeast of the jump-off point. Company A moved through Company C at the lead point and attacked frontally, while Company B delivered fire support and Company C tried to flank the hill on the right. But the three platoons of Company A were stopped cold at the base of the hill by heavy enemy machine gun fire. The company commander, Lieutenant Joseph A. Schimmenti, was

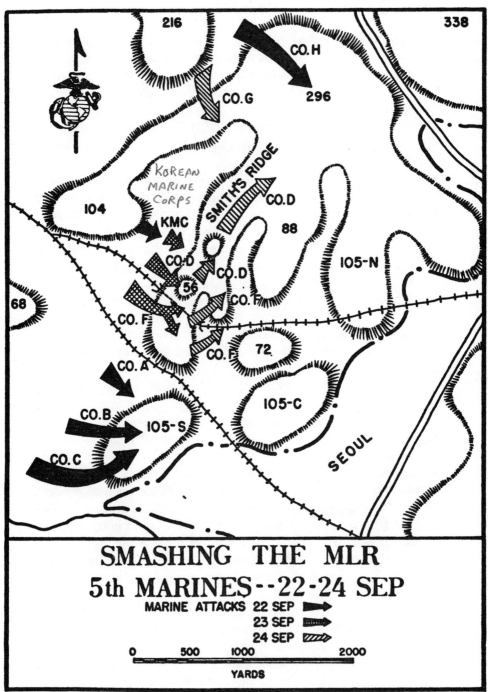

216

338

CO. H

296

CO. G

KOREAN
MARINE
CORPS

SMITHS RIDGE

CO. D

104

88

KMC

CO. D

CO. D

105-N

56

CO. F

68

CO. F

CO. F

72

CO. A

105-C

CO. B

105-S

CO. C

SEOUL

SMASHING THE MLR
5th MARINES--22-24 SEP

MARINE ATTACKS 22 SEP

23 SEP

24 SEP

0   500   1000   2000

YARDS

Map 16.

wounded and Lieutenant Nathaniel F. Mann was killed before they had established a foothold on the lower part of the hill. Company C was also under heavy fire from the hill and from Hill 105-C behind it. That company was seven hours in reaching the far side of the hill and closing in. Then came a heavy artillery bombardment of the hill, plus heavy mortaring and several air strikes. Company B then passed through Company A at the base of the hill and gained the top in fifteen minutes. The 1st Battalion had lost twelve men killed and thirty-one wounded that day.

As the day ended, one company of the battalion had to move back to Hill 68 (see Map 16) because the Korean marines had been stopped cold, and had to withdraw to Hill 104, whence they had set out that morning. The regimental line was in the shape of a V lying on its side, with the 3rd Battalion prong far out on the left and the 1st Battalion out on the right. Hill 68 protected the 1st Battalion flank as well as the right flank of the Korean marines.

On the morning of September 23 the Korean marines attacked again to try to straighten out the line. The two 5th Marine battalions were ordered to stay on their hills on left and right and support the Koreans with as much fire as they could deliver. The point of impact was Hill 56 where a powerful force of North Koreans lay entrenched. The South Koreans took heavy casualties and still made little progress.

At Colonel Murray's regimental command post on Hill 104 he and Lieutenant Colonel Roise of the 2nd Battalion conferred. They assumed that the reason for the Korean marines' setback was inexperience, so they withdrew the Koreans from the line and sent up the 2nd Battalion. The artillery was called in to drop a barrage on Hill 56, and the colonel ordered up a platoon of tanks to support the attack.

It was midafternoon and the marines were in a hurry to take the height before nightfall. Company F led off on the right, south of the railroad (see Map 16), which tunneled through a part of the hill. Company D moved out on the left along a sunken road to hit Hill 56 north of the tunnel.

First, Company F moved through rice paddies, and here the tanks were of no help at all. The lead tank bogged down in a ditch and was out of action until it could be hauled free. The four remaining tanks of the platoon divided; one remained in the paddy area to give support fire to the infantry against the hill. The three others sought the hard ground of the railroad track. But as the men of Company F moved across the flat ground, the machine guns, mortars, and rifle fire of the North Koreans brought down many casualties. Without support even from their own mortars (the mortar platoon did not get the message to engage) the assault platoons engaged the North Koreans in hand-to-hand fighting on the slope of Hill 56. Company D marched along the sunken road with virtually no opposition and then emerged on the slope of Hill 56 in the north. The 1st Platoon then turned left to take the long ridge the men named Smith's Ridge in honor of their company commander, Lieutenant H. J. Smith. But what Colonel Murray and Lieutenant Colonel Roise did not know was that this whole ridge line was the enemy's main line of resistance and every knoll bristled with guns. The 1st Platoon immediately came under heavy fire. The platoon commander, Lieutenant Ray Heck, fell with a mortal wound. That put Staff Sergeant T. Albert Crowson in charge, but not for long. He was shot in the leg and fell. In the next few minutes fifteen men were hit. Lieutenant Smith came up himself to bring his platoon out of trouble, while the other two platoons fought along the northeast slope of Hill 56. It was growing dark, and the enemy on Smith Ridge was too powerful. Smith stopped and dug in on Hill 56 for the night, out of contact with the rest of the battalion.

Meanwhile, on the other side of the hill, Company F was having real difficulties. Lieutenant Tilton A. Anderson's 2nd Platoon moved up against strong North Korean positions just beyond the tunnel. The fire was very heavy, Anderson estimated the enemy to be at least in company strength. He had lost several men during the traverse of the paddy fields, only twenty-seven were now left. They assaulted the hillside positions with grenades and small arms and wiped out the enemy, but when the fight was over only seven marines were on their feet. They withdrew then to the company position south of the tunnel, with their wounded and dead, and combined forces with the battered 2nd Platoon, which dug in about fifty yards from the 3rd Platoon. Company F was also isolated that night on the shoulder of Hill 56.

The two companies fully expected enemy counterattacks that night against their slender resources, but nothing happened. Perhaps that was because the marines of the other two battalions of the regiment gave support fire all day long, and so did the artillery. So did marine air. VMF-14 flew six close support missions that day for the infantry, breaking up one counterattack on Hill 105-S and keeping the enemy off balance. And when night came the sky was bright with the flashes of the 11th Marines' howitzers as they plastered the North Korean defenses.

That day, September 23, the 7th Marines, the third rifle regiment of the 1st Marine Division, came into the line, moving across the Han to the rear of the 5th Marines. The regiment was green, composed of men shifted from other duties or newly trained. General Smith decided to work them in gradually to give them experience without enormous responsibility. They were assigned to cover the division's left flank, along a ridge line running north from the ferry crossing at Haengju.

On the southern flank of the X Corps line, the 7th Division's 32nd Infantry captured a main objective on September 23; a hill three miles below the Han River, and seven miles south of Yongdungpo, which dominated the approaches to the Han River and Seoul from the southeast.

And farther south, along the Pusan Perimeter, the North Koreans had begun their withdrawal everywhere. The speed with which the Americans had taken Inchon and Kimpo and Yongdungpo was an obvious warning to the North Korean high command that a hundred thousand troops were threatened and might be cut off and pounded between the two arms of the UN force. This knowledge, not any sudden surge of superiority by the beleaguered Eighth Army, led to the North Korean move northward.

General MacArthur was still not very pleased with the Eighth Army, particularly since at 160,000 men it vastly outnumbered the North Korean force around it. Three days after his shipboard appraisal that called for a new landing on the west coast because of the Eighth Army's inability to move, the army still had not made any significant progress. But on September 21 came information that indicated the enemy was withdrawing all along the line. The information came from Colonel Lee Hak Ku, chief of staff of the NK 13th Division. Very late at night, Colonel Lee drove from his headquarters to the village of Samsan-dong, south of Tabu-dong which had been the scene of so much bitter fighting. He found two American soldiers of the 8th Cavalry Regiment, sound asleep on the roadside. He shook them awake and then surrendered to them. Taken back to headquarters, the colonel gave a full picture of the situation of the North Korean 13th Division. It was down to 1,500 men, he said, no longer an effective unit and its men were fleeing toward Sangju. All the division's tanks were destroyed and it had left only two of sixteen self-propelled guns. There was still some artillery and some ammunition, but rations had been cut in half. The colonel also had observations about other North Korean units and all of them indicated a desperate situation around the perimeter. When General Walker learned all this, he prepared to move.

On September 22 General Walker issued orders for a general offensive— every unit was to prepare to strike the enemy, envelop the units, and try to destroy them. The I Corps was to move up the main roads from Taegu and then Taejon, to meet the 7th Division at Suwon. The 2nd Division and the

25th Division were reorganized into the IX Corps under Major General John B. Coulter. The 2nd Division was to attack toward Chonju. The 25th Division was to take Chinju and then be ready to move west or northwest as needed. The ROK forces on the east were to march up the east coast.

The only southern force that actually got into operation against the enemy on September 22 was the British 27th Infantry Brigade which was attached to the U.S. 24th Division. The brigade was across the Naktong and ready to attack before daylight. At dawn the 1st Battalion of the Middlesex Regiment seized Plum Pudding Hill (their name for it) on the right of the highway, three miles south of Songju. The battalion did not stop there but immediately attacked high ground to the northeast, which the British called Middlesex Hill. Supported by American tanks, they took the hill against heavy opposition and were in control before darkness fell. That was the real beginning of the Eighth Army's breakout.

Also on September 22, Task Force 777 began to move. This task force was led by Lieutenant Colonel William A. Harris. He had been assigned by Major General Hobart Gay, commander of the 1st Cavalry Division, to lead the pursuit of the enemy. The 3rd Battalion of the 7th Cavalry was to take the lead, supported by the 77th Field Artillery Battalion and the 70th Tank Battalion. This force was called Task Force Lynch, after Lieutenant Colonel James H. Lynch, the commander of the cavalry battalion.

On the night of September 21 Task Force Lynch had been involved in a fight with a large but disorganized North Korean force of stragglers who had been caught below Tabu-dong by the course of events. At 8 A.M. on September 22 the task force moved out nevertheless, virtually surrounded by small groups of disorganized North Koreans, as the tanks led the way up the road. Flights of fighter planes zoomed low above the road strafing fleeing groups of North Koreans.

When the advance tanks reached a point near Naksong-dong where the road curved around a hill, suddenly the lead tank was stopped by enemy fire. No one could see the guns, but General Gay, who was with this group, ordered the other four tanks of the unit to speed around the hill firing their guns, and they did. In the course of the rush they overran the two antitank guns around the corner which had been causing the trouble.

A little further on, the column was again stopped by a small group of North Koreans who held them up with a grenade attack. But it took no more than ten minutes to disperse this group, and the column went on.

After some confusion involving the point at which the task force would cross the Naktong, that evening Task Force Lynch moved toward Naktong-ni. It was a bright night as the tanks rolled. Five miles along the road the column began moving through burning villages. The North Koreans were scorching the earth behind them, killing prisoners and civilians. One large group of retreating North Koreans was captured, offering no resistance. At ten thirty that night the lead tanks halted on the cliff overlooking the Naktong River crossing down below at Naktong-ni. There was activity down there, and the lead tank fired at an antitank gun. The shell missed but struck an ammunition truck that was concealed nearby. The ammunition went up with an enormous flash and roar, and in the light the men of the column could see dozens of abandoned North Korean vehicles on the bank of the river, and hundreds of men either on the edge or swimming. The tanks and the machine gunners began firing on the enemy below and killed several hundred of them. The rest of the night was spent rounding up prisoners and captured equipment on the southeast bank of the Naktong.

The 24th Division was also supposed to start moving, but was delayed. On September 22 enemy artillery destroyed the only raft at the Naktong River ferry and cut the footbridge. This prevented the ferrying of vehicles and supplies. Anything that came across the river that night was brought by Korean civilians on their heads and backs.

On the morning of September 23 the British were driving forward again. The Scottish Highlander Argyll Battalion attacked Hill 282 beside Middlesex Hill. They climbed up and surprised a North Korean unit at its breakfast. In an hour it was all over. Then the Highlanders looked across the way, at Hill 288, which dominated the area. They moved to attack, but the North Koreans who occupied the hill were also moving up to attack the Middlesex Regiment on its hills. The North Korean attack was supported by artillery and mortar fire. The British were supported by American artillery until, for some unknown reason, the American artillery support was withdrawn around noon. This left the British in a pickle. They called for an air strike. The P-51 fighters came in. The British put out their white recognition panels. So did the North Koreans. The P-51 pilots guessed wrong and plastered the Argyll position. It was a perfect air strike—if you were a North Korean. The Highlander position was wrecked, men scrabbled off the hill to escape the terrible napalm. Major Kenneth Muir, the executive officer of the Argylls, saw that a few men still held the top of the hill and he found about thirty uninjured soldiers to go with him to help them. But the North Koreans were coming up the other side, and when Muir's men got to the top they were mowed down by automatic fire. Muir was mortally wounded. Only a dozen men were still on their feet. With so few men and little ammunition, Major A. I. Gordon-Ingraham, the Highlander commander, had to order a retreat. At three o'clock in the afternoon the Argylls were down at the bottom of the hill and the North Koreans were on the top. A nose count showed that the battalion had lost eighty-nine men, sixty of them to the P-51s.

That September 23, the 24th Division started its drive up the road toward Seoul. The 21st Infantry led the way toward Kumchon, but soon stopped. The reason was the NK 105th Armored Division which had set up a system of minefields, guarded by camouflaged tanks dug into the ground, and many antitank guns. The Americans brought up a company of the 6th Medium Tank Battalion (Patton M-46 tanks) and these engaged the enemy. The Americans lost four tanks while destroying three.

On the south the 27th Infantry prepared to move to the Nam River and attack through Uiryong to Chinju. (See Map 15.) At the same time the 35th Infantry was to attack at the Chinju Pass. The 27th Infantry did not get going that day, and the 35th Infantry was held all day at the pass by troops of the NK 6th Division.

In the area of the Naktong Bulge, so well known to the 5th Marines, three North Korean divisions began their western retreat on September 22. The next day the 38th Infantry followed, but was stalled by a delaying force in the hills around Chogye.

On the night of September 23 General Smith realized that the North Koreans were making their major stand in the hills northwest of Seoul where the 5th Marines were engaged. The matter came up in a conference at X Corps Headquarters. General Almond was pressing again for the capture of Seoul by September 25—that political issue once more. He was unhappy with the progress of the marines. He suggested that General Smith send the 1st Marines around to the southeast to attack Seoul from another angle, while the 5th Marines continued the assault from the northwest. But Smith said that if the 1st Marines were thus detached it would be much harder to take the city. It could mean street fighting in Seoul itself, which would again mean more time lost. Further, the strength of the North Koreans northwest of Seoul indicated another regiment had to be employed to break the defense.

General Almond did not like this suggestion at all. He knew that General MacArthur would be unhappy if Seoul were not taken by September 25; to take it would give MacArthur another of those prized opportunities for the polemics he managed so well. In a manner that the marines could not help but regard as threatening, Almond announced that they could have one more day, twenty-four hours. If they did not then capture Seoul, Almond would bring the 7th Division and its 32nd Regiment into the battle for Seoul, in the southeast, to envelop the city.

Thus it was settled on the night of September 23. The marines had one more day. The 1st Marines would continue their approach from Yongdungpo to join the 5th Marines in the assault. And as the two regiments broke into the city, the 7th Marines would come down from the northwest to add the final bit of strength that would topple the North Korean defense.

The conference broke up then with very little good feeling between army and marine commands.

9

A Ridge Named Smith

On the morning of September 24 the attack began again. General Smith had a pretty good idea now that he was facing the enemy main line of resistance outside Seoul. He still did not know that he was facing Major General Wol Ki Chan, a Soviet-trained officer, with the 5,000-man 25th Brigade, made up of officers and noncommissioned officers who had learned their trade with the Chinese Communist armies in the fight against the Japanese and then against the Chinese Nationalists. The 25th Brigade was strictly a firepower outfit. It had only two infantry battalions. The rest were machine gun battalions with heavy machine guns, mortar battalions, a 76 mm artillery battalion, and an engineer battalion skilled in the use of mines. General Wol had been brought down from Chorwon with the specific task of organizing a defense of Seoul northwest of the city. He had been given other troops, including the NK 31st Rifle Division of 3,500 men. So up on those hills were 10,000 tough North Korean soldiers ready to fight. And opposing them at this moment were the 5th Marines. The hill the Koreans call An-san, Hill 296, was the key to the defense.

Even though not all this was known to General Smith on the night of September 23, the 1st Marines were now ordered to move up on the right flank of the 5th Marines and turn to the northeast, attacking through the heart of Seoul. The 7th Marines closed up on the 5th Marines' left flank, to prevent

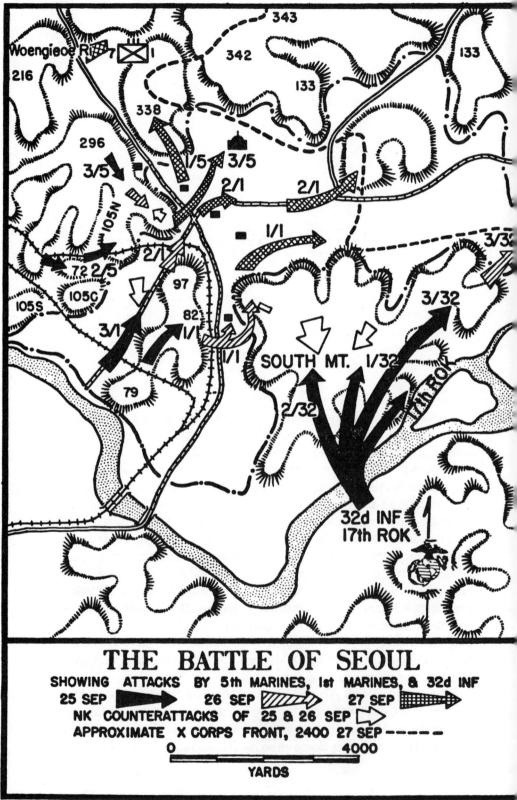

343

342

133

216

Woengieoe Ri 7 1

133

338

296

1/5 3/5

3/5

105N

2/1 2/1

1/1

3/32

72 2/5 2/1

105C

97

3/32

105S

82

3/1 1/1

1/1 SOUTH MT. 1/32

79

2/32

17th ROK

32d INF
17th ROK

THE BATTLE OF SEOUL
SHOWING ATTACKS BY 5th MARINES, 1st MARINES, & 32d INF
25 SEP ➤ 26 SEP ➤ 27 SEP ➤
NK COUNTERATTACKS OF 25 & 26 SEP ⇨
APPROXIMATE X CORPS FRONT, 2400 27 SEP - - - - -

0   4000
YARDS

Map 17.

the enemy from escaping. The 5th Marines would drive ahead against the hills.

On Hill 56, Company D and Company F still clung to their small perimeters. They had heard the North Koreans bringing up supplies and digging in around them during the night. All three of Company F's platoon officers had been wounded the day before, but all had refused to be evacuated.

The order that morning called for the 2nd Battalion to continue its attack until it reached Hill 105-N. That meant the two companies were to move against about 2,500 enemy troops who were heavily armed with automatic weapons, mortars and artillery, and dug in on the ridge near Hill 88, Hill 296, and Hill 105-N. (See Map 17.)

The 3rd Battalion was to support the frontal attack with a flanking movement along the eastern spur of Hill 296. The 1st Battalion would occupy the positions vacated by the 3rd Battalion and protect the flank.

The action began that night of September 23–24 in the fashion that the North Koreans had learned so well from the Chinese Communists—the night harassment attack. As darkness fell, the enemy machine guns kept up a heavy fire against the positions held by the 1st Battalion. They were somewhat discouraged by a night fighter plane from VMF (N)-542 that roamed about over Seoul, the Han River, and Yongdungpo, but the plane could not be everywhere at once. Late that night North Korean troops came quietly up the hillside occupied by Company C, in their rubber shoes, and overran one platoon, killing the crew of a machine gun and taking the gun off with them. They moved down to the base of the hill. They would fire a burst, which lighted up their position, then move and fire another. Captain Francis Fenton of Company C warned his men not to reply. This inactivity spurred the North Koreans to carelessness. They came up very close to the marine positions. The marines could hear them moving about, scraping, panting, muttering as they moved the machine gun. Then came the right moment, on command every marine in the line threw a grenade toward the noise, and almost simultaneously they exploded. There was no more noise. "That discouraged the enemy and he withdrew," wrote Captain Fenton in his After Action Report.

The enemy tactics continued the same.

On September 24, the action began before dawn in the 3rd Battalion sector of Hill 296. One small counterattack was repelled but was followed almost immediately by another.

But the main action was to be from the 2nd Battalion. Captain Peters' F Company was now down to about ninety men, and some of them had been wounded. Corporal Weldon D. Harris had been wounded twice the day before, in killing three North Koreans in hand-to-hand combat. He had refused evacuation to fight on. Still, Captain Peters had to weed out those too badly hurt to fight, no matter what they said. He sent Lieutenant Harry Nolan to the rear, and Lieutenant Anderson commanded what was left of the 2nd and 3rd platoons—about twenty riflemen. Lieutenant Albert Belbusti's 1st Platoon was about the same size. The rest of the ninety men were machine gunners, mortarmen, and ammunition carriers. Lieutenant Smith's Company D was better off. He had two platoons almost intact. Lieutenant Colonel Roise planned to bring up Company E, the reserve, between the other two to capture Hill 105-N.

Shortly after dawn, the 11th Marines' artillery again began working the guns that had hardly cooled all night. At 6:10 A.M. the guns began a twenty-minute barrage. At the end of it, VMF-323 staged an air strike with 500-pound bombs that they laid down within a hundred yards of the marine line.

The marines jumped off then, trying to take the high ground. Company F, in the wake of that close air support, did manage to achieve a superior position on the lower part of the ridge.

Company D was bothered by a low ground mist that cut down visibility and by smoke from burning huts in its area. Company D moved forward to the northeast, to take the wooded hill and ridge. Visibility was terrible. Before the marines knew it they were on top of the enemy. Both were surprised. The enemy began firing automatic weapons from the ridge and soon had Company D pinned down. (See map 17.) For the next two hours they were stuck. Tanks moving up the road in support came under enemy artillery fire and one tank hit a box mine, which knocked off a tread. A second caught a direct hit from a mortar shell on the motor hatch and it squealed to a stop.

Lieutenant Smith was stuck below a large knob that crossed the sunken road from Hill 56. It had to be taken so that Smith could move forward to that troublesome ridge and clear the enemy out of the woods there.

When the attack stalled, Smith called up every man to the line, including the company clerks.

For a time then the fight was machine gun against machine gun, mortar against mortar and grenade against grenade. The North Koreans tried a flanking movement. They were driven back by the marines. Lieutenant George C. McNaughton's platoon was in the lead. He was wounded in the shoulder but he kept going. He sent a squad under Sergeant Robert Smith to flank the enemy on the left and work up the reverse slope of the hill on the east. Sergeant Smith and his men made the ridge line, but were promptly brought under fire from high ground across the way. In ten minutes seven men were killed and four were wounded. A pharmacist's mate, James Egresitz, started up to help the wounded but was shot down and died. The fire continued. Finally one BAR man and two riflemen came back down the ridge line. All were wounded. They were the survivors of the flank attack.

At ten o'clock that morning Lieutenant Smith sent a message to battalion headquarters to ask for reinforcement. Lieutenant Colonel Roise said he had none to send. The only reserve, Company E, was committed to the final attack on Hill 88 and Hill 105-N. So it was win or die. The marines tightened up the defense. When Lieutenant George Grimes' 60 mm mortar section ran out of shells, the mortarmen picked up their rifles.

The North Koreans launched an attack against the marine right flank. The marine machine guns opened up. The two machine guns out front kept up a steady fire. The NCO in charge of the gun section was shot down, but a squad leader took over and the guns kept firing. Some of the gunners were casualties, then ammunition carriers took over the guns. Lieutenant Karle Seydel served as ammunition carrier for those machine guns and made five round trips under fire to keep them supplied with ammunition. Despite the fact that he was a constant target he was not hit.

Lieutenant Smith had tried the right flank and it did not work. He sent Lieutenant Lee Howard out on the left flank, but Howard was wounded and the marines were driven back.

At about 10:30 A.M. the smoke and mist began to clear, and then battalion could do something for them. Lieutenant Karl Wirth, the forward observer for the 11th Marines, began to see targets. The guns of the 11th Marines began to speak up, accompanied by the 81 mm howitzers of the battalion weapons company. Lieutenant Colonel Roise ordered an air strike, and four planes of VMF-323 roared in with bombs, rockets, and the wicked napalm.

Fire was coming in from three directions, the only part free was west, where the men of Company F were slowly winning their battle. The going was hard. Corporal Harris got his third wound, and this one was fatal. Other men fell, but Captain Peters' company was moving up. Having reached the east side of the ridge, Peters found the casualties fewer and the going easier. One reason was the great help of VMF-214, whose Corsairs screamed in with bombs and napalm and rockets. That day VMF-214 launched five aircraft every two hours to support the attack. VMF-212 put up twelve flights of four planes each. The Company F attack consisted of two long firefights, and the second was more a slaughter than a fight. The marines had taken most of the ridge when Captain Peters sent Lieutenant Anderson's men forward to eliminate an enemy strong point that was firing on them from a distance. Anderson's men took cover behind a stone wall and peppered the enemy who retreated into an open field. Then the slaughter began.

As Lieutenant Smith made ready for another assault, he counted noses. He had forty-four men left on their feet, and four officers, including the wounded McNaughton and Lieutenant Wirth, the artillery observer. Just after 10:30 A.M. they moved out across terrain studded with North Korean foxholes and trenches. They came across scores of North Koreans, but most of them were dead, victims of the artillery, the mortar shells, the rockets, and the napalm. The going was much easier than anyone had expected. Halfway up Lieutenant Smith stopped to regroup his skirmish line, and then he led his men to the top of the ridge. They made it, but there Smith was killed, five other men were hit, and when they reached the last line, Lieutenant McNaughton, the acting company commander, had only twenty-six men still on their feet. At the top they found three enemy officers and more than a company of North Korean troops, but they were in flight. The marines paused and began to shoot. Their BARS and machine guns followed the enemy down the hillside as they fled toward Seoul, and North Koreans began to fall under the onslaught. At one o'clock that afternoon, Lieutenant McNaughton was able to tell the battalion command post that the objective was secured. Two hours later Company F made a similar report about its gains. Captain Peters reported the death of his machine gun platoon commander, Lieutenant Wiley J. Grigsby, and three others. Three men were wounded.

When Lieutenant Colonel Roise learned that both companies had taken their objectives and the way was clear, he committed Company E to its attack. The time was about three o'clock in the afternoon. Hill 88 and Hill 72 barred the way to Hill 105-C and Hill 105-N. Captain Jaskilka's company was to clear the way. He set off in midmorning and by noon had taken Hill 88, backed up by the artillery. But Hill 72 still stood out there, able to enfilade the other high points. Jaskilka had to go after Hill 72 before Hill 105-C could fall. He discussed the area to be fired on with the artillery. They could not find Hill 72 and asked for map coordinates. Map coordinates? What map coordinates? "Just look out there," said Jaskilka. "It looks like Nellie's tit. . . ."

The artillerymen looked, and they saw.

Under heavy artillery support Captain Jaskilka's men moved up to the skirmish line, led by tanks. They ran into heavy machine gun and mortar fire. The tanks ran into a minefield. One was knocked out by a mine and the other by a mortar. The three other tanks were stalled until Staff Sergeant Stanley B. McPherson of the 1st Engineer Battalion cleared a path for them under fire. It seemed impossible that he was unhurt, but there it was. When he had made the way safe, the tanks sped ahead and swiftly knocked out two antitank guns and rolled over several machine gun positions. Hill 88 fell. Hill 72—Nellie's Tit—remained. And until it was taken, the Hill 105 would remain a problem.

From its height the enemy could fire down on both these hills and the valley that surrounded it. But the trouble was that it was growing late for another assault. Lieutenant Colonel Roise ordered the marines to go into perimeter defense for the night and await the following day to attack again.

Company D had gone into the battle with 206 officers and men. At the end, 152 of these had fallen: 36 dead, including the company commander, 116 wounded seriously enough to demand evacuation. Twenty-six of the survivors were also wounded but continued to fight to the end. The marines counted the enemy dead that day, they numbered some 1,500 on Hill 56 and the ridge, and 1,750 on the Hill 296 defenses. Some of these, of course, were killed by the infantry and the tanks, but the vast majority had fallen to the artillery and the air strikes.

Now the marines held most of the defense line, including that troublesome ridge Hill 105-N that had cost Company D so dear. And in their fashion, the men of Company D honored the dead commander who had led them up there. Forever after the tree-lined height would be known to marines as Smith's Ridge.

10

Seoul and the Nutcracker

On that morning of September 24 the 1st Marines were stirring long before dawn. The North Korean engineers had done a good job of mining the area around Hill 105-S. Company C of the 1st Engineer Battalion set about undoing what the enemy had done. By dawn they had cleared a site on the southwest bank of the Han at which the 1st Marines would cross the river. This place was about a mile and a quarter southwest of Hill 105-S.

There were still delays. The troops continued to encounter mines cunningly laid, and the engineers had to root them out or explode them. It was eight in the morning before the first elements of the regiment were on the water in the LVTs.

The 2nd Battalion crossed first. On the other side of the Han they met virtually no opposition, which was just as well because they had no tank support since they had no ferry yet. Even nine days after the initial landing at Inchon the desperate nature of General MacArthur's gamble was still readily apparent. The X Corps, faced with bridging rivers, had no bridging equipment. Luckily the enemy opposition was so slight that they were able to move immediately toward Hill 79. (See Map 18.) By afternoon the 1st Marines were in contact with the 5th Marines and moving abreast of them on a 1,500-yard front against Hill 79.

While this crossing was occurring, General Almond was visiting General

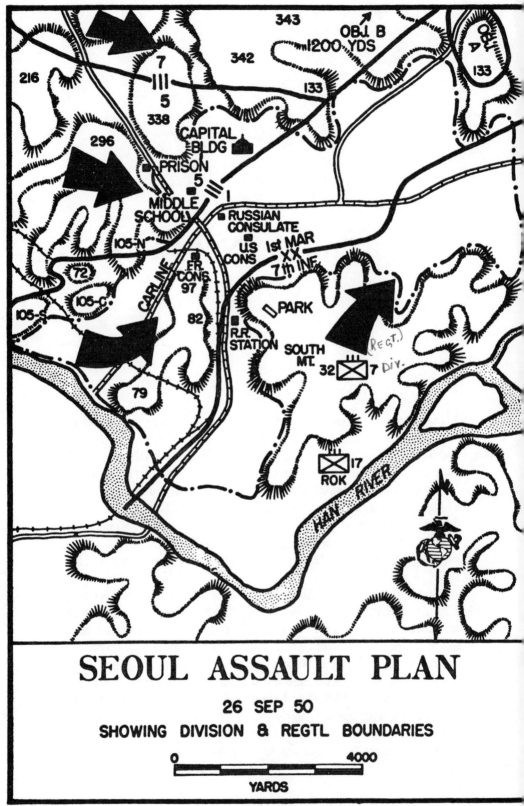

SEOUL ASSAULT PLAN

26 SEP 50

SHOWING DIVISION & REGTL BOUNDARIES

0   4000

YARDS

Map 18.

Barr of the 7th Division. General Almond was still concerned that the marines were not doing their job, and he decided that he would not wait the twenty-four hours but would send the army in to help. He ordered General Barr to use the ROK 17th Regiment (again a political move) and the Army's 32nd Infantry to cross the Han and attack around from the southeast into Seoul. They would be taken across the river by the marine amtracs as soon as the 1st Marines were through with them. That would be on the morning of September 25. Having made that decision and communicated it to General Barr, General Almond then visited Colonel Puller of the 1st Marines at his command post and Colonel Murray of the 5th Marines, and he informed them of his new orders, without first informing General Smith, the division commander.

That afternoon of September 24, General Smith discovered this change when he and other commanders met General Almond for a conference at the Yongdungpo traffic circle near the city hall. He announced that General Barr would move at six o'clock the next morning. Then, the X Corps commander told General Smith that he had gone over his head and issued orders directly to the marine regimental commanders.

General Smith was furious. He requested—in a tone that meant demanded —that General Almond refrain from interfering with his command. General Almond backed water and denied that he had done so. But Smith already had the word from Murray and Puller that the X Corps commander had indeed issued orders to them. Thus in his haste to take Seoul for General MacArthur's greater glory, Almond committed an unpardonable breach of military courtesy and cast serious aspersions on the abilities of the marines. He tried to brush it all aside but the fact was that he had opened a wound that would remain, and the always uneasy command relationship between marines and army had become as bad at the end of the first three months of the Korean War as it had been only after three years of the Pacific War.

While this wound began to fester, Colonel Puller was very busy. Second unit of the 1st Marines to cross the Han that day was the 1st Battalion accompanied by regimental headquarters. As they crossed over, Colonel Puller told Lieutenant Colonel Hawkins that he had better drive east along the river and pass through the 2nd Battalion to make his attack. The 2nd Battalion by that time was far ahead, and Hawkins indicated that this pass through might be a little difficult.

"You'll just have to advance a little faster," said Colonel Puller.

Whereupon Lieutenant Colonel Hawkins put his men into double time and they literally ran along the river to find and overtake the 2nd Battalion.

The marines were moving fast, so fast that in the areas they ran through small pockets of enemy troops were left behind. There was a price for this speedy movement: it meant casualties. In the case of the 1st Marines that day the casualties were fifteen men killed or wounded in "friendly" territory by enemy stragglers. But General MacArthur would have Seoul on September 25, and this was part of the price.

At one o'clock on the afternoon of September 24, the 1st Battalion passed through the 2nd Battalion and continued the attack, supported by artillery and 4.2-inch mortars. They reached Hill 79 which was located in Seoul proper at three o'clock and raised the American flag atop it. The rest of the afternoon was spent in consolidating positions. The 3rd Battalion came up and cleared the stragglers off Hill 105-S at dusk. All three battalions then settled down for the night, prepared to battle for Seoul the next day.

In the south, the forces of the Eighth Army were moving, but not nearly so expeditiously as General Walker had hoped or General MacArthur had earlier expected. On September 23 it had become apparent all along the line that the North Korean strength was now very spotty in the south. Some divisions were virtually destroyed and their men reduced to stragglers. Other units remained strong in power and morale. The only way to find out was to move up and attack.

On the day that General Coulter assumed command of the IX Corps— September 23—he moved the 27th Regiment around from the south to the northern edge of the 25th Division. To speed the move, General Kean formed a new task force, Task Force Torman, under Captain Charles J. Torman. This unit was to take the spearhead in clearing the way for the 27th Regiment, and it did, leading the regiment along the coastal road toward Chinju. Next morning the task force moved up to the Nam River bridge there. Captain Torman was wounded when a tank ran over a box mine and he was hit by fragments. He was out of the battle and on his way to the hospital in an hour.

On September 24, the 35th Regiment, which had been delayed by a skillful action of the NK 6th Division at the Chinju Pass, consolidated its position there instead of moving up. Too little and too late. That night the commander learned that the North Koreans had crossed over the Nam bridge at Chinju and then blown it. The plan had to be changed. The 35th would have to cross downstream, and it had best get moving. So it moved, and at two o'clock on the morning of September 25 the 2nd Battalion of the regiment crossed the river two and a half miles southeast of Chinju and attacked. The battalion was supported by fire from Task Force Torman's tanks on the other side of the river.

About three hundred NK 6th Division troops staged a rear guard action in

Chinju and again delayed the 35th Regiment. It was midafternoon on September 25 before the other two battalions crossed over the river into the town. Later Task Force Torman came across on an underwater bridge made of sandbags by the engineers in the North Korean fashion. The 65th Engineer Combat Battalion then spent the whole night of September 25 repairing the highway bridge so that it could carry vehicular traffic. And sixteen miles downstream from Chinju engineers and Korean refugees worked to build another underwater bridge across the Nam. These people were under fire most of the day.

All this, of course, was a long, long way from Seoul and what was happening here had nothing to do with the "anvil effect" wanted by General MacArthur.

General Walker tried to invigorate the movement. On September 24 he ordered IX Corps to make unlimited attacks, to seize Chonju and Kanggyong. General Kean tried to comply. He set up two task forces both built around armor, both designed to be speedy in the fashion of General George Patton's 3rd Army forces of World War II that drove so vigorously through France. They were Task Force Matthews and Task Force Dolvin. Each was to begin its drive from Chinju. Task Force Matthews was to drive north along the coastal area to Kunsan. Task Force Dolvin was to take the inner road winding up at Kanggyong on the Kum River. If these two forces could get rolling, in a day they could reach their objective and perhaps give General MacArthur a sense that the Eighth Army had gotten out of its bog after all.

But once again, the North Koreans had done a good job of balking the American advance. Three well-blown bridges west of Chinju delayed Task Force Matthews. And for the same reason Task Force Dolvin didn't get going on September 24 and 25. So much for General Walker's hopes for speed in an end run around the southwest corner.

Farther north, opposite the old Naktong Bulge, the 38th Infantry and the 2nd Division faced troops of the NK 2nd, 4th and 9th divisions in the Chogye area. The fighting was quite spirited on September 23. The next day the 23rd Infantry from the southeast came up to assist the 38th Infantry in a double envelopment of Hyopchon. About two battalions of North Korean troops were still in the town. The 23rd Infantry came up the road from the south while the 38th Infantry put a roadblock across the road leading to Kumchon. The 38th Infantry waited, the 23rd Infantry entered Hyopchon, and the North Koreans spilled out on the road to the northeast. It was a "turkey shoot" for the 38th Infantry then, and the Americans claimed to have killed about three hundred North Korean troops at the roadblock.

All along the roads in this area, North Korean troops were fleeing northward. They were harried all day on September 24 by P-51s of the Fifth Air Force, and in the fifty-three sorties flown that day in that area several hundred enemy soldiers were killed. The rest were reduced to mobs, large and small, scrambling out of the way of the diving aircraft, moving off the roads and onto trails that led up into the mountains.

That night of September 24, part of the 38th Infantry moved down into Hyopchon from the north. On the morning of the 25th, the 38th Infantry started northwest from Hyopchon. But they soon bogged down on the road. The NK 2nd Division had gone ahead of them, toward Kochang, abandoning its heavy equipment as it ran out of gas or broke down. The road was choked with enemy wreckage and immovable equipment. Trucks, motorcycles, antitank guns, artillery pieces, and mortars all had to be dealt with. Prisoners had to be taken, and that day four hundred and fifty were rounded up. Enemy troops that still had fight in them had to be killed, and about two hundred and fifty were that day. By day's end the NK 2nd Division was no more. What remained was a disorganized rabble of about twenty-five hundred men scattering into the mountains where they would become an enormous nuisance. Their commander, Major General Choe Hyon, was with them, hoping to restore them to a fighting force.

The 23rd Infantry was supposed to take an alternative route to Kochang, parallel to the road of the 38th Infantry. But although the road existed on a map, it did not exist on the ground. Again, delay and confusion, and the unit was slow in getting moving.

Despite the difficulties of being bombed by the Americans, the British in the Songju area kept moving north. Their pluck impressed the American 19th Infantry, and attacking south from Pusang-dong on the Waegwan–Kumchon road, that unit captured Songju at two o'clock on the morning of September 24. The British were below the town. Next day, September 24, the Allies mopped up enemy remnants in the Songju area.

The NK 10th Division had been fighting the holding action in the Songju area. But with the fall of the city, the unit withdrew. Its situation was desperate. Most of its vehicles were nearly out of gas. Most of its artillery was out of ammunition. To keep the Americans and British from capturing the guns, the artillerymen buried them—hopeful that the day would come when they would once again ride triumphantly, down this road and recover their lost arms.

This day for the first time the North Korean I Corps commander admitted that something was very wrong, and he ordered a general retreat of the NK I Corps northward.

The U.S. 24th Division was retracing the steps it had taken southward in what sometimes seemed eons ago, sometimes seemed only yesterday. This time they were moving north along the Taejon–Seoul highway, the sweet smell of victory in their nostrils instead of the acrid stink of defeat. After the tank battle of September 23, the 5th Regimental Combat Team took the lead and drove on until it reached an eminence known as Hill 140, north of the road. Here dug-in enemy troops stopped the movement forward, a rear guard action to permit thousands of other troops to escape northward. The NK I Corps order called for the NK 9th Division to fight the rear guard action, and it diverted to Kumchon to hold up the UN forces. The North Koreans still had a handful of antitank guns and tanks from the ranks of the 849th Independent Anti-Tank Regiment and the 105th Armored Division. These were thrown into the Kumchon struggle, and they moved into and south of Kumchon to meet the Americans. In the battle that followed on September 24, the Americans lost six Patton tanks and the North Koreans lost eight T-34s. The Fifth Air Force made the difference, for its planes destroyed five of those enemy tanks. The 5th RCT had a hundred casualties, the North Koreans had far more. At the end of the action the 849th Independent Anti-Tank Regiment had ceased to exist for all practical purposes. There was one other element of this battle that surprised everyone involved. Lieutenant George W. Nelson of the Fifth Air Force was piloting an AT-6, or "mosquito," as they were called in Korea. This lightweight plane was used to spot enemy troops and vehicle concentrations and call down attacks by the fighters and bombers. Lieutenant Nelson was flying over the Kunsan area and he spotted some two hundred enemy troops on the ground. They seemed to be disorganized. He scribbled a note on his knee, ordering them to lay down their arms and assemble atop a nearby hill to surrender. He signed it "MacArthur," swooped down, weighted the note, and dropped it. As he circled he saw the troops beginning to comply and soon they were all marching docilely up the hill. Nelson flew around until he spotted a 24th Division patrol, and he dropped another note telling them to go back and pick up the prisoners. They did. Thus a Fifth Air Force pilot captured some two hundred prisoners for the first such feat of the war. The air force wreaked a great deal of damage on the retreating enemy. The debriefing officers totaled it up as of September 24 and found that some eight thousand enemy soldiers had been destroyed in the past few days. No one was inclined to doubt their figures, the carnage on the roads lent credence to the claims.

Once again, the ragged nature of the fighting left behind many small units of North Korean troops who harried the following American units. But at least the 5th RCT was moving, and that night of September 24 the 21st Infantry swung north of the highway to make a flanking attack on Kumchon.

But the most spectacular movement of the Eighth Army forces was that of Task Force Lynch. Having reached the Naktong-ni crossing site of the Naktong River and blown up an ammunition truck, the task force began to cross the Naktong. Colonel Lynch ordered the crossing at four thirty on the morning of September 23. An hour later his advance companies had secured the far bank. That day Major William O. Witherspoon, Jr., led the 1st Battalion on ten miles to Sangju, which had been hurriedly abandoned by the enemy. Task Force Lynch was rolling. The only problem, as usual, was transportation across the rivers. Still no adequate bridging materials had appeared. But the engineers put together a ferry and a raft that were capable of moving tanks and on September 24 they put about four hundred South Koreans to work rebuilding one of the old North Korean underwater bridges. Before noon on the 24th tanks were rolling on the far side of the Naktong and hurrying to catch up with the infantry at Sangju. When they got there, Captain John R. Flynn moved out with a platoon of tanks and Company K of the 7th Cavalry. They moved swiftly to Poun, which was less than fifty miles from Chonan, the important road center. But they could not go beyond Poun, orders forbade it. And so there they stopped. The marines had already breached the door to Seoul, but the Eighth Army was still a hundred miles away.

On the east coast of Korea, the ROK Army was making far better progress. Part of the reason, of course, was the exhaustion of the North Korean forces they faced. Part was the terrain, which, though mountainous, did not have so many rivers to cross. But part of it must be attributed to the courage and eagerness of the South Korean soldiers. Their units did not travel by truck, they marched northward on foot, and yet in some areas they were outdistancing the motorized American forces on the other side of the peninsula.

Moving out of Taegu, the 6th Division gained sixteen miles on September 24, approaching the rugged Sobaek mountain range, coming up to Hamchang. The 8th Division on the east moved toward Andong, and at midnight on September 24 advance elements were in that city. But here there had to be a fight. The NK 8th and 12th divisions were retreating through Andong just then. The 12th Division had just about gone through, but the 8th Division arrived to find that the ROK troops had beaten them, and they had to detour around the city. They did so, but they mined and booby-trapped and set up rear guard actions that cost the 8th Division two important days.

On the far eastern side of the peninsula, the ROK 3rd Division was advancing on September 24, aided by Rear Admiral C. C. Hartman's American naval units, which kept a heavy pall of smoke from their guns over the enemy. The retreating enemy was forced off the coastal road and began to retire along inland trails. The ROK troops approached Yongdok.

On the night of September 24, as the marines and the army's 7th Division prepared in and near Seoul for the next day's fighting, it was apparent that the anvil effect was not going to be an important factor at this stage of the war. The North Korean 5th, 8th, 12th and 15th divisions had broken on September 23 and permitted the advance of the six ROK divisions in front of them. The ROK forces were driving hard in the east. And in the west Task Force Lynch had driven about thirty miles north. But the gap between the northern and southern commands was still far too great. The break had not come quickly enough. General Almond's X Corps was going to have to take Seoul and seal off the enemy's line of supply and escape, if it was to be done.

11

Seoul

September 25, 1950. Just three months earlier the North Korean People's Army had rolled across the 38th parallel and with almost contemptuous ease had pushed the Republic of Korea military forces along ahead of them. In two days they had captured Seoul, and then inaugurated a reign of terror which ended in the deaths of thousands of South Koreans. Anyone whose actions indicated a loyalty to the Republic of Korea was suspect and liable to "people's justice," which generally meant accusation followed by shooting. At best, the adherents of the republic could expect trial before a People's Court and summary punishment.

Just now, in September, Seoul was going through another bloodbath. On September 20 instructions of Pyongyang came to district headquarters in South Korea calling for the evacuation of prison inmates to North Korea. If the prisoners could not be taken north, then the instructions said they were to be shot on the spot. So as the marines moved up on Seoul, in the mountains and in the prisons hundreds of people were being killed, others suffering new nightmares—men like Koo Chul-Hoe. Koo, a South Korean newspaper reporter and politician, had been arrested by the North Koreans almost immediately after the invasion and continually imprisoned after that time. In midsummer he was held in the West Gate Culture House (culture house was the North Korean euphemism for prison), in Detention House No. 1, Cell No.

10, Second Floor, with nineteen other cellmates. Koo fell ill and was moved to the infirmary. It was hardly better than the cell he had vacated, with thirty inmates, sleeping on the floor with dirty blankets. The "patients" received virtually no medical care and one or two died every day.

On the morning of September 15, Koo learned that something was in the wind. The officials in charge of his prison suddenly began rushing about excitedly, holding meetings and paying no attention to the prisoners. The next day, the North Koreans began preparing the prisoners for a change. They asked them how they could stand a march of twenty-five miles or so. The implication was that the prisoners were to be taken out to help in the harvest of crops. But Koo and some others sensed that this was far from the truth. For the next three days the jailers moved several thousand prisoners out, on the road north. On September 20 it became apparent that the UN forces were advancing; in Koo's jail he could hear the rumble of gunfire day and night. On September 21 Koo and his friends saw North Korean soldiers with branches on their heads climbing the hill behind the prison. They were headed for the front. The next morning at ten the Political Security Bureau men (the secret police) came to the prison and began checking the names and crimes of prisoners. Ten minutes later Koo heard noise in the prison yard and, looking out of his building, saw prisoners running in every direction while the guards fired at them. The guards shot them down with burp guns. Koo and three friends tried to escape. They got out of their building, but the guards spotted them and began shooting.

That night the shelling of Seoul took on a new urgency. Shells dropped around the prison yard. Koo and his friends took refuge in a hiding place in the rafters of their building. Thus they escaped murder. They hid until hunger forced them down from the hiding place—it was September 23, the day the marines were assaulting the "Main Line of Resistance" on the other side of the mountain. One of Koo's friends went to the kitchen. The "instructors" were not around, so the kitchen help gave him some white rice and dried fish that had obviously been meant for the captors, not the captives. When Koo and his friends came down they found that most of the guards had left. Where they had gone they did not know. They knew that there were still enough "instructors" to retain authority. That night they were told they would be taken north. North Korean officers and men came into their room and tied the hands of the four prisoners and tied their arms together in pairs. Koo was tied together with Choo Yung-sup, an old friend from his home town.

"We are taking you to the army hospital to protect you," said the officer. "If we left you here, you may be massacred when the Americans and the remnant National army come."

The officer left them then, tied up.

An hour passed. The captives lay there in the dark, waiting. Koo spent the hour freeing his hands, but he was careful to leave the ropes on so they would pass a cursory inspection. They heard the sound of heavy leathery footsteps and saw lights from flashlights. Their captors were returning. There were seven of them, the officer who had ordered them tied, two armed instructors, and four North Korean soldiers. The North Koreans announced that the car was ready to take them north and demanded that the prisoners come out. They herded the prisoners to the front of an L-shaped air raid dugout shelter next to the prison doctor's office. Then, without a word, they aimed their guns at them. At that second Koo realized the air raid shelter was to be their grave. Reflexively, Koo dropped into the dugout, freeing his hands from those of his companion Choo. He ducked around the corner of the shelter. The shots began. Choo and the other two jerked, fell, and lay still.

The officer flashed his light on the bodies.

"One scoundrel isn't there," he said.

The lights flashed again, and fell on Koo. More shots, but they all went high. Koo lay perfectly still as another light played on his knee. He heard a voice:

"Let's put the rest in and cover them up."

The officer led the soldiers back to the infirmary to get more prisoners.

Koo got to his feet and made his way to the main cell area of the prison. The cells were empty. Everything was silent. Then he heard the sounds of gunfire again near the infirmary and he knew that more of his friends were dying. He prayed for them. He heard doors close. The prison was silent again, silent as the tomb it had become.

He tried to find a place to hide. He went into the flower garden which the "instructors" had maintained. He got into an oil drum in a corner, but felt it was too exposed. He got out. He heard someone call:

"Comrade Choo, have you seen a man going in this direction?"

Koo knew that someone had seen him and now they were hunting for him. He cowered under some plants as he heard footsteps coming his way. Then above he saw a parapet on the next level, and somehow, exerting a strength he did not know he had, he managed to climb up and hide behind it. The footsteps approached, the man lingered in the garden, obviously searching everywhere. He heard other voices, and then the footsteps and the voices died away.

Koo stayed for two nights on that rooftop, afraid to move. He was screened from the hot sun by the tall branch of an apricot tree. But he had neither food nor water. At the end of the second night he was so wild from thirst that he decided he would go down, if it meant dying, to have a drink of water. From his catbird seat he had been a spectator as the battle for the mountain raged. The North Korean troops came forward with their burp guns and held the ridge of the hill. The sound of firing grew louder that morning, and suddenly a figure appeared on the ridge that was not dressed in the gray-green of the North Korean People's Army. Then came another figure and another, and he watched as the North Koreans fled down the hill.

On the morning of September 25, the 1st Marine Division was ready to launch the first divisional attack of the war, with all three regiments abreast. On the left were the 7th Marines, in the middle the 5th Marines, and on the right the 1st Marines.

Farther south, prepared to move east and north, was the army's 32nd Infantry Regiment of the 7th Division, and about to wheel off to the south toward Suwon to meet Task Force Lynch was the 31st Infantry.

On the night of September 24 the marine amtracs of the 1st Amphibious Tractor Battalion and the 56th Amphibious Tank and Tractor Battalion prepared to take the men of the army's 32nd Infantry across the Han. With them, to help liberate Seoul, were troops of the ROK 17th Regiment, called The Seoul Regiment. Altogether about five thousand Americans and South Koreans would cross. The objective was the 900-foot mountain called Namsan, which extended from the river two miles deep inside Seoul to within a mile of the main railroad station and two miles from the Government House. The regiment's second objective was to seize Hill 120, two miles east at the southeast edge of Seoul. The third objective was Hill 348, a large mass five miles east of Seoul which dominated the eastern highway and rail line. The crossing was to be made at the Sinsa-ri ferry site, three miles east of the old rail and highway bridges across the Han. At four o'clock in the morning of September 25 General Almond and his staff came down from X Corps headquarters at Ascom City to watch the show. Major General Barr moved up to an advanced observation post near the river. There was not much to see because the whole river was bathed in heavy fog. At six o'clock the artillery and mortars began a thirty-minute barrage across the river. The barrage ended at six thirty and the 2nd Battalion of the 32nd Infantry boarded the amtracs and started across the river. Company F was in the lead.

One 76 mm gun fired a few rounds at the amtracs, and some small rounds bounced off the steel sides of the tractors.

The entire battalion moved across the river in the shelter of the fog and left the beach without a casualty. The men climbed out of the amtracs and stopped. At about seven thirty the fog lifted and then Corsairs from VMF-214 conducted air strikes on the enemy dug in on South Mountain and Hill 120, which was to be taken by the 1st Battalion. Those troops crossed the river and at eight thirty began moving east along the riverbank toward Hill 120. In midmorning, General Almond crossed the river to see how things were. He found the 2nd Battalion stopped, for no apparent reason. Nobody was shooting at them. General Almond spoke harshly to Lieutenant Colonel Charles M. Mount and Mount got his troops going. They climbed the cliffs which were thirty to sixty feet high, and then they advanced to the slopes of South Mountain. The 3rd Battalion crossed the river just after noon, and then came the ROK 17th Infantry which moved to the right flank and prepared for a night attack on Hill 348.

The army found South Mountain only lightly defended. By three o'clock in the afternoon, the 1st Battalion had reached the summit and was digging in. It had not attained its objective; Mount was supposed to link up with the 1st Marines and he did not make it.

It was apparent that General Wol, the North Korean commander, had not expected this crossing, for only the ROK 17th Regiment, which crossed last, ran into any concentration of fire. It had taken the general most of the day to get organized to meet this new threat from the southeast.

General Wol's efforts were concentrated that September 25 on attempting to prevent the marines from breaking into Seoul.

The attack began at seven o'clock that morning. The 1st Marines and the 2nd Korean Marine Battalion were to seize the high ground inside Seoul about six miles from their morning position, with South Mountain on the right and the Duk Soo Palace on the left. (See Map 18.) The Korean marines were to follow behind and mop up, thus preventing those unpleasant incidents of enemy attack in an apparently pacified zone.

The 5th Marines, along with the division reconnaissance company and the 1st Korean Marine Battalion, would take that part of Seoul's highlands overlooking the road to Uijongbu. This sector included the northwestern section of the city and the Government House. Again the Korean marines would come up behind to mop up.

The 7th Marines would protect the left flank of the division and take the high ground on both sides of the road to Kaesong, six miles northwest of the center of Seoul.

The remainder of the Korean marine regiment would remain behind as division reserve and would prepare to make a triumphal entry into Seoul for General MacArthur's high political purposes.

One new element had been added to the plan: the 187th Airborne Regimental Combat Team, which had recently landed at Kimpo airfield. Its 3rd Battalion would guard the left flank west of the Han River.

Before the troops moved that morning, the artillery paved the way with a barrage, and planes from VMF-214 on the carrier *Sicily* came in to smash the enemy positions on the Hill 296 defense complex. They were still very tough positions, and that included the antiaircraft gun positions manned by the 19th Antiaircraft Regiment of the North Korean army. This North Korean unit had established an excellent air defense around Seoul. The marine pilots called it a "flak trap." On September 24 ten F4Us had flown in support of the attack on Smith's Ridge, and five of them had been hard hit by flak.

This next day was a bad day for marine air: Lieutenant Colonel Walter Lischeid, the squadron commander of VMF-214, ran into flak on the first air strike of the morning. He jettisoned his 500-pound bomb and headed for Kimpo, but he never made it. Just as he was ready to enter the approach pattern, his plane exploded and crashed into the ground in flames. Two hours later two other squadron commanders were shot down. Lieutenant Colonel Richard W. Wyczawski of VMF-212 escaped his disaster with relatively minor injuries. Lieutenant Colonel Max J. Volcansek of VMF (N)-542 was wounded on his first pass at the enemy positions, but he kept on and made two more. The plane was hit again and again, and when he brought it limping back to Kimpo airfield he discovered that the F7F was so sorely hurt that it had lost most of its aerodynamic qualities, and he could keep it in the air only by flying at about 200 knots, which was just twice the approved landing speed of the aircraft. Landing at 200 knots in that plane would have been suicidal, so Volcansek decided to bail out. He waited almost too long. When he ejected the canopy he was at 1,000 feet. He tried to climb out of the cockpit but at this low altitude the slipstreams from the twin engines pinned him against the coaming. He kicked the stick forward with both feet, the aircraft lurched downward and literally spat him out of the cockpit. The tail of the plane came rushing up, apparently to decapitate him, but missed by a couple of inches. He pulled the ripcord on his parachute, it opened, and a few seconds later he hit the ground. He was picked up by a helicopter and flown back to Kimpo.

After the artillery barrage and the air strikes, the 2nd and 3rd battalions of the 5th Marines attacked side by side against the battered North Korean defenses of Hill 296. The 2nd Battalion's immediate objective was Hill 105-N. It was supported by fire from the 3rd Battalion.

Company E led the attack supported by tanks but the marines ran into heavy enfilading fire from the well-prepared North Korean defenses on Hill 72. Lieutenant Deptula's platoon took the brunt of it and suffered a number of casualties. The fighting was brisk until just after one thirty in the afternoon when Deptula's men drove the last of the North Koreans from the hill and took over.

What remained of Company D after the heavy losses of the day before was led by Lieutenant Seydel. That company started from its position on Smith's Ridge that morning, and before one thirty in the afternoon it had taken Hill 88.

Company F moved up to occupy Hill 72. Company E turned to Hill 105-N, and an artillery bombardment was laid down to give them a hand. By midafternoon that strong point was diminished and the hill secured.

Compared to the last few days of fighting for the 2nd Battalion, this attack was easy going. But not so for the 3rd Battalion on the left. Company G and Company H attacked against the remaining positions of the enemy on a spur of Hill 296. In the beginning they were harried by firing from Hill 338 on the left and Hill 105-N on the right. Colonel Murray held the battalion up for a while so that the 2nd Battalion could take Hill 105-N and make the going a little easier. As the resistance on Hill 105-N died down, the 3rd Battalion began to move once more and in two hours had taken its objective and was in communication with the 2nd Battalion on the right.

Company H had a bad time on the left flank. At about five o'clock in the afternoon Company I began to move through Company H to continue the attack. Just then about two hundred North Koreans made a counterattack, supported by mortars, machine guns, and artillery. The fighting was very hard and both companies of marines suffered. But the enemy's strength was soon depleted. So brave were they that they had marched right into the marine guns. With a half of the North Korean number fallen, the remainder retreated and left the field to the marines. Company I kept the front line, and Company H, which had been fighting all day, went into battalion reserve and moved back.

So as night closed in, the 3rd Battalion of the 5th Marines was ready for the fighting of September 26, when it expected to move along the spur on which it had its perimeter, right down into the heart of Seoul.

The 1st Battalion had moved around to the left flank to link up with the 1st Korean Marine Battalion and guard the approaches to Hill 216 and Hill 296. These were the troops and this was the hill that Koo Chul-Hoe saw from his place on the roof of the prison that day.

The brunt of the attack on Seoul on September 25 was placed on the shoulders of Colonel Puller's 1st Marines. They had done very well in those few days since they came off the ships at Inchon. By now General Smith averred that they were every bit as good as the more experienced 5th Marines.

They certainly would have a chance to prove it this day, with the pressure on from X Corps and Tokyo to capture Seoul.

During the night, in preparation for the next day's attack, Lieutenant Colonel Ridge's 3rd Battalion moved forward to the east, through the 2nd Battalion. Then it turned north, toward the heart of the city. The 1st Battalion on Hill 79 lined up so that it could coordinate its attack with that of the 3rd. Seoul lay dead ahead.

Theoretically the attack that morning was to have tank support, but, in fact, the tanks did not arrive, being engaged in a firefight on the way that delayed them until too late.

Two platoons of tanks from Company B of the 1st Tank Battalion had crossed the river at the Haengju ferry on the afternoon of September 24, accompanied by engineers who were looking out for mines along the way up to the front. They also had along a battered platoon of infantry from the 5th Marines, from Company F, under Staff Sergeant Arthur Farrington. On this afternoon because of the hard fighting, a gap existed between the 5th Marines' line and the 1st Marines, and the tanks and these fifty foot soldiers entered the area. They had traversed about half the distance to the front when they began taking fire from the slope of Hill 105-S. Theoretically, Hill 105-S had been cleaned up by the 1st Battalion earlier in the day. Actually, the movements had been so rapid that pockets of resistance had been left behind and these apparently had been consolidated. Lieutenant George Babe, of the engineers, who was senior of the foot soldiers, was wounded. Technical Sergeant Pasquale Paolino took charge, but the North Koreans outnumbered them at least three or four to one. The tank commander, Captain Bruce Williams, thought it might be a good idea to open up the hatches and take all these men on foot into the protection of the tanks and, as the marines sometimes said, "get the hell out of there." But then he thought of another idea. Why not bring up a flamethrower tank and outflank the enemy? He did just that. Staff Sergeant Marion Altaire's M-26 led the flamethrower around the enemy's left flank along a trail that moved south from the railroad line. The flamethrower tank came up on a North Korean position lined with trenches, its ugly snout looking down along the trench lines. The operator began to sear the trenches with bursts of burning napalm that clung with hellish intensity to the clothes and skin of the enemy soldiers. Men began to scream and other men to run. Those who were not too horribly burned in the first blasts of flame fled down the slope, where the other M-26 tanks were waiting with their machine guns spitting.

At the time that all this was occurring, Sergeant Paolino and Sergeant Farrington moved their men along the railroad embankment. Paolino noticed that enemy grenades were coming from three thatched huts below those North Korean trenches. As they went closer they saw that one of the huts concealed a cave that went back into the hillside.

Paolino banged on the tank of Lieutenant Cummings and indicated the mouth of the cave and the huts. The tanks began throwing 90 mm shells into the huts and soon they were blown up or blazing, destroyed. Cummings was shifting his fire to the cave, when suddenly eight North Korean soldiers appeared with their hands up. They managed to surrender unharmed, and immediately afterward a whole file of men began emerging from the cave. Altogether the tanks and infantry took 131 prisoners and killed about 150 North Korean soldiers on this hill that had been deemed "safe."

The hillside also yielded prisoners. One "tree" suddenly stood up and held its rifle over its head. The "tree" was ordered to strip and did. So did all the other prisoners—the marines had already suffered enough from North Koreans who "surrendered" only to pull out a grenade or a pistol and start their private war. In the stripping of the prisoners down to the buff two females were discovered. They claimed to be nurses, but the marines swore they had been using weapons. Someone found two pair of long underwear for the ladies and they were soon properly if not stylishly dressed.

Captain Williams then organized his party, the American foot soldiers outnumbered almost three to one by the enemy. The prisoners were lined up three abreast between two M-26 tanks and the march toward Seoul continued.

The infantry attack by the 3rd Battalion of the 1st Marines could not wait for the dilatory tanks and it jumped off on schedule. The marines moved fast until they got to the intersection of the railroad line with broad Ma Po Boulevard, and here the fighting became intense. Colonel Puller came up and established his command post here. But without the tanks, the job of rooting out enemy soldiers was enormous, it meant fighting street by street, alley by alley, house by house.

It was noon before Captain Williams and his strange column came up to the intersection. Williams wanted to explain but Colonel Puller was gruff. This was no time for swapping "sea stories" the colonel said, there was dirty work to be done. The tanks were sent immediately into action, up both sides of the wide boulevard, with the infantrymen of the 1st Battalion. The enemy had prepared his defenses, two of the tanks were knocked out temporarily by mines.

The marines moved forward slowly but doggedly. The North Koreans contested every street and every intersection with a roadblock. The roadblocks were built of rubble and rice bags filled with earth. They were reinforced with rails torn up from the streetcar tracks. They were manned by North Koreans with machine guns and burp guns. Some of them had antitank guns. More machine guns and mortars were placed on the rooftops of buildings.

The progress was "foot-by-foot." Every entry was a potential trap for the marine riflemen. They moved cautiously, firing their rifles, spraying the doorways. They broke through walls from one building to the next. The engineers crawled forward ahead of the tanks, exploding mines. The tanks came up then and forced the barricades, with 90 mm shells, machine guns, and bulldozer blades. Behind, the artillery fired on call, and the calls were frequent. The marine Corsairs were called down to strike particularly trouble-some spots.

Doggedly the marines moved ahead, their officers mindful of the enormous pressure from General Almond to take Seoul that very day.

Captain Barrow's Company A moved up the high ground overlooking the railroad station and yards. Down below lay the low ground and the railroad embankment. It seemed empty, until an artillery observer saw motion. When he trained his glasses on that part of the embankment he saw more. He called for artillery and mortar fire from the rear. Captain Barrow moved his machine guns up to cover the embankment. The heavy fire came in, and literally hundreds of North Korean soldiers began rushing out from behind the embankment. To go down into that sort of situation would be foolhardy, but the pressure from General Almond was being felt all up and down the line. From the 1st Battalion command post came orders for Company A to advance. Captain Barrow turned off the radio and sent an officer back to battalion to argue his case. The officer brought Lieutenant Colonel Hawkins up forward and when he saw the situation he was convinced that to advance at that moment would be foolhardy.

Under the pressure, the marines did advance a long way. By day's end Colonel Murray's 5th Marines occupied the mountain called An-san on the edge of the city. But occupation of this height did not mean there were no enemy troops left on the fringes of the hill. There were hundreds of them, and they were still men of General Wol's toughened 25th Brigade fighters who made the "foot-by-foot" advance as expensive as possible.

By nightfall Lieutenant Colonel Hawkins' 1st Battalion of the 1st Marines held Hill 82. Lieutenant Colonel Ridge's 3rd Battalion, on the left, held Hill 973. One battalion of the army's 32nd Infantry was dug in on South Mountain (Nam-san) where it had sat all afternoon. As noted, the 7th Marines' mission was to cover the left flank of the 5th Marines and deny the

North Koreans use of the main road to Pyongyang, the North Korean capital. One battalion was atop a hill overlooking this road.

Altogether the marines held almost half the city as night fell, and the darkness was broken only by the flash of guns and the crackling flames of the fires set in the wooden buildings. It had been a hard day for the marines, but General Smith was satisfied that they had done their job.

12

"Enemy Fleeing. . . .
You Will Attack NOW"

General Smith was pleased with his marines and their progress on the night of September 25. They had fought their way deep inside Seoul, and he anticipated a coordinated attack the next morning that should complete the investment of the South Korean capital.

But the same could not be said of General Almond back at the headquarters of the X Corps. Almond had promised General MacArthur Seoul on a platter on that three-month "monaversary" of the North Korean invasion. He was nearly frantic because the impossible had not been achieved, and he was easy prey to any sort of rumor or tale that would make victory look even better than it was. He was prepared to clutch at any straw.

The opportunity General Almond sought came in the form of an air report that enemy troops were streaming out of the city on the road north toward Uijongbu. Almond immediately sent a message to the Far Eastern Air Force command in Tokyo requesting a flare mission to illuminate the roads so that night fighters could attack the enemy troops. A B-29 flew over the area of northern Seoul and dropped flares for two hours. The night fighters attacked. What they attacked no one was quite sure. The North Koreans, as noted, were moving prisoners out of Seoul to the north. Refugees were fleeing the city to get away from the fighting. The NK 18th Division had come up from the Yongdungpo area after the battle there and was moving north toward

Uijongbu. But General Wol and what remained of his NK 25th Brigade and all the extra troops he had rounded up were still very much in the fighting.

General Almond, cloaked in the security of his ignorance and goaded by his understanding of General MacArthur's ego, chose to believe that the North Koreans had been routed, that the troops were fleeing the city, and that, after all, he could give MacArthur Seoul for the three-month monaversary that he prized so much because he knew its media appeal. So General Almond ordered the weary marines to stage a night attack and drive the enemy from Seoul.

When that message reached the headquarters of the 1st Marine Division, General Smith was having his dinner, a can of C ration. The message was received by Colonel Alpha L. Bowser, the division operations officer. The order was so unlikely that Bowser immediately telephoned Lieutenant Colonel John H. Chiles, the X Corps' operations officer, to verify it. He asked how a night air observation could determine the nature of the people crowding the roads. There was no response to that question. The order to attack was repeated.

Colonel Bowser then walked to General Smith's quarters and gave him the alarming news. General Smith called Major General Clark L. Ruffner, chief of staff of X Corps, and again questioned the sanity of the order. There was no indication on the marines' front that the enemy which had been holding the town block by block was prepared to do any less now. No one in the line had seen any signs of retreat or a growing weakness. In fact, although General Smith did not have that information at the moment, the North Koreans were just then preparing for a series of night attacks.

General Ruffner did not argue. He simply told General Smith that the order had been dictated personally by General Almond. The marines were to attack at once. The only unit that was not going to attack was the 32nd Infantry sitting on its hill far from the action. Perhaps General Almond's confidence in the army troops had been shaken by his experience of the morning.

There was no recourse for the marines. What General Ruffner did not say was that General Almond was just then writing a communiqué for the press which would be given out at about midnight. Seoul had been "liberated," said General Almond, just as General MacArthur had promised, and on the 25th of September, the third month to the day, that the evil North Koreans had breached the 38th parallel.

If the marines had known of the communiqué they would have understood that if necessary they were to be sacrificed for General MacArthur's ego. Since they did not know, they found General Almond's action hard to understand.

But orders were orders and it was not the first time the marines had been sent to fight against all logic. General Smith issued the orders to his regimental commanders. He also told them to be careful.

At about ten thirty that night, while General Smith was telling Colonel Murray that the high command had demanded an attack against the "fleeing enemy," word was coming in to 5th Marine headquarters about a counterattack staged against the 3rd Battalion at that moment. A reinforced company of North Koreans had moved up and begun a probe. Lieutenant Colonel Taplett and his men in the line were fighting it off. And next door, the 3rd Battalion of the 1st Marines was getting ready for trouble. Company I, on the right, held Hill 97, which would soon be called "Slaughterhouse Hill." Company G held a roadblock and high ground on Ma Po Boulevard. Company H stood between the two. Lieutenant Colonel Ridge was expecting trouble that night, and so he had sited his heavy weapons to cover every bit of his front. Riflemen manned the roadblock. The road in front of it was mined. Lieutenant Harold Savage was in command and he had placed a heavy machine gun section, a 3.5-inch bazooka squad, and a 75 mm recoilless gun in the roadblock. The battalion's 81 mm mortars were also placed to fire in that area.

The word to attack filtered down from above. Lieutenant Colonel Ridge was aghast and protested loudly. It did not help. But as it turned out, before Ridge's men could attack, they had to defend themselves from the North Koreans who were "fleeing" the wrong way.

On getting the word, Major Simmons of the 1st Battalion sent a patrol to make contact with the 5th Marines. The patrol leader was Corporal Charles E. Collins. He had with him seven marines and three Korean civilians. The patrol went out. It made contact—not with the 5th Marines but with a strong force of enemy troops retreating the wrong way. The force included tanks and self-propelled guns, making ready for an assault up Ma Po Boulevard to hit the U.S. roadblock.

Corporal Collins and his men nearly blundered into the massing attack. But not quite. Collins saw what was coming, sent his patrol back immediately to report, and covered their going with his own rifle fire.

The Almond order to attack "at once" had led General Smith to set a rapid-fire timetable. Both regiments were to attack at one forty-five that morning of September 26. There had been a little delay—fifteen minutes— because of the need to register the artillery on the new line. It was a most fortunate delay, for at one thirty the marines in the line began to hear the clanking sound of tank treads not far away. The enemy was coming. The marines did not know it but the attack was staged by a reinforced battalion of the 25th Brigade.

The patrol sent out from the 1st Marines to make contact with the 5th Marines returned to report on the massing enemy force. And then, in a few minutes, the enemy was upon the roadblock. One of the T-34 tanks fired the first shot. It killed a radioman. Then the shooting broke out in earnest as the Americans returned fire. One T-34 was knocked out immediately. The other took cover around a corner of the boulevard.

Lieutenant Savage was wounded. Sergeant Robert Caldwell took charge.

Back at division headquarters General Smith had the word that this counterattack was no feint but a direct drive by a powerful force. He deferred the jump-off of the night attack, and the artillery concentrated its efforts on assistance to the roadblock, and Colonel Taplett's defense against the continuing attack in his sector. In the second attack on the 3rd Battalion of the 5th Marines, two hundred enemy troops struck the line at about this same time.

The duel of tanks and artillery continued until two fifteen that morning, and then the marines in the roadblock area had unmistakable indication of a North Korean infantry advance. The primary weapons of the North Koreans were grenades and burp guns, and the sound of both increased in crescendo as the foot soldiers moved up against the roadblock.

The marine artillery then had its hands full. Three battalions of the 11th Marines' howitzers were supporting the roadblock, and the rest of the guns were firing against the North Koreans out in front of Lieutenant Colonel Taplett's position.

The roadblock was the scene of the heaviest attack. The enemy force was led by a dozen tanks, the strongest armored force the North Koreans had employed since the Inchon landing. They were accompanied by two self-propelled guns and many 120 mm mortars. The artillery of the 11th Marines increased the tempo of their firing until they nearly burned out their howitzers. The attack was stopped cold by three fifteen. Then, however, the marine gunners had to stop shooting to let the howitzers cool a little, and when they did, the North Koreans surged forward. The marines ordered up every mortar in sight, and they fired as fast as they could. Nevertheless, for a time on the line the future of the roadblock looked very grim indeed.

Earlier in the day as the 1st Marines had moved forward, their advance had been supported by the army's 31st Field Artillery Battalion. That night the field artillery battalion had reverted to army command but the observer who had been with the marines all day long was still with them. He called up his artillery in this time of crisis and asked for a barrage. He got it, 360 big 155 mm shells came hurtling in on the enemy in front of the roadblock. They brought a noticeable diminution of the strength of the attack.

When the 11th Marines' howitzer tubes had cooled, they took over once more. The fight continued. The ammunition supply of the battalion began to run very low. Lieutenant Colonel Ridge organized a jeep brigade to go to the rear and pick up rifle, machine gun, and mortar ammunition. Back and forth they rode, often under fire, bringing up the supply. Dawn neared and the enemy still tried. No one could say they were not persistent. In Lieutenant Colonel Taplett's sector, the last attack was staged at 4:45, and it was fought off.

At about this same time, another battalion of General Wol's shock troops advanced to attack Lieutenant Colonel Mount's 2nd Battalion of the army's 32nd Infantry on top of South Mountain. The army men were ready for trouble. Since ten thirty they had been hearing the sounds of fighting down below and they expected something to come their way. The first indication was the sound of tanks rolling along the road below the mountain. Then came the enemy infantry up the mountain. First they hit Company E on the peak of the mountain, and Company E threw them back. But down below on another protuberance was Company F and here the enemy penetrated and overran the company's position. Mount called up Company D, his reserve, and put it against the enemy here. The fighting was very vigorous.

When it ended Lieutenant Colonel Mount counted a hundred dead North Korean soldiers *inside* the American perimeter. Elsewhere on the sides of South Mountain were another three hundred dead.

At about this same time, before five o'clock in the morning, yet another North Korean unit attacked the 1st Battalion which was occupying a ridge line of South Mountain. Again a firefight broke out, with the enemy using grenades and burp guns, and the Americans replying with machine gun fire, BARs, M-1s, grenades, and mortars.

One of the most active and dangerous enemy was the crew of a 76 mm self-propelled gun that was firing on the roadblock. The shells came uncomfortably close, low overhead, just missing. Major Simmons worried because the misses were so near. He figured that when the first light of dawn came, the enemy gunners would see what was happening and adjust their gunsight. That could be very bad medicine for the marines at the roadblock. So Simmons ordered up one 75 mm recoilless rifle, and placed it beside the house he was using as a command post so that it looked down Ma Po Boulevard. As the gray of dawn lightened the sky, the gunner spotted the self-propelled gun and fired one shell that blew the gun apart. The recoil blast also blew the side off the command post house.

For all effective purposes the fight ended at six thirty when the last two enemy tanks were knocked out. At about that time Corporal Collins, who was assumed to be dead long since, returned to the land of the living dressed in the white robes of a Korean civilian. He had spent the night in no-man's-land dodging fire from both sides.

As the morning light strengthened and the sound of gunfire was reduced to an occasional popping, the marines got their heads up. Outside Lieutenant Colonel Taplett's perimeter lay another hundred dead enemy soldiers.

He sent a patrol then down the hillside to Ma Po Boulevard to make the contact with the 1st Marines who had been cut off by the night's fighting. The patrol ran into strong enemy fire and retreated. The North Koreans had been knocked back from that counterattack, but they were far from finished.

Colonel Puller came along the boulevard from his regimental command post on the edge of the city to inquire about the night's work.

"You had better show me some results of the alleged battle . . . ," he said to Lieutenant Colonel Ridge. The battalion commander showed him eighty-three North Korean prisoners and led him out to look at seven dead T-34 tanks, the remains of the two self-propelled guns, and eight blasted antitank guns. The bodies of dead North Korean soldiers sprawled all around the roadblock and the streets beyond. Someone had counted them: more than four hundred. And the wounded—perhaps twice as many—had been taken away.

It was not long before the media correspondents showed up at the scene. They looked it all over, and someone asked Colonel Puller about the "fleeing enemy" reported by X Corps headquarters the night before.

Colonel Puller was restrained and he spoke in a very low key.

"All I know about a fleeing enemy," he said, "is that there's two or three hundred out there that won't be fleeing anywhere."

As for the rest, the correspondents could see for themselves.

Back at X Corps headquarters, General Almond had nothing to say about the fleeing enemy this morning. He tried to turn the attention of the press elsewhere.

"Nothing could have been more fortunate," General Almond said, "than the tank-led enemy counterattacks. It gave us a greater opportunity to kill more enemy soldiers and to destroy his tanks more easily than if we had had to take the city house by house."

Somehow it sounded as though Almond had planned it that way. And his remarks would have been quite a surprise to Lieutenant Lawrence O'Connell of the 3rd Battalion of the 5th Marines, who had led that patrol down to meet the 1st Marines that morning and was reduced to fighting his way back house by house. They made it, but poor O'Connell got one souvenir he would never forget. While moving carefully through a dark courtyard so as to avoid the "fleeing enemy," he fell through rotten planking into a cesspool and came up redolent of secondhand kimchee and other noxious substances.

But back home in America, General MacArthur had his carefully planned if completely unwarranted triumph. For Supreme Headquarters in Tokyo reported on the night's fighting just as it pleased, with an assist from General Almond, and no regard for the facts.

"Three months to the day after the North Koreans launched their surprise attack south . . . troops of X Corps recaptured the capital city of Seoul. . . . By 1400 [2 P.M.] 25 September the military defenses of Seoul were broken. . . . The enemy is fleeing the city to the northeast."

General Smith would have been very happy if that were only true. General Wol would have been very surprised to hear it.

Meanwhile the marines set out to really capture Seoul, street by street, alley by alley, and house by house.

13

The Long, Long Day

On the night of September 25, back in the southern area of Korea where the Eighth Army was operating, the engineers worked through the night to repair the highway bridge near Chinju, and on the afternoon of September 26 tanks and trucks began crossing. It made all the difference in the world.

General Walker had been feeling very much neglected. He had not been given the engineering support he felt he needed to bridge the Naktong and the Nam rivers and thus move his armor across to drive north as General MacArthur had ordered.

"We have been bastard children," he had observed gloomily a few days earlier to Major General Doyle Hickey, MacArthur's deputy chief of staff. At that point General Walker had only two bridges. Now, on September 26, he had another. He could move.

Downstream the engineers finished the sandbag underwater bridge across the Nam, too, and before dawn on the 26th the 1st Battalion of the 27th Infantry crossed the river. The Eighth Army was moving; the 27th Infantry attacked toward Uiryong and captured the town just before noon. (See Map 15.)

To be sure, Walker continued to have his engineering problems. Task Force Matthews was still stalled behind the river by three blown bridges west of Chinju. But Task Force Dolvin was not. Lieutenant Colonel Welborn G.

Dolvin led the force out of Chinju at six o'clock in the morning of September 26, headed for Hamyang. He was hot on the trail of the NK 6th Division which was retreating up this road, and he was traveling fast. Two companies of the 89th Medium Tank Battalion were in the lead, the tanks of each tank company carrying one infantry company of the 35th Infantry Regiment. For the first three miles the column sped along. Then the lead tank struck a box mine laid by the enemy, and the whole column skidded to a stop. Engineers came up to check the minefield. They found and removed eleven more mines. The tanks revved up again and started going.

But the North Koreans, they found, knew how to retreat. Half a mile along the road another tank hit a mine and was damaged. The column stopped. The engineers came up again and removed more mines. The column started. Half a mile further along the road another tank hit a mine. This time they were coming close to the retreating force, and a rear guard of about a platoon was dug in behind the minefield. It took the infantry an hour to disperse the enemy concentration. The column went on. They began passing antitank guns, abandoned trucks which had carried troops, and abandoned truckloads of ammunition. They were getting very close to the retreating NK 6th Division. The column sped on toward the Hamyang. They were in estuary country, the land mass cut often by long narrow inlets from the sea that crept forward like fjords. By late afternoon they had reached Hajon-ni. They pressed on. Then from a distance they heard an enormous explosion. The enemy had just crossed over and blown the bridge across the estuary three miles north. The NK 6th Division was only half an hour ahead of them, but the blown bridge let them get safely away. Dolvin had to stop on the bank and wait all night while a bypass was built.

On the morning of September 26, elements of the 38th Infantry entered Kochang, and there they captured a North Korean field hospital which held about fifty of the enemy's wounded. The prisoners said that four North Korean divisions were to have assembled at Kochang for a defense, but that the Americans had moved so fast they had been unable to pull themselves together and that the retreat was becoming a rout. The abandonment of the hospital was a good indication of the state of affairs with the enemy.

While the men of the 38th Infantry were sorting things out at Kochang, the 23rd Infantry appeared there, having taken the long road to the north, having fought three engagements the night before, and having rebuilt four short bridges that had been destroyed by the retreating enemy. That afternoon the 23rd Infantry moved on fourteen miles to Anui. They found desolation. Hours earlier the North Koreans had murdered hundreds of South Korean

Marines storm ashore at Inchon in the amphibious landing of September 15, 1950. (U.S. Marine Corps)

Leathernecks mop-up heights on Wolmi Island. (U.S. Marine Corps)

Waterfront at Inchon blazes as marines pour in from landing craft, and an LST pushes up on shore. *(U.S. Marine Corps)*

One bulldozer pulls another through the muddy shore of Wolmi Island, as equipment is unloaded from LSTs. *(U.S. Army)*

(above) Major General Oliver P. Smith, commanding 1st Marine Division, returns civil government to the mayor of Inchon on behalf of the United Nations. *(U.S. Marine Corps)*

(right) Marine Colonel "Chesty" Puller studies the terrain before advancing to another enemy objective beyond Inchon. *(U.S. Marine Corps)*

Navy corpsman, attached to the marines, treats wounded prisoners as they are rounded up in Korean fighting. *(U.S. Marine Corps)*

Colonel Lee Hak Ku, North Korean 13th Division chief of staff, captured by Company B, 1st Cavalry Division, near Taegu, sits in a military police jeep that will take him to 1st Cavalry Division headquarters. September 21, 1950. (U.S. Army)

Douglas MacArthur, commander in chief, UN Forces in Korea, attends a briefing session at the 1st Marine Division headquarters, Inchon, on September 17, 1950. *(U.S. Army)*

Men of the 9th Infantry Regiment advance up Hill 201 on the Pusan Perimeter. *(U.S. Army)*

Men of the 9th Infantry Regiment aid a wounded soldier while under heavy North Korean fire. September 18, 1950. *(U.S. Army)*

Heavy trucks of the 21st Infantry Regiment cross the Kumho on an underwater crossing, consisting of rocks and sand bags reinforcing the river bed. *(U.S. Army)*

U.S. tanks move through a roadblock on Ma Po Boulevard, Seoul, on September 25, 1950. *(U.S. Army)*

U.S. troops moving to forward positions five miles east of Inchon, on the way to Seoul, pass three North Korean tanks knocked out by marine air action. *(U.S. Army)*

An aerial view of Seoul showing the capitol building in the center. Behind are the hills that the marine and army troops fought for to get at Seoul. (*U.S. Army*)

(above) While street fighting continues in Seoul, residents have unfurled the United Nations and Republic of Korea flags in a shell-torn building high above marines. *(U.S. Marine Corps)*

(below) United Nations troops fighting on the outskirts of Seoul. September 20, 1950. *(U.S. Army)*

(above) Syngman Rhee inspects troops of the 1st Marine Division and a platoon of Korean marines. Major General John T. Seldnen is with Rhee. *(U.S. Marine Corps)*

(right) The first Jewish Sabbath service in liberated Seoul. *(U.S. Army)*

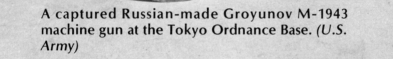

A captured Russian-made Groyunov M-1943 machine gun at the Tokyo Ordnance Base. *(U.S. Army)*

Two captured Russian-made self-propelled SU-76s. The guns are 76 mm on full-tracked vehicles with medium armor. *(U.S. Army)*

(above) A member of the 61st Middlesex Regiment stands watch as troops search the houses of the burning village of Yangsong-ni, Korea. October 27, 1950. *(U.S. Army)*

(right) Members of the Task Force Indianhead set up hot coffee on the capitol grounds, less than twenty-four hours after the capture of the North Korean capital of Pyongyang. *(U.S. Army)*

Graves of American prisoners of war shot by North Korean forces found beside an abandoned train where the unburied bodies of others were discovered. October 27, 1950. (U.S. Army)

After the battle. The wreckage of the town of Kumchon in North Korea. (U.S. Army)

(above) Foot soldiers of the ROK 3rd Division march past the Diamond Mountains at Yangjin-ni on their northwest drive toward Wonsan. *(U.S. Army)*

(below) First UN troops to cross the 38th parallel hold a sign-posting ceremony to let all know that the ROK 3rd Division made the historic crossing. *(U.S. Army)*

YOU ARE CROSSING
THE 38th PARALLEL
COURTESY of 3rd R.O.K. DIV.

men, women, and children and buried their bodies in a shallow trench. This was the deadly work of the North Korean Security Police, the KGB of the People's Republic. The dead were loyal South Korean citizens, victims of the vengeance of a defeated enemy. The enemy had flooded the rice paddies, which meant the Americans had to stick to the roadway and the streets of the town. This was not the most comfortable of positions on which to build a perimeter, but the infantry dug in for the night.

With the fall of Kumchon to the 5th Regimental Combat Team and the 21st Infantry on September 25, the 24th Division began moving rapidly up the highway toward Taejon. On September 26 the 2nd Battalion of the 19th Infantry captured Yongdong, which had been deserted by the retreating enemy. They found three American prisoners of war in the town jail. The regiment hurried on toward Taejon and was still moving at midnight. But they had to stop to refuel the tanks and give the men some sleep.

As they slept for a little, the North Korean Security Police were busy about their grisly work in Taejon. After this city had fallen to the North Koreans in July, it had become a political center for the North Koreans. Hundreds of political prisoners had been packed into the jail. It overflowed and the North Koreans made a jail of the Catholic Mission. Military prisoners, South Korean and Americans, were held in other places in the city. As the retreat of the North Korean People's Army began, the security forces began to execute their prisoners. The prisoners were taken out to fields in groups of one or two hundred, bound together with their hands tied behind them. They were led to trenches dug by the soldiers, and then were shot and tumbled into the trenches.

General Gay and the staff of the 1st Cavalry Division found it hard to understand why they had orders from I Corps not to advance further than Poun. This was another administrative foulup, caused by an inelasticity of the military system. The 1st Cavalry Division had been assigned a zone of operations in the beginning of the breakthrough. It had now reached the end of that zone. Gay asked I Corps for permission to move on past Poun. It was denied. So the 1st Cavalry Division's drive was stalled. General Gay also sent a tank-infantry team down the road from Sangju toward Kumchon where the 24th Division was having hard going on the Waegwan–Taejon road, faced by determined North Korean defenders. The 1st Cavalry force managed to make contact with the 24th Infantry and could have been very helpful in the fight, but some staff officer at I Corps ordered the 1st Cavalry men to withdraw because they were outside their zone of operations. This is the sort of military idiocy that loses wars; fortunately the North Koreans were by now so disorganized that it did not matter a great deal.

General Gay concentrated his division in the Sangju–Naktong-ni area, and fretted. His advance unit, the 7th Cavalry, was stalled at Poun. On the night of September 25 he received another radio message from I Corps forbidding him to advance farther—although back in Taegu General Walker was irritable and wondering why his forces were so slow in linking up with X Corps up north, and in Tokyo, MacArthur's staff had quite given up hope.

Finally General Gay sent a message to Eighth Army headquarters asking what was going on. No one ever told him. Just before midnight on September 25 he had a message from General Walker that it was all right for him to go all the way up to Seoul to link up with X Corps if he could do it.

On the morning of September 26, General Gay called a meeting of his regimental commanders at Sangju. He told them the division was finally unleashed and that at noon they would start marching north and would not stop until they linked up with X Corps. The 7th Cavalry would lead, up the road to Osan, passing through Chongju and Chonan, those familiar places where the Americans had suffered ignominious defeat in the first few weeks of the war.

When Lieutenant Colonel William A. Harris of the 7th Cavalry had this word, he ordered Colonel Lynch at Poun to take his task force north just as fast as he could. Somewhere near Suwon, he told Lynch, he ought to make contact with the 7th Division.

So at eleven thirty on September 26, the 3rd Platoon of tanks from the 70th Tank Battalion moved out of Poun, with the regimental Intelligence and Reconnaissance Platoon. Their orders were to move at best speed and not to fire unless fired upon. They moved along at a nice clip, seeing no enemy soldiers, but evidence that the North Koreans had retreated ahead of them. Hundreds of Korean civilians lined the road and waved and smiled as the armored column passed by. In midafternoon they reached Chongju and found that the enemy had left the place just hours earlier. A few civilians remained. Then it was back on the road, speeding towards Osan, with the civilians cheering them on.

On the right, the ROK II Corps was moving as fast as were the Americans (courtesy of the turbid situation at U.S. I Corps). On the night of September 25, the ROK 6th Division reached Hamchang and moved on. Further east the ROK 8th Division was still fighting the retreating NK 12th and 8th divisions outside Andong. On September 26 the division secured Andong and its advance troops reached Yechon, twenty miles to the northwest.

Still farther east the ROK Capital Division was pursuing scattered elements of several divisions, which were beginning to organize as guerrillas. The Capital Division was nearing Chunyang in the middle of the mountain country of the east.

On the east coast the ROK 3rd Division captured Yongdok on September 25. The advance was aided by supporting fire from the American naval task group off the shore. The ROK 3rd Division caught the North Koreans in Yongdok by surprise. When they entered the town they found that the NK 5th Division had fled, leaving trucks with the engines running and horsecarts filled with supplies, the horses tied to trees. A number of fieldpieces were still in place for a defense that was never attempted, with piles of ready ammunition nearby. That was the end of the NK 5th Division. The soldiers fled into the mountains with a few supplies, split them up and formed themselves into bands to become guerrillas, a change that would create a good deal of difficulty for the United Nations' forces later on.

Gradually, reluctantly, the contempt in which the Americans held the Republic of Korea forces gave way to a grudging respect. Why the Americans had expected the South Koreans to be any better than themselves in the early days of the war is inexplicable. Washington had denied the South Koreans tanks and decent artillery, and their training had been minimal; it had been General MacArthur's belief that the South Korean defense force should be kept in the status of a police organization, not an army, and that is the policy that had been followed until June 25, 1950. It had taken the South Koreans three months to clear away the dead wood in their military organization and to put together fighting teams. Now, with increased American supplies, they were performing ably. With the fall of Yongdok, General Walker remarked:

"Too little has been said in praise of the South Korean Army which has performed so magnificently in helping turn this war from the defensive to the offensive."

The general was quite right. His generosity was another indication of the change that had occurred in the war, a change so swift and so vast that all concerned were having difficulty in accommodating themselves. His magnanimity of voice was accompanied by change of action: the South Korean army was now being equipped with 2½-ton troop-carrying trucks and accompanied by American armor, which made its task considerably easier and increased the ROK Army effectiveness.

On the morning of September 26, in Seoul, General Smith ordered a

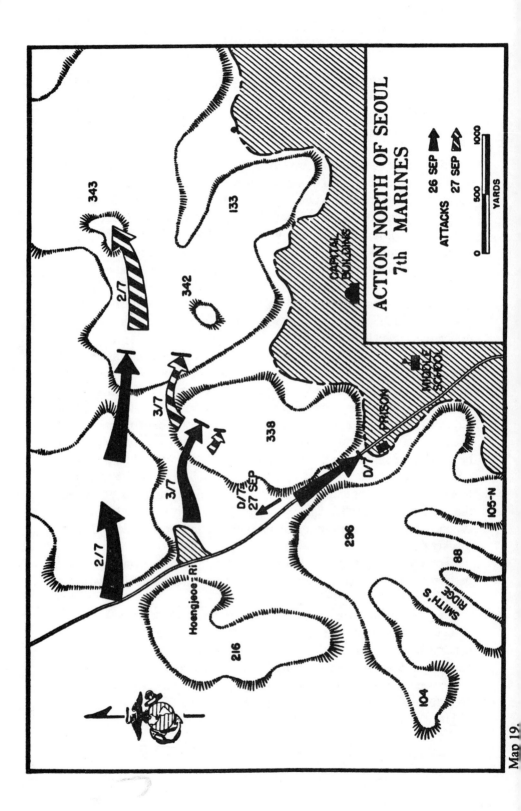

ACTION NORTH OF SEOUL
7th MARINES

ATTACKS 26 SEP
27 SEP

YARDS
0   500   1000

343

133

342

CAPITAL
BUILDINGS

2/7

3/7

3/7

338

MIDDLE
SCHOOL

PRISON

D/7

D/7
27 SEP

296

105-N

88

SMITH'S
RIDGE

104

Hoengjeoe Ri

216

Map 19.

continuation of the attack that had begun the day before, with the addition of the 7th Marines to the roster. (See Map 19.) The 7th Marines, accompanied by the Korean 5th Marine Battalion, were to move up from the left, and gradually pinch out the front of the 5th Marines, linking up with the 1st Marines for the drive through Seoul.

The 1st Marines and the Korean marines' 2nd Battalion were assigned to drive ahead through the center of the city and to turn to the right to the northeastern outskirts. Having been pinched out by the 7th Marines, the 5th Marines were to go into reserve for a rest.

The army's 32nd Infantry was to drive about two miles northeast, almost to the highway leading east out of Seoul.

Thus the X Corps front was a sort of scoop running from the northwest end of Seoul around to the southeast. The marine and army drive would tend to push the enemy out of the city moving to the northeast.

At 6:30 in the morning of September 26, Colonel Litzenberg ordered Company D of the 7th Marines to move southwest along the Kaesong–Seoul highway, to make contact with the 5th Marines on the right and push forward into Seoul.

The advance in the beginning was more a triumphal entry. Thousands of citizens of Seoul lined the highway to cheer the Americans in. Leading the column was Lieutenant William F. Goggin. It was hard not to feel like Caesar entering Rome that day, with the shouts and cheers of the crowd around them, some holding little American flags, others Republic of Korea flags, these dredged up from Lord knew where, having to have been hidden during the Draconian days of the North Korean occupation. There was no way the marines could put out flankers as they ought to have done, because of the crowds on the road. But there seemed no need. There seemed to be no resistance in Seoul. The company passed through Hoengjeoe-ri. Up above on the right was the height of Hill 296, which had cost the 5th Marines so much in the past few days. Up on their left was Hill 338. The marines moved through the narrow valley below. Up ahead on the right they could see the Sodaemun Prison. (See Map 19.) Up ahead was the Arch of Independence.

Suddenly from a tower about a quarter of a mile away came a burst of machine gun fire. Lieutenant Goggin was the first to fall, and several other marines were hit. The rest of the company disappeared onto the sides of the road as more machine guns and many rifles opened fire from positions only a hundred yards away on the hillsides. Company D had been caught in that most uncomfortable of positions, between enemies dug in on high ground, while they were trapped in the narrow pass.

It was bad enough at first, with fire from both hills on the front. But soon the

fire began coming also from the lower·slopes of the two hills on the flanks of
the marines, and it seemed they would be encircled and trapped. In the face of
this emergency Captain Richard R. Breen, commander of Company D,
ordered an attack on the high ground around the prison. At the same time,
Lieutenant Paul Sartwell put two 60 mm mortars in operation on the road. He
was exposed to enemy fire, but it was worth it: in a few minutes his men had
knocked out one of the enemy machine gun positions. Sartwell was wounded,
and wounded again, and then wounded a third time, which put him out of
action. The mortars kept on firing.

Lieutenant Edward H. Seeburger led the 2nd Platoon toward the prison.
Lieutenant Paul V. Mullaney took the 1st Platoon up the slopes of Hill 338 on
the other side. Lieutenant James Hammond kept his 3rd Platoon on the road.
So the marines had improved their position slightly, with an oval perimeter
that moved away from the road concentration. But it was still a dangerous
position, and they had no artillery support. They did have the help of marine
air, which sent air strikes against the enemy on the hillsides and prevented the
company from being overrun. But the company could not have any
reinforcement—the other units were occupied—and so Captain Breen organized himself for a siege. He brought his wounded into a diminished perimeter
on the best ground he could find. The enemy closed in. The marines dug in
and fired from the foxholes. The air force sent over transport planes carrying
ammunition, food, and medical supplies. The enemy made life very hard for
the fliers. One transport was hit so hard by ground fire that it crash-landed at
Kimpo airfield. Marine Corsairs were ordered in to attack the North Koreans
around the perimeter and their attacks relieved the pressure. The North
Koreans fired on the company with machine guns and mortars. The marines
fired back. In late afternoon Captain Breen had a call by radio from regimental headquarters asking about his situation. Breen said he could hold. He did
not tell regiment that he was wounded. Regiment said it was sending help and
dispatched a small column led by tanks. But by the time it reached the area the
North Koreans had closed around the company and the relief column turned
back. The men of the company expected an assault by infantry and maybe
tanks but there was no assault. Company D had stumbled into a section of the
final main line of defense of General Wol's 25th Brigade, but that brigade was
feeling so much pressure on other sectors that the men could not be spared to
try to overrun Company D in force.

During the night a convoy of ambulances came through the enemy lines to
pick up many of the wounded. It was a long night for Captain Breen and his
men; at any moment they expected one of the North Korean night assaults.

The other units of the 7th Marines moved out farther north and toward the east. (See Map 19.) The 2nd Battalion moved to take Hill 343 but was stopped by heavy fire from Hill 338. The two companies making the assault stopped there and dug in, waiting for help on the right flank. Company G of the 3rd Battalion provided it. Captain Thomas Cooney ordered two of his platoons to attack Hill 338 and they gained control of the north summit. However, there were still many North Koreans on that hill and they stopped the other platoon from taking the rest of the hill. The presence of these marines on the north side of Hill 338, however, helped keep the North Koreans from trying an assault on Company D down in the valley near the prison.

Following that long night of September 25 and the abortive North Korean counterattack on the 5th Marines and on the 1st Marines, when morning came those two regiments were slated for more action.

Ma Po Boulevard, which had been the scene of much of the night action, was the epitome of a handsome street just ravaged by battle. The flower shops and food shops along the broad avenue were wrecked and burning. Broken pots, unrecognizable pieces of cloth, other bits of the debris of civilization had rolled out along the road. Smoke and flame still rose from the wreckage. Dead North Koreans, not yet bloating, lay alongside buildings or in the road. The body of one was burning—the result of a hit from a white phosphorus shell.

Having sent off his glowing report of the capture of Seoul to Tokyo, General Almond bestirred himself from his headquarters to visit the marines this morning. General Smith did not record their discussion of the previous night's order to "attack the fleeing enemy."

Still the commander of X Corps must have gotten an indication of what the enemy was really up to: the North Koreans were staging a house-to-house defense, just as he had said they were not doing.

From Tokyo that day came more disinformation:

"Seoul, the capital of the Republic of Korea, is again in friendly hands. United Nations forces, including the 17th Regiment of the ROK Army and elements of the U.S. 7th and 1st Marine Divisions, have completed the envelopment and seizure of the city."

Just about then the 2nd Battalion of the 1st Marines was fighting what the marines called "The Battle of the Barricades" and moved in to pass through the 3rd Battalion and carry the fighting along Ma Po Boulevard. They moved upward, northward, along the railroad track, Company E and Company F in the front, led by six Sherman tanks, commanded by Lieutenant Cummings.

Cummings' tank had gone forward only a few yards when an explosion knocked it off center, killing a number of marines and North Koreans in front of them. It had struck an American mine, laid the night before in front of the roadblock and overlooked by the engineers groping through the rubble of battle the following morning.

House by house, alley by alley, they moved. About every two hundred yards, those "friendly hands" of the North Koreans had built rice bag barricades across the avenue. The barricades were eight feet high and five feet thick. They stretched across the entire width of the street. They only way to breach them was to smash them with the tanks. And of course behind each barricade the marines had to expect to find an antitank gun that must be spotted and destroyed before it could knock out the tank.

The engineers crept ahead, looking for and exploding enemy mines. The infantry moved up the sides of the street covering the engineers with rifle and BAR fire. They needed eyes in the backs and tops of their heads. For some, asbestos suits would have been welcome, since the heat and the smoke of the fires in the buildings along the avenue made the going rough.

There might be a North Korean in the upper story of any building, on any roof, in any doorway, any side street, any alley. He might have a rifle, or a burp gun, or a handful of grenades, or a mortar. Yes, they were "friendly hands" all right. And that morning they still held half of Seoul.

The tanks moved up the center behind the engineers. The tanks reached the barricades and crashed through. They took one barricade. Almost immediately afterwards the marines clearing up behind the wrecked bastion were astounded to see a detachment of about fifty North Koreans dragging an antitank gun up to the position, still in the belief that they held the barricade. The shock lasted only seconds, then the marines turned automatic fire loose on the North Koreans. Most of the enemy died on the pavement of Ma Po Boulevard. A few dragged themselves off to the cover of the buildings.

The progress, as Colonel Puller put it "was agonizingly slow." Every block or so the marines would come across people, dirty, frightened civilians, women and children, huddled in the rubble. These had to be moved out of danger, another delaying factor.

In Peking and Moscow the newspapers carried reports of the "heroic defense" of Seoul staged by the North Koreans. It was true. No matter their politics, these men were soldiers, and they gave their lives courageously.

On Ma Po Boulevard the North Koreans fought to the death. They had also taken a page from the Japanese book of World War II. One unit of North Koreans had been designated to destroy tanks. The Americans first became aware of it when a single soldier came charging out from behind a building and hurled a satchel charge onto the engine compartment of a flamethrower tank. Marines watched in paralyzed fascination as the soldier darted back to cover safely, and the tank blew up. Fortunately the crew of the flamethrower tank escaped, but that was not the last such incident of the day. Several more times in the afternoon, single soldiers came rushing forth with satchel charges. The marines were now primed, however, and every one of the North Koreans heroes was cut down before he could succeed in his mission.

Slowly the marines advanced. Captain Goodwin C. Groff's Company F approached an intersection at the foot of Hill 97. Here Company F was supposed to follow the rail line and Company E, coming up behind, was to turn right and move down the avenue. But once more, Company F had run into a major North Korean defense point and could not knock it down. It took the additional effort of Company E to wipe out enemy resistance here, and in the fight, Captain Norman Stanford, commander of Company E, was hit. By nightfall the 2nd Battalion of the 1st Marines had advanced less than a mile, about a quarter as far as they had come the day before.

If Seoul had been "liberated" on September 25, as one reporter wrote that day, the remaining North Koreans did not know it.

On the right of the 2nd Battalion of the 1st Marines that September 26, the 1st Battalion had the task of "liberating" the railroad station, around which the enemy had built a nest of defenses. The marines of Company C came down Hill 82 in a column and formed up in a line along the stream that paralleled the railroad yard. The North Koreans seemed to be everywhere, in between railroad cars, around the corners of the buildings, in positions around the station itself. By nightfall the marines had taken the railroad yard and the surrounding area. They held South Mountain and its lower slopes, including a big park at the bottom. When they drove the last of the enemy from the passenger station and went inside they found a few bodies of North Koreans and a dozen bodies of Korean women and children in a heap. They had been shot down by the North Koreans.

The 5th Marines were to clear the last resistance from Hill 296. That task was given to the 3rd Battalion, after preparatory barrages by the artillery and the 81 mm mortars. Company I would run down the hill driving the enemy before them into the heart of Seoul. Company G on Hill 105-N would drive down against the flank of the enemy. But like the men of the 7th Marines, those of the 5th Marines did not realize that they were going up against General Wol's main line of resistance, or what was left of it. The lower slopes of Hill 296 were swarming with North Korean positions, all the way down to the prison area.

Company I called off the barrage and went charging down the hill, expecting to reach the bottom. But the North Koreans stopped them with an enormous volume of machine gun and small arms fire. The two assault platoon leaders were wounded.

Captain McMullen then took over, fighting the company as a unit. They charged ahead across the bare ground on this slope. There was no cover, no way to hide, the best way for a man to save himself was to move ahead, fast. The men of Company I did and soon were assaulting the line of trenches and bunkers built up by the North Koreans. The fury of their charge pushed the enemy out of the trench line and the marines occupied it. But they were growing short of ammunition.

The North Koreans counterattacked uphill. Company I held, until it seemed the equal fury of the North Korean attack would drive them out of their ridge line. Some marines were down to their last cartridge. Then, at the blackest moment, up came Lieutenant Williamson with a supply party, bringing ammunition and more fire support. The arrival of this reinforcement tipped the scale, and the North Koreans were driven back down the mountain. At the end, Company I was a shadow of its former self. Captain McMullen was wounded and had to be carried from the ridge.

On the eastern side of Seoul that day, the 32nd Infantry was to attack. The 3rd Battalion moved out from a position east of South Mountain to capture Hill 106, which was two miles away. At the base of the hill the men of Company L routed a North Korean force from a strong defensive position. Then the drive up the hill was relatively easy. When Company L reached the top, they saw a column of North Koreans marching out of Seoul, going northeastward along the highway. They called for an air strike and the planes came in to scatter the enemy troops. Company L drove down the hill and put up a roadblock on the highway to stop off the escape route.

The 32nd Infantry and the ROK 17th Infantry spent most of the day clearing up isolated groups of enemy. The main line of defense was northwest of them, but the eastern side of Seoul also had to be cleaned out, and it was dangerous and deadly work. They suffered more than a hundred casualties. But as the day ended, South Mountain and the area to the east were secure. Even so, that night of September 26 at X Corps headquarters must have been a difficult one for General Almond, who had already captured Seoul on September 26. Now, September 27 loomed up and still General Wol's defenders did not know they were beaten.

14

Linkup

Task Force Lynch was heading northward at full clip to join up with the 31st Infantry of the 7th Division, which was heading south along the Suwon road. In the forefront were Lieutenant Robert Baker's platoon of tanks from the 70th Tank Battalion. Out ahead were the jeeps of the 7th Cavalry's Intelligence and Reconnaissance Platoon. They left Chongju and went on, until six o'clock in the night of September 26, when they ran out of gas at the village of Ipchang-ni. They had traveled sixty-four miles since noon. The fuel truck had not kept up with the tanks.

Lieutenant Baker found enough gasoline among the jerry cans of the column to fill up three tanks. They were still waiting when a party from the I and R platoons came back from the security post up the road to announce that a North Korean tank column was approaching. The three fueled tanks got ready to fight. But instead of T-34 tanks, the approaching column turned out to be three North Korean fuel trucks. They came up to Task Force Lynch before they realized that these were American tanks, not North Korean. The drivers panicked. One ran into a jeep. They all jumped out of their trucks and ran for the hills. The Americans found enough fuel in the three trucks to refuel the other three tanks and at eight o'clock that night the column was ready to go again. This time Baker's three tanks led the procession, with the other three bringing up the rear. The vehicles now traveled with lights on to speed their progress.

Just after eight thirty the task force moved onto the main highway to Seoul, south of Chonan. As they moved through the outskirts of Chonan they saw North Korean soldiers who paid no attention, believing these were North Korean tanks. The Americans came to an intersection where main roads seemed to go off in all directions. Lieutenant Baker did not know what to do. He saw a North Korean soldier standing on the street. He stopped his tank, pointed in one direction.

"Osan?" he asked.

The soldier nodded. Then he recognized the white star on the American tank and ran off down another street.

Lieutenant Baker led the column through Chonan then, past scores of North Korean troops who stood along the way in little knots and watched them go. They did not shoot at the Americans and the Americans did not shoot at them.

Outside Chonan, the column began to encounter larger groups of North Koreans who did shoot and the tanks shot back with their machine guns. After a few miles the three lead tanks began to step out ahead of the rest of the column. The problem was that the tanks went through enemy positions so fast that the North Koreans were caught by surprise. But after the tanks had sped through, the North Koreans realized that these were Americans, and as the rest of Task Force Lynch came up, the enemy was ready to fight. So the column was being delayed by little actions along the road, and the distance between the tanks at the point and the rest of the column continued to widen.

Colonel Lynch lost track of Baker and his tank platoon. He tried to reach them by radio, but there was no response. So Lynch formed another point, of infantry in trucks. The lead truck carried a .50 caliber machine gun on a ring-mount and a 3.5-inch bazooka team. They kept reaping the results of Lieutenant Baker's whirlwind ride: they would be contested by a small enemy force, they would stop and quiet it down, they would go on, and meet another spatter of fire, stop again, fight, and then board the trucks and go on.

When they were about ten miles south of Osan, Colonel Lynch heard the sounds of tank and artillery fire. He ordered the column to put out its lights.

In the exhilaration of the run, Lieutenant Baker did not realize how far ahead of the column his three lead tanks had gotten. They came charging into Osan at full speed, but outside the town he began to see T-34 tank tracks on the road. He stopped. Then he heard the sound of vehicles and thought that the task force must be just behind him.

He started up again. Three miles north of Osan the tanks were fired on by enemy troops. They ran through the fire and on northward. Baker saw tank tracks, but these were M-26 tracks, not T-34. More fire came in, and this was serious. A crewman in the open turret of the No. 3 tank was decapitated and the ring of the .50 caliber machine gun was knocked off by a high-powered shell. Unfortunately this was "friendly fire" from the guns of the U.S. 31st Infantry column that had headed south on the morning of September 26.

Lieutenant Baker ran on. His tank moved through the American lines. American tanks were in position, their guns trained on the road. The tank commander let the first tank through, intending to blast the second and then turn back to the first. But then he saw the white star on Baker's tank and stopped his platoon in time. By a very narrow margin Lieutenant Baker and his men were saved. It was 10:26 P.M. They had established the first contact between X Corps and the Eighth Army.

But contact was not linkup, and there were many North Koreans between Colonel Lynch's task force and the contact point. In fact, Lieutenant Baker seemed to have a charmed life that night—he ran right through a North Korean armored force of ten tanks south of Osan. They had not shot at him because they thought his tanks were their own until they had gone by. He then ran through the North Korean defense position north of Osan, without being destroyed by the antitank guns. Finally he ran through the American lines and only there received his casualty at the hand of friends. The American engineers had just removed the mines they had earlier placed in front of their position and were preparing to attack. Another fifteen minutes or so and Baker would have appeared in the midst of a pitched battle.

When Lieutenant Baker made his miraculous run through three fighting positions almost unscathed, Colonel Lynch was far behind, about ten miles south of Osan. The task force reached the village of Habong-ni, and the point went on through. Colonel Lynch saw a T-34 tank, about fifty feet off the road. Knowing that Lieutenant Baker's tanks had gone through here before his point had, the colonel assumed that this was a dead tank. It must have been knocked out by the air force earlier, he told Captain Webel, the regimental operations officer.

Just then, the "dead" tank came to life, spouting machine gun and 85 mm cannon fire. A second tank, hitherto hidden, appeared and opened fire on the column as well. Task Force Lynch ground to a sudden stop and everyone bounced out of the vehicles and headed for the ditch.

Lieutenant John G. Hill, Jr., hurried up ahead to stop the lead truck and bring back the 3.5-inch bazooka team. They came back and the bazooka knocked out the first tank. The second revved up and careened onto the road, then ran south on the road through the Task Force Lynch vehicles, running over several of the jeeps, and firing into the trucks. Outside the village, it turned off the road into a rice paddy, but still continued to fire the 85 mm gun. A 75 mm recoilless rifle with armor-piercing ammunition was brought up. The tank ran over a vehicle, got stuck, and was immobilized. Captain Webel went up to the tank, intending to climb on top and drop a grenade down the periscope tube, when suddenly the tank wrenched loose from the vehicle it had caught up on and very nearly ran him down. The 75 mm recoilless rifle got in a good shot and the tank was immobilized. But the gun could still fire and did. The 3.5-inch bazooka was brought up, but its firing mechanism failed. Captain Webel went to one of the jeeps and got a five-gallon jerry can full of gasoline. He moved up to the tank, poured the gasoline on the hull, concentrating particularly on the engine hatch. A shot started the fire and the explosion blew Webel off the tank and he landed twenty feet away. He got up with two broken ribs and superficial burns. He ran back to the road and watched the tank burn. It lit up the whole area with its flames.

At the head of the column Colonel Lynch heard the sound of tank engines coming down from the north. They could be Baker's tanks, of course, returning for some reason, perhaps to reestablish contact with the column. That was one guess. The other was that they were enemy. As they came down the road in the darkness it was impossible to tell which.

Colonel Lynch ordered his driver, Corporal Billie Howard, to move the lead truck across the road and block it off. This took a little doing; Corporal Howard got into the truck and moved it, and then he jumped out. By this time the lead tank was less than a hundred yards away, followed by another. The tanks screeched to a halt just yards from the truck roadblock. A figure appeared in the hatch and a Korean voice shouted:

"What the hell is going on down here?"

Colonel Lynch's men replied with a burst of small arms fire.

Down slammed the hatches on the tanks, and the guns started spitting. The first victim was the truck blocking the road. It caught fire and burned.

The three M-24s at the rear of Task Force Lynch's column came up to engage the enemy tanks. Eight more North Korean tanks rumbled down from the north to help their compatriots. The Americans destroyed one T-34. In turn, the North Koreans knocked out two American tanks. That was no way to win a battle. The future of Task Force Lynch looked grim.

Then up came Captain Webel, fresh from his encounter with the single tank in the field to the south. On his way to the battle he ran across a group of American soldiers who had just pulled a 3.5-inch bazooka and a number of rockets from a wrecked truck. The trouble was they were not bazooka men and did not know how to operate the weapon. Webel grabbed the bazooka and told one man to act as loader and others to bring up rockets. He zeroed in on one tank and knocked it out. He came up on another and knocked it out. As the enemy tankers got up through the hatch to escape he fired on them with a Thompson submachine gun and knocked them out.

Captain Webel's initiative prompted some other heroic actions. Sergeant Willard H. Hopkins picked up a handful of grenades, got up on another tank and began dropping them through the hatch. That tank was knocked out with all its crew dead.

Hopkins then found a bazooka and organized a bazooka team of his own. In the next hour they were credited with destroying three more tanks.

Six enemy tanks down, four left, and only one American tank still in action. One of the enemy tanks ran straight down the road, knocking over American vehicles like ninepins. But at the end of the column a 105 mm howitzer stood in the path, and the crew of that weapon opened fire at a point-blank range—twenty-five yards. Sergeant Hopkins had also followed this tank down its path of destruction, trailed by his bazooka crew. He opened fire. He was caught in the crossfire between the artillery position and the tank and killed. But bazooka rockets and 105 mm armor-piercing shells finished off that tank. Now there were three. Their commander decided they had enough of fighting for the moment and they rumbled off to the north. What had appeared for a few minutes to be disaster for Task Force Lynch had been turned into victory by a handful of men. Two men were killed, twenty-eight were wounded, and two tanks and fifteen other vehicles were destroyed. But for that price the Americans had knocked out seven T-34 tanks and killed most of the crews.

So far it had been a hard night. Colonel Lynch opted at this point to stop and rest a while and wait for morning before moving on north into the face of those three enemy tanks and whatever else might be up there. When dawn came the Americans prepared to move and at seven o'clock were on the road. The surviving vehicles were brought up behind, the infantry led in a skirmish line along and on the sides of the road. Within in a few minutes after leaving the starting position they encountered one of those enemy tanks. It opened fire with its machine gun, but a 3.5-inch bazooka silenced the gun and destroyed the tank.

Nearby a machine gun opened up on the column. Lieutenant William A. Woodside led a charge against the gun. They killed all the gunners. Further on the column came upon the last of the night's tanks, and both of them they found deserted. They blew them up with grenades.

And then, an hour and a half after starting out that morning, at a small bridge north of Osan the leading element of Task Force Lynch, with Platoon Sergeant Edward C. Mancil at the point, met men of the 31st Infantry. The X Corps and the Eighth Army had linked up, with no important enemy elements in between.

15

Scouring the South

The confusion and cross-purposes of commands in Korea was not confined to the usual uneasy relationship between army and marines. The various army units, too, seemed to be unable to cooperate, a factor that caused unnecessary casualties and loss of time.

On the morning of September 27 the 31st Infantry Regiment attacked North Korean forces on the hillsides north of Osan. Although Task Force Lynch was inside X Corps' lines, the 31st men did not ask for its participation. When General Gay came up to Osan shortly before noon, he saw the battle in progress in the hills, and he offered to send the 8th Cavalry Regiment around on the flank as an enveloping force. He also offered the use of the 77th and 99th Field Artillery battalions and a tank company. The offer was made to the senior 31st Infantry officer present, a battalion commander. Quite in the military tradition, he replied that he would have to ask for permission from higher authority to accept. Presumably he sent the message to Colonel Richard P. Ovenshine, the commander of the 31st Infantry.

What happened next?

No one knows. What did not happen was the concurrence of higher authority. The 1st Cavalry, having met up with the 31st Infantry in the 31st's zone of operations, sat idly by and watched while the 31st Infantry took two days to win a victory that could have been won in a few hours with help.

General Barr, the commander of the 7th Division, said he had never been told. Obviously, then, General Almond had never been told. And obviously also, no one had ever thought to issue a general order to the effect that when the Eighth Army came up, it was to fight.

So why all the rush for the Eighth Army to link up? This costly waste of men and effort was a classic high level foul-up of the sort that was all too familiar in the Korean War.

But if the lead element of the 1st Cavalry that got all the publicity was misused by the high command, at least the other elements of the division were allowed to perform. On the day before when Eighth Army allowed General Gay to fight, the general had sent the 8th Cavalry to move on Ansong, via Koesan. The 5th Cavalry was ordered to take up a rear guard action with the central points at Chochiwon and Chonan. It was to stop and defeat any part of the North Korean army that tried to break through toward the north.

They did a fine job. They captured many troops of the NK 105th Armored Division. They captured many stragglers from other units. They destroyed seven more T-34 tanks in conjunction with air strikes by fighter bombers. They ambushed a number of North Korean units trying to work their way north, such as a party of fifty men in nine Soviet-built jeeps, caught near Taejon.

Also, the ROK Army 1st Division, which was at that point the most experienced and effective fighting unit in the ROK Army, crossed the Naktong at the Sonsan ferry site and began operating from the Poun–Hamchang area and moved north. So in spite of the failure of the high command to make effective use of the linkup, the drive northward of the Eighth Army paid off. While the Americans were converging on the Seoul area, the South Koreans were rushing up the center and east side of the peninsula toward the 38th parallel.

The night of September 26 was relatively quiet—as compared to the night before when all hell had burst loose along Ma Po Boulevard. Even Company D of the 7th Marines, isolated in the pocket between Hill 296 and Hill 338 was not disturbed by enemy attack. But the fact was that still Seoul was not liberated, a matter that had become something of an embarrassment to General Almond.

On the morning of September 27, however, the marines sensed a different atmosphere. General Wol's men were still fighting, but there were no "Mansei" attacks, no concerted effort to drive the marines out of the city. Undoubtedly it was because the 25th Brigade had been badly mauled and was thoroughly disorganized. One indication of the problem of General Wol was the war materiel captured by the 7th Marines: four machine guns, six rifles, and six hundred bayonets. The North Koreans in Seoul were fighting with all the materials at hand, and obviously there was not much left.

At dawn on September 27, a task force of infantrymen and tanks and engineers advanced along the Kaesong road from the northwest to rescue the men of Company D. They met little resistance, came upon the company and brought them back to the 7th Marine command post at Hoengjeoe-ri. At the same time the 3rd Battalion of the 7th Marines attacked the northern part of Hill 338 which had produced so much trouble the day before. Company H ran into trouble—heavy fire from above as it marched along a draw. Captain Shields tried to break through but could not. There were still many North Korean soldiers on that highland. They were dug in deep and they firmly resisted the efforts of Company H and Company G to push them out. Company G was ordered off to another mission and Company I arrived to participate. Still, at the end of the day, the North Koreans clung to the north end of Hill 338.

Company G's new mission, ordered in midmorning, was to capture Hill 342, which stood high above the capitol building. What happened next was an indication of the trend of the fighting and its effect on the Korean civilian population of Seoul. For three months the civilians had lived in a reign of terror imposed by the North Korean Security Police. They walked the streets in fear of the soldiers. But in the past three days the attitude had changed. The men of Company G were setting out to capture the hill when they came to a minefield, which had been marked off and identified by unknown civilian friends of the Americans. So there was not a single casualty incurred there.

But Hill 342 itself was a different proposition. As Captain Cooney's men approached the hill they were immediately engaged in a firefight. The North Koreans they faced were old hands: in a few minutes Cooney had lost several officers and noncommissioned officers, singled out by the enemy riflemen. The fight continued until nightfall, and still the marines did not have control of this important feature.

The 1st Battalion of the 7th Marines was in reserve, blocking off roads and waterways northwest of Seoul in the Haengju area. What happened there on September 27 was another measure of the situation of General Wol's Seoul defenses. Obviously he had called for help from all outlying units. At about noon a company of North Korean soldiers came down from the northern hills to attack through Haengju and harry the marines in Seoul from behind. (See Map 11.) But Company A had been detailed to man a crossing of the Han at

Hill 125. Further support was available from Company B and Company C. All of it was needed, for the North Koreans seemed determined to break through. The fighting was brisk for a couple of hours. Then the local North Korean commander must have seen that he could not overpower the marines or break through and he called off the action. As quickly as they had come, the North Koreans moved back and disappeared toward Kaesong. They also must have picked up all the other units nearby and told them Seoul was lost, for this was the end of the marine fighting in the area.

The 2nd Battalion of the 7th Marines moved farther around to the northeast, attacking Hill 343. Again they ran into the ragged remnants of the North Korean main line of defense. Company E and Company F fought on that hillside all day long, their gains measured in feet and yards. But by the end of the day they had advanced a mile and a half and held the top of Hill 343.

The keys to Seoul were held by Colonel Murray's 5th Marines and Colonel Puller's 1st Marines, who were advancing along the streets of the city toward the capitol and business district. How many of the marines were carrying American flags in their packs is unlikely ever to be known, but there were certainly a lot of them. After it was all over the army liked to jeer at the marines for their flag-raising proclivity. But Colonel Puller had the answer for them: a marine with a U.S. flag in his pack, which he was bent on putting up somewhere, was not likely to "bug out" in the fighting. As if to prove that, on this day the drive into Seoul seemed to be a race between the 5th Marines and the 1st Marines to raise flags over public buildings.

The day started out with all the usual concerns. The 3rd Battalion of the 5th Marines kicked off at six forty-five, expecting to have the same sort of trouble against the eastern spur of Hill 296 that they had been having for two days. But instead of a greeting of heavy automatic and rifle fire, as they advanced they were met only by sporadic sniping. In forty-five minutes Company G and Company I had captured the high ground and moved down into the streets of the western side of Seoul. Here they ran into the expected, minefields and barricades. But once the minefields were cleared, the barricades proved to be scarcely manned. So the progress was much swifter than it had been the day before. Less than three hours after the start, Company G made contact with the 1st Marines on the right. Both regiments were heading for the capitol building, the prize that would symbolize the fulfillment of General MacArthur's premature announcement—the liberation of the South Korean capital.

At 10:30 the 3rd Battalion of the 5th Marines had reached the Middle

School. (See Map 19.) At noon the capitol building loomed ahead, flying two red flags of the North Koreans high above. On the right the men of the 2nd Battalion of the 1st Marines were racing toward that goal, and they had some help from Richard J. H. Johnston, a correspondent of *The New York Times* who had lived in Seoul in the first postwar years. For Johnston it was the second liberation—the first having been made with Lieutenant General John R. Hodge's XXIV Corps in the late summer of 1945. He knew the streets and alleys of Seoul, and he led the 1st Marines quickly to the French Consulate. The gate opened. The place was deserted. Quick as a peddler a marine pulled an American flag from his pack and they ran it up the flagpole.

Lieutenant Cummings in his tank then led Company D toward the main intersection of Seoul near the Middle School, where the major streetcar lines crossed. Here the marines ran into the remnants of the organized defense of central Seoul. Cummings' tank destroyed two North Korean self-propelled guns which had been situated in the middle of the intersection. Then he ran into a mine, and his tank was put out of action. The infantry moved up. A North Korean truck tried to escape, hauling a howitzer. Staff Sergeant Arthur MacDonald's Sherman tank put two 90 mm rounds into the truck and it stopped, a total wreck. The marines captured the howitzer and its crew. The tanks smashed the barricades and marines swarmed across the breach. The North Koreans seemed to lose heart and fled.

Lieutenant Colonel Newton's 1st Battalion climbed rocky Hill 338. Company A led the way after a barrage from the artillery and mortars and an air strike. The 1st Platoon seized a piece of high ground. The 2nd Platoon moved forward along an ancient wall that led to the top of the hill. The dug-in North Koreans stopped the platoon with mortar and machine gun fire. Marine Corsairs came in to rocket and machine gun the North Koreans' positions. The marines on the ground used 60 mm and 81 mm mortars. The 1st Platoon advanced to higher ground and covered the 2nd Platoon as it advanced along the wall. The 3rd Platoon came up on the right and smashed the last resistance on the summit and the hill was quiet.

The 3rd Battalion moved up Kwangwhamun Boulevard toward the capitol building, led by a flamethrower tank. Just after three o'clock they burst inside the Government House grounds, and more marines rushed for the flagpoles. Down came the red North Korean banners. Up went the Stars and Stripes.

And so it was everywhere in downtown Seoul. Correspondent Johnston led his batch of Company E marines to the Soviet Embassy, which was also abandoned. Up went Old Glory here. They reached the American Embassy and raised the flag there. At that point from the roof of the Duk Soo Palace nearby came a badly aimed sniper's shot. Several marines saw the enemy sniper. One marine took one shot to knock him off the roof of the palace.

On September 27, the 32nd Infantry held its positions on South Mountain and the lesser heights, waiting for the marines to join up. At four thirty in the afternoon the 2nd Battalion of the 1st Marines moved along the streetcar line south of Government House. The enemy fought street by street, and the marines were supported by Corsairs. Tanks came up to add their fire to the fight. This was the last important North Korean defense, and it collapsed just after four thirty. There were still enemy troops in Seoul, and they had to be routed out one by one or in small groups. The potshots of snipers popped for hours. But the organized resistance was over. The marines marched to the eastern part of the city, and there they dug in for the night. Seoul was indeed liberated, only two days after General MacArthur claimed.

16

Clearing the Rubble

On September 27 much of the Eighth Army was engaged in mopping up small clots of North Korean resistance below Seoul. What remained of the NK I Corps organization in the south was trying desperately to stage holding actions so the remnants of the proud divisions could escape northward.

Those blown bridges west of Chinju delayed Task Force Matthews until September 27. That day Captain Charles Matthews led the advance unit out of Chinju with the 25th Reconnaissance Company and Company A of the 79th Tank Battalion. Behind came the rest of the 24th Infantry.

Matthews' advance force reached Hadong at five thirty that evening. There they learned that a group of American prisoners of war was being taken northward, and that the North Korean force holding them was just about two hours ahead. Then a captured North Korean told them some of the prisoners were just half an hour ahead, on the road to Kurye. Task Force Matthews hurried along the road, and at the village of Kondu, ten miles north of Hadong, they ran across the North Korean jailers and liberated the prisoners. There were eleven Americans from the 3rd Battalion of the 29th Infantry Regiment. They were in bad shape. Most of them could not walk.

On the morning of September 28, the task force crossed the Nam, or part of it did. Sergeant Raymond N. Reifers of the recon company gunned his tank and made it across, but the next vehicle got stuck. The others piled up behind the stuck vehicle, while Sergeant Reifers plowed ahead in to Namwon.

There he discovered that he had stumbled into an enemy concentration. Hundreds of North Koreans were in the town. They had been watching a pair of F-84 jets which were strafing and rocketing the North Korean positions and vehicles and they did not see the tank until it burst into town and came rumbling up the main street. North Koreans scattered like bugs, over fences, into houses, anywhere to get away from the approaching enemy. Sergeant Reifers was a little unnerved himself, to discover suddenly that he and his tank crew were the only Americans in sight. Then he heard voices shouting in English.

"Don't shoot. Americans. GIs . . ." and a gate burst open and out of a courtyard streamed a line of ragged American prisoners.

Reifers got on the radio:

"SOMEBODY GET UP HERE! I'm all alone . . . this town is full of enemy soldiers and there are American prisoners. . . ."

Lieutenant Robert K. Sawyer got his tank across the stream and sped to Reifers' assistance. Soon other vehicles were in Namwon. They cleared the town of the enemy while the medics took over the former prisoners. There were eighty-six prisoners in this group.

That afternoon Task Force Dolvin arrived in Namwon. Task Force Blair then moved up to Chongup, and Iri, where it was stalled by another destroyed bridge. On the night of September 29 the 24th Infantry captured Kunsan on the Kum River estuary. Task Force Dolvin and other elements of the 24th Infantry and 35th Infantry moved through rugged country called the Chiri-san region, which lies in a rectangle bounded by Chinju, Hadong, Namwon, and Hamyang. It was notable for its steep mountains and precipitous valleys. It had long been a haven for escaped North Korean units and guerrillas. There were thousands of North Koreans in this area, including many guerrilla bands of two hundred to four hundred men, and elements of the NK 6th Division.

Task Force Dolvin moved toward Hamyang, hampered by blown bridges and minefields all the way. On September 27 it ran through a ridge line manned by about six hundred enemy, but was stopped by another blown bridge. That night the engineers built a bypass. The next day the task force met part of the 23rd Infantry east of Hamyang. Then the Americans came to another blown bridge and had to stop for three hours while engineers and Korean laborers built a bypass. The NK 6th Division was fighting a delaying action, and doing a good job of it, but the Americans were learning how to deal with the situation. That day a liaison pilot informed the task force that the enemy ahead near Hamyang was preparing to blow another bridge. The leading tanks sped up and came to the bridge with their machine guns spitting. The North Koreans who were placing the demolition charges on the bridge fled and the tankers captured the bridge intact. The North Koreans ahead were caught off base, and the task force was able to speed along, killing enemy soldiers along the road, capturing others, and sending still others off into the mountains. In the middle of the afternoon Task Force Dolvin entered Namwon, to be greeted by Sergeant Reifers and his friends.

Task Force Dolvin then went on, traveling through the night and in the morning reached Chonju to find that the 38th Infantry was already there. Along behind the task force came infantrymen to mop up. On September 29 the ROK marines captured Yosu on the south coast. So by September 29 the southern area of the Eighth Army front had been partly cleared and the lines of communication established, even though many North Koreans still roamed the hills.

Further north the enemy continued to give trouble. On the morning of September 27 a heavy enemy barrage hit the 23rd Infantry at Anui. One round did particular damage in the 3rd Battalion command post: it killed the battalion executive officer, the intelligence officer, the assistant operations officer, the motor officer, the artillery liaison officer, and an air force liaison officer. It wounded the battalion commander and twenty-five enlisted men.

At the 3rd Battalion command post the war was very real that day, but also that day the last organized North Korean unit east of the Naktong River, the NK 10th Division, withdrew from positions near Hyongpung and crossed over to the west side of the river to retreat northward. At four o'clock in the morning of September 28 the 38th Infantry started for Chongju, seventy-three miles away on the coastal plain. The 25th Division was also approaching Chongju from a different direction, but the 38th Infantry got there first, having covered the seventy-three miles in a little over nine hours. At Chonju the Americans found about three hundred North Korean soldiers, they killed a third of them, and took most of the rest prisoner.

The advance was moving faster than the supply train. The IX Corps had only a handful of trucks to resupply all the units that were fanning out across South Korea in pursuit of the North Koreans. The supply chain ran almost two hundred miles back to Miryang, the railhead for the line that led back to Pusan port. The average time for a trip from Miryang to the front was forty-eight hours. At Chonju the 38th Infantry ran out of gas and had to appeal for help. A liaison plane pilot reported the trouble to IX Corps, and gas was hurried up to the line on an emergency basis, arriving twenty-four hours later. The advance could go on. In the middle of the afternoon of September

29 the fuel arrived and then the 3rd Battalion of the 38th Infantry moved on to the town of Kanggyong on the Kum River.

Taejon was a key point in the North Korean plan of retreat. The line of defense on September 27 was along the heights west of Okchon. The purpose was to hold as the frayed elements of the seven divisions of the NK I Corps from the Waegwan area moved northward. On the 27th the U.S. ground forces and air forces destroyed a number of tanks in the Taejon area—a total of about thirty was claimed, but this is entirely too high to be accurate. The claims do show how vigorous the fighting was. On September 28 the 19th Infantry attacked the heights at Okchon, only to discover that the enemy had moved out during the night. Air force planes reported a long column of troops marching north out of Taejon that morning, estimated at eight hundred. Another large group was seen near the railroad station. Another force estimated at a thousand men was seen in the afternoon west of the city. The air force attacked steadily, with napalm and rockets, and reported the infliction of many casualties.

At four thirty that afternoon, scouts of the 19th Infantry entered the outskirts of Taejon, and the engineers came up to clear mines. An hour later tanks trundled along the road leading the infantry, and before dark a liaison plane landed on the Taejon airstrip, the first to arrive since that July day so long ago when Major General William Dean's 24th Division had evacuated the city, and Dean had been captured. Now the division had retaken the city. The 19th Infantry Regiment, which did the job, was the unit that had been last to leave Taejon in the days of American retreat.

At Taejon the Americans discovered more grisly evidence of the North Koreans' brutality to their enemies. In one grave near the airstrip they found the bodies of five hundred ROK soldiers, hands tied behind their backs, victims of mass execution. In fact, the North Korean Security Police were carrying out executions almost to the minute that the American tanks rolled into the city. Hundreds were shot that day, including a number of Americans. When the U.S. soldiers were checking the graves, they discovered two Americans and three Korean civilians still alive. They had feigned death and been buried alive, still wired to their comrades. One of the Americans survived by punching a hole in the earth with a lead pencil, the other with his hands. The Koreans saved themselves in similar ways.

Other troops coming into Taejon had more horror stories to tell of North Korean atrocities in the towns. At Sachon the North Koreans burned the jail as the Americans approached, and about three hundred South Korean officials, police, and landowners perished.

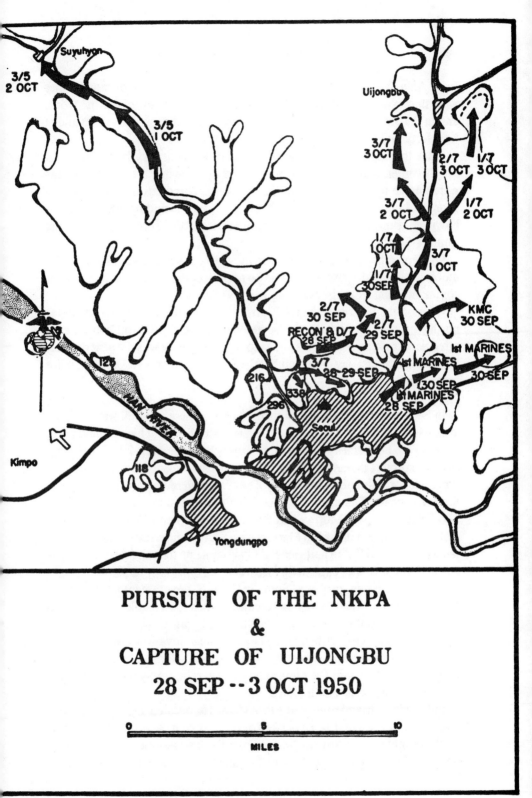

PURSUIT OF THE NKPA
&
CAPTURE OF UIJONGBU
28 SEP -- 3 OCT 1950

0   5   10

MILES

Map 20.

At Anui, Mokpo, Kongju, Hamyang, and Chonju, hundreds more bodies were unearthed from their shallow graves. Taejon, however, was the worst, and in the days just before the capture about seven thousand Koreans and at least forty American soldiers were murdered there.

Since the capture of the city by the North Koreans they had used it as a supply center. When the Americans moved up so swiftly the North Koreans were unable to destroy many of these supplies. Hundreds of prisoners were taken and many guns and other bits of equipment, including four American howitzers captured by the North Koreans from the 24th Division in the summer fighting.

On September 29 the 24th Division moved its headquarters to Taejon once more. Its task at the moment would be to protect the Eighth Army's lines of communication from the Naktong River to Seoul.

Over on the UN right, the ROK Army was making tracks, moving faster northward than any others. On September 29 the ROK 3rd Division captured Samchok, and sped on. (See Map 15.) Kangnung was the next destination and on the last day of September the South Koreans were only five miles below the 38th parallel.

In Seoul the marines still had their troubles. There was still some sniping inside Seoul. The 7th Marines spent September 28 seizing high ground north of Seoul on both sides of the road to Uijongbu. (See Map 20.) The enemy fought to protect that escape route. The 1st Marines spent the day clearing the remainder of Seoul of enemy troops. They encountered many mines, but they finished the task. That night Colonel Puller put his command post in the Duk Soo Palace, Colonel Murray had taken over the Women's University, and Colonel Litzenberg of the 7th Marines was in far less impressive quarters off to the west. General Smith and General Craig came up to make their headquarters at Seoul too. The capital was secure.

Now came a new problem. Some in the U.S. government establishment believed that President Syngman Rhee was much too volatile to be returned to power in South Korea. Those who held this view could recall his saber-rattling in the days before the North Korean invasion. And they knew that not all the incursions across the 38th parallel by far had been carried out by the North Koreans. They hoped somehow to dump Syngman Rhee and start all over again in South Korea.

But General MacArthur had other ideas. He decided that he personally would escort President Rhee back to Seoul. When he was informed that he must not make any efforts to "restore" the Rhee government without direction from Washington, he said loftily that there was no question of restoration, the Rhee government had remained in Korea all during the war and in political control and it was simply a question of taking them back home. This was hardly true, the Rhee government had been restrained at one point from fleeing from Korea by way of Pusan. But in another sense, MacArthur was right; a power vacuum could not be allowed to exist; just such a situation at the end of World War II had led to the mess Korea found itself in, in 1950. Since there was no other government than that of the North Koreans, who were on the run, Rhee had to be brought back if continuity was to be retained and order restored. President Truman's political advisors were extremely leery of Syngman Rhee, but there was no real alternative.

The Korean War was just then approaching a point of crisis. From the beginning, General MacArthur had announced that it was his intention not only to drive the North Koreans back onto their own side of the 38th parallel, but to go all the way north, defeat the North Korean People's Army, destroy the North Korean People's Republic, and unify Korea under a government acceptable to the United States. When MacArthur had first enunciated this personal policy in discussions with representatives of the Joint Chiefs of Staff in the early days of the invasion of South Korea, not too much attention had been paid to his words. The Joint Chiefs were more seriously concerned about the immediate problem of the war: getting the materiel to Korea to fight the North Koreans before time ran out and the South Koreans and Americans were pushed into the sea.

But early in September, as the time for the Inchon landing drew near, MacArthur's words began to have a different ring. In Washington President Truman had to develop an American policy toward the war to be followed after the liberation of Seoul and the driving of the North Koreans into their own territory.

The President faced serious problems regarding the armed forces and Korea policy. Defense Secretary Louis Johnson had proved to be a disaster. He talked too much and too wildly to the press, often subverting the President's policies. He also undercut Truman's China policy (although the President did not then know it) by passing secrets of state to Wellington Koo, the Nationalist ambassador to Washington. Johnson had been the one bad cog in the wheel when the decision about the defense of Korea had to be made that June night after the invasion from the north.

In the first week of September 1950, President Truman was thinking about firing Johnson and replacing him with General George C. Marshall, who had been commander of the army during the World War II years and then Secretary of State. There had never been any question of Marshall's loyalty to the President. There was much question about Johnson's.

Truman was also having troubles with General MacArthur, who seemed
bent on having his own views become the Asian policy of the United States.
Under his hat as commander in chief, Far Eastern Forces, MacArthur had
made a trip to Taiwan late in July. It was embarrassing to the State Department and to the President, because MacArthur exuded (without saying so
much) the view that the U.S. must back Chiang Kai-shek to the hilt, just at the
time that the Soviets and the Chinese Communists were claiming that the U.S.
was preparing to use Taiwan as an American base. For Truman, who was
trying to maintain an arms-length policy with Taiwan, the MacArthur visit
was a great annoyance. Then, late in August, MacArthur had issued a
statement to the annual convention of the Veterans of Foreign Wars which
again emphasized the importance of Taiwan and again embarrassed the
administration. Truman demanded that it be withdrawn. Secretary Johnson
jibbed at issuing such an order to MacArthur, and Truman then made the final
decision to fire Johnson.

As for MacArthur, Truman considered replacing him in the Korean War
with General Omar Bradley, but he did not, largely because the Republicans
would have made an enormous issue of the matter. The Republicans had
already created serious difficulty in the management of foreign relations,
stemming from their view that the Truman administration was responsible for
the victory of the Chinese Communists over the Chinese Nationalists. The
Republican right would continue, even until the 1980s, to believe that the
United States could force its way of political life on all countries save those of
the Communist bloc, which was the declared enemy. And MacArthur's views
were the Republican views; most of them were derived from him. In a
nutshell, MacArthur believed that the United States could and should destroy
communism in North Korea and in China and he was willing to risk World
War III to do so.

On August 23, with the fate of the Pusan Perimeter still hanging in the
balance, General MacArthur had made his views crystal clear in a military
conference at his headquarters in the Dai Ichi Building in Tokyo. He was
touting his plan for the Inchon landing against some opposition from General
Lawton Collins, the army chief of staff. MacArthur, with his corncob pipe,
stood up before the big situation map in the conference room, and spoke:

> The prestige of the Western world hangs in the balance. Oriental
> millions are watching the outcome. It is plainly apparent that here in Asia
> is where the Communist conspirators have elected to make their play for
> global conquest. The test is not in Berlin or Vienna, in London, Paris, or
> Washington. It is here and now—it is along the Naktong River in South

Korea. We have joined the issue on the battlefield. Actually we here fight Europe's war with arms, while there it is still confined to words. If we lose the war to Communism in Asia, the fate of Europe will be gravely jeopardized. Win it and Europe will probably be saved from war and stay free. Make the wrong decision here—the fatal decision of inertia—and we will be done. I can almost hear the ticking of the second hand of destiny. We must act now or we will die.

The MacArthur rhetoric overwhelmed his listeners as it so often had done in the past. Shorn of its trimmings it was a sweeping statement of the MacArthur philosophy: the war against communism had to be fought to the death and the sooner the West got on with it the better. This position put MacArthur on a collision course with the Truman administration.

Further complication, of course, came from MacArthur's massive ego, but by this time the difficulties between the earthy President Truman and the patrician, power-loving general were more fundamental than simply a personality clash.

MacArthur understood the psychology of the crowd; he always had, as his remarkable public relations operation had shown all through World War II and the occupation of Japan. Now he announced that he was going to come to Korea and he wanted to ride from Kimpo airport to Seoul by limousine.

Someone pointed out that there was no bridge across the Han River.

Then build one, said MacArthur.

It could be done. Just recently, now that the need was over, the command had brought in bridging materials. So the marines, who had moved a division across the Han on rafts and amtracs, now had to stop what they were doing, which was winning a war, and build a bridge for the American Caesar. They did it. They broke up the rafts they had built from pontoons and they brought other pontoons from Okinawa. By midnight on September 28 they had finished the bridge.

Another factor in the equation at Seoul was the eagerness of MacArthur's sycophants to please the general. When General Almond learned that MacArthur intended to come to Seoul to deliver the capital into the hands of President Rhee, he decided that if his boss was coming to Korea he ought to be met in style. Almond ordered the marines to provide an honor guard to meet the general at Kimpo and another to meet him at the capitol building in Seoul. The rest of the marines were to stand at attention along the route from Kimpo to the capitol. The marine band would play for the general's pleasure. To be sure that everything went well, all battalion commanders were to drop the war and report to Almond's headquarters for a night conference.

When General Smith had this word he balked. The battalion commanders still had a war to fight. They would not appear to listen to General Almond.

This lese majesty might have created a real problem, except that for once MacArthur agreed. There would be no honor guard, no cordon of troops, no marine band. MacArthur's reasoning, of course, had nothing to do with General Smith's. MacArthur, the master showman, wanted the Koreans to have the show as soon as he was through with it. He would conduct the ceremony. The Americans would be in the background. The Korean marines would be in the front. There would be some Americans in the honor guard, but they would be army. The marines were so annoyed that they all agreed to appear in battle dress, making a mute statement of what they thought of the proceedings.

The day—September 29—did not open very auspiciously. Just before five o'clock in the morning about a hundred North Koreans attacked the observation post of the 2nd Battalion of the 1st Marines, on a spur of hill in the city's outskirts. The point was defended only by a rifle platoon and the fighting was brisk before the enemy was driven off. Half an hour later another group of North Koreans hit the left flank of the battalion with grenades and burp guns. The marines suffered thirty-two casualties but they killed forty-eight North Koreans. And all during the day, the 7th Marines fought on around the northern perimeter of Seoul.

At ten o'clock in the morning of September 29, the MacArthur plane, the SCAP (Supreme Commander, Allied Powers, which was MacArthur's title as head of the Japanese occupation) landed at Kimpo airfield. The door opened and out stepped General MacArthur and Mrs. MacArthur. He was dressed in his beautiful field costume. He stretched elaborately and, to show that he was really one of the boys, he remarked, "This is just like old times," which it was not in any way. Inchon, Kimpo, and Seoul had been left intact at the end of the Japanese war; now they were largely wreckage.

Five olive drab staff cars stood waiting, one with the five stars of a general of the army on the license plate. Behind them stood a train of forty spanking clean jeeps. The MacArthur nobility filled up the staff cars, and the lesser lights (press and line officers) were relegated to the jeeps. The procession then hurried toward MacArthur's bridge.

There was no trouble. Two of Colonel Puller's battalions and two of Colonel Litzenburg's were still fighting in the outskirts of Seoul but three battalions of marines, carefully kept out of sight, lined the route and made sure there was no interference.

The South Korean capitol building was little more than a shell, having been bombed, rocketed, and shelled until part of it burned. The windows were broken and the glass roof shattered. MacArthur said the building bore the smell of death and he was quite right, the last of the dozens of corpses there had been hauled out just hours before his arrival. The audience the general faced was very much a mixed bag: half a dozen generals, four admirals, Ambassador Muccio, marines in their battle dress, ROK officers in fatigues, British naval officers in white shirts, shorts, and long white stockings and white shoes, and the army Military Police all dressed up with their shoes shined. About an hour after the general arrived, President Rhee and the South Korean contingent came into Kimpo airfield in another plane and were driven across MacArthur's bridge into Seoul.

The ceremony was held in the National Assembly Chamber, which was hung with mulberry-colored drapery. At high noon MacArthur and President Rhee came in, arm in arm, and the audience stood in silence. MacArthur went to the lectern and delivered another of his emotionally charged speeches:

> Mr. President: By the grace of a merciful Providence our forces fighting under the symbol of that greatest hope and inspiration of mankind, the United Nations, have liberated this ancient capital city of Korea. It has been freed from the despotism of communist rule and its citizens once more have the opportunity for that immutable concept of life which holds invincibly to the primacy of individual liberty and personal dignity.

As the general spoke, an artillery piece not far away sent off a round in support of the 7th Marines, and the concussion shook the building. Glass tinkled down from the broken roof, and brave men flinched. But not MacArthur. In his heroic style he did not move a muscle to give credence to the fright.

And having finished his peroration, he called on all to say with him the Lord's Prayer, and they did. The general had worked himself up into such a state that tears ran down his cheeks. Then with the timing of a Barrymore, he turned the government over to President Rhee.

> My officers and I will now resume our military duties and leave you and your government to the discharge of civil responsibility.

President Rhee was also nearly overcome. He grasped the general's hand. "We admire you," he said, "we love you as the savior of our race. How can I ever explain to you my own undying gratitude. . . ."

So it ended. Seoul was liberated. The ROK Army was on the 38th parallel. The North Koreans were fleeing toward Pyongyang. The big question was, what would the UN forces do next?

17

Crossing the Parallel

For a long time President Truman and his advisors in Washington had anticipated the day when the UN forces would be on the march and Truman would have to decide how far they should go in punishing the North Koreans for their ignoble adventure in aggression.

No one questioned the right of the UN forces to reach the 38th parallel. (See map, p. 10.) The advisors cited the United Nations Security Council resolution of June 27, 1950, which called on the U.S. to come to the aid of South Korea and "... to restore international peace and security in the area." But what did worry some of President Truman's advisors was the possibility of a Soviet or Chinese Communist countermove. Secretary of State Dean Acheson called the question of crossing the parallel "explosive."

That concern prompted Truman's angry reaction when General MacArthur had suddenly appeared in Taiwan to counsel with Generalissimo Chiang Kai-shek. The gesture had to appear to the Soviets and the Chinese Communists as a provocation and indication of unfriendly American intentions toward the Peking government.

All during the summer of 1950 the Truman administration had considered the problem: how to proceed without setting off World War III. It was apparent that the North Korean government was the pawn of the Soviets. (The North Korean invasion was the first step in a policy of using satellite nations to carry out aggression that was to continue as a cornerstone of Soviet activity for the next three decades.)

President Syngman Rhee had not helped much. Seeing the war as a godsend for his own ambitions, he had announced on July 13 that the North Korean attack had wiped out the 38th parallel issue. A few days later he told the world that the South Korean government would not be bound by any settlement of the war that left his country divided. This view was echoed in the United States by John Foster Dulles, who at the time was one of Truman's advisors, and by John Allison, then director of the Office of Northeast Affairs, both of whom advocated a military solution to the problem in Korea. Allison made one point that appealed to President Truman: the North Koreans must not go unpunished for their transgression, because such failure would encourage other potential aggressors.

The State Department's policy planning staff suggested that to move above the 38th parallel would be most dangerous. Allison called that policy appeasement—and so did a number of Republican members of the congress. Allison found it easy to accept the danger of starting World War III. He thought the American people ought to be told "why and what it will mean to them."

At this point the hawks so bullied the doves with talk of "appeasement" that the doves retreated in confusion, and the talk about stopping at the 38th parallel died. The fact was, of course, that the policy planning staff was far more prescient than Dulles, Allison, or the other hawks.

By midsummer General Collins and Admiral Forrest Sherman of the Joint Chiefs of Staff were convinced that MacArthur was right, that the North Korean forces should be totally destroyed. The Defense Department's thinking was exemplified by a draft memorandum of July 31 which suggested that the unification of Korea under the UN auspices (read U.S.) would show the Japanese that Soviet expansionism could be checked, and would tend to push the Chinese away from the Soviets. "Skillfully manipulated, the Chinese Communists might prefer different arrangements and a new orientation." The implication here is that the Peking government might be brought around to a pro-U.S. attitude. This suggestion ignored every action the United States had taken since 1945, when it had definitely backed the Chinese Nationalists in the civil war and, after Chiang Kai-shek had fled to Taiwan, the United States had embraced him and protected his regime there, and by this policy the United States lent authority to Chiang's claims that he would soon invade the mainland. Is it possible that the policymakers in the Pentagon did not understand in 1950 the enormous weight the Peking government gave to the continued U.S. backing of Chiang? This seems to be quite certain; one of the most serious American failings seems to be a total lack of understanding or even cognizance of the perception other nations have of U.S. policy and aims, based on its actions and on the public statements of so-called responsible individuals.

The above suggestion certainly indicates what many suspected, that the American military establishment had a faulty understanding of Asian affairs. Also, at this time, the realists of the State Department had been driven underground by Senator Joseph McCarthy's wild claims to having seen Communists under every regional desk. In the hysteria of anticommunism that had held America in bondage for four years few were brave enough to disagree with the hawks, and those who did disagree were almost entirely put down or ignored. George Kennan's is a case in point. As director of the policy planning section Kennan opposed crossing the parallel. And, surprising as it may seem in the 1980s when the CIA has so stained a reputation, on August 18 a CIA memorandum suggested that crossing the parallel would create "grave risks" for the United States. The Chinese might well enter the war, said the CIA.

Fewer and fewer of the top officials were listening. Secretary of State Acheson came around to the view that MacArthur ought to be allowed to go anywhere he wanted to destroy the North Korean army. Dean Rusk, then Assistant Secretary of State for Far Eastern Affairs, favored the crossing. John K. Emmerson, a senior advisor on Asian affairs, and John Allison led the hawks of the State Department. They suggested that there was a growing sentiment in the United States in favor of a "final" settlement of the Korean problem instead of any sort of "deal." The Republicans certainly were tending toward the greater involvement. General Dwight D. Eisenhower, then president of Columbia University, suggested that it might be necessary. Much of the press adopted a similar tone. On August 25 Secretary of the Navy Francis P. Matthews came out in a speech in Boston in favor of "preventive war" with the USSR. Hanson W. Baldwin of *The New York Times* said this speech was a "trial balloon" sent up by Secretary of Defense Johnson, who had been making this sort of remark around Washington for months. President Truman disavowed the sentiments, but what were the Soviets and the Chinese to think?

The next day George N. Craig, national commander of the American Legion, urged the Truman administration to warn the Soviets that "further aggression" by its satellites would be "the signal for our bombers to wing their way toward Moscow."

Ambassador Philip Jessup on August 27 answered Matthews for President Truman in a radio broadcast, saying that "the destruction of war is so catastrophic that no stone must be left unturned in the effort to maintain our security and our highest values by peaceful means."

And on September 1, Truman felt he had to order the firing of General Orvil A. Anderson as head of the Air War College because Anderson was teaching courses advocating preventive war. That day Truman felt it necessary to do what he virtually never did: speak to the nation on the problem. He told a nationwide radio audience that "We do not believe in aggressive or preventive war."

But Truman was not sure what he should do, and that is certain because he continued to support General MacArthur as commander, knowing full well that MacArthur wanted to carry the war as far as the Kremlin if necessary.

Even in September, the experts in Washington were still hedging—the National Security Council would not offer a final recommendation. Wait and see what the Russians and the Chinese did, it said. Unification of Korea (forcible, that is) was a fine idea if it did not mean general war. But who knew? MacArthur should be allowed to cross the 38th parallel, but not to run the risk of war. Obviously, these conclusions were in conflict, but the experts simply did not know what to do and they passed the buck to President Truman. Finally they did make a specific recommendation: that barring Chinese or Soviet intervention, MacArthur should be allowed to advance as far as the Yalu River, the border between Korea and China, and the Tumen River, the border between the USSR and Korea.

So, after all the hemming and hawing, the hawks would have their way. The quiet demeanor of the Soviet representatives to the UN was regarded as definitive; the Soviets did not want to extend the conflict. That was the conclusion drawn by the Americans. President Truman approved the recommendation. The Joint Chiefs of Staff drew a directive to be sent to General MacArthur, and it was approved by President Truman, Secretary Acheson and Secretary Marshall.

The die was cast.

Consequently, by the first of September the Truman administration was split into two camps. The hawks had convinced themselves and much of the media that (a) it was necessary to clean up Korea and put an end to the North Korean People's Republic, and (b) that there was no indication this would bring either the Chinese Communists or the Soviets into the war. A finer example of conviction through wishful thinking and myopic argument would be hard to find.

So as the summer ground along the opinion in Washington was solidifying in favor of the march up the Korean peninsula to destroy the North Korean People's Army and the government of President Kim Il Sung.

By September 1, the matter of a definite long-range policy toward the Korean War was still officially undecided. The President's political advisors now accepted the idea that if the UN forces crossed the 38th parallel the North Koreans would invite the Chinese Communists into the war. If this happened, then the next step was to tell General MacArthur to resist the Chinese, while taking the matter to the UN once more to have them condemned as aggressors.

The alternative could be a Soviet entry into the war to support North Korea directly. If this happened, the advisors said, General MacArthur would have to go on the defensive while Washington decided what to do. One thing was certain, the U.S. political and military establishment did not agree with MacArthur's contention that the issue between the United States and the USSR had been joined on the battlefield of Korea and had to be fought out there to the end. Neither Truman nor his advisors had any intention of fighting a general war over Korea.

The Truman administration did not, however, agree with a growing sentiment among the non-U.S. allies of the UN that the time had come to call a halt to the war. The dissidents wanted the United States to stop at the 38th parallel and turn the future over to the diplomats. But the pressures to do the reverse were enormous. President Truman knew that the Republicans were completely prepared to make a partisan issue of the conduct of the war. The newspaper columnists were telling him so every day, and so were such Republican leaders as Senator William Knowland of California, a hawk and supporter of Chiang Kai-shek. Even within his own administration Truman had his problems, only the worst of which was the conduct of Defense Secretary Johnson.

President Truman, knowing that he had been betrayed by Johnson, fired him but the process took some two weeks at the height of the Korea discussions. When, on September 21, General Marshall became Secretary of Defense General Marshall's first task was to define a policy for Korea that President Truman could accept. His task was made infinitely easier because Truman trusted Marshall implicitly. Marshall biographer Leonard Mosley does not even mention Marshall's part in the final decision, but the fact is that Truman esteemed Marshall's military opinions more highly than those of any other man. Marshall and Acheson both approved the final directive drawn by the Joint Chiefs of Staff, and if Marshall had not approved, it seems most unlikely that Truman would have allowed it to go out. That directive was specific authorization for General MacArthur to carry the war into the territory of the enemy:

> Your military objective is the destruction of the North Korean armed forces. In attaining this objective, you are authorized to conduct military operations north of the 38th Parallel in Korea. Under no circumstances however will your forces, ground, air, or sea, cross the Manchurian or USSR borders of Korea, and as a matter of policy, no non-Korean ground forces will be used in the North East provinces bordering the Soviet Union, or in the areas along the Manchurian border. Furthermore, support of your operations north or south of the 38th parallel, will not include air or naval action against Manchuria or against USSR territory. When organized armed resistance by the North Korean Forces has been brought substantially to an end, you should direct the R.O.K. forces to take the lead in disarming remaining North Korean units and enforcing the terms of surrender. Circumstances obtaining at the time will determine the character of occupation of North Korea. Your plans for such an occupation will be forwarded for approval by the Joint Chiefs of Staff.

This order was sent to General MacArthur on September 27. When he returned from the triumphal Seoul entry "to resume" his military duties, his answer was already in the hands of the Joint Chiefs of Staff:

> Briefly my plan is: (a) Eighth Army as now constituted will attack across the 38th Parallel with its main effort on the Pyongyang axis with the objective of seizing Pyongyang; (b) X Corps as now constituted will effect amphibious landing at Wonsan, making juncture with the Eighth Army; (c) 3rd Infantry Division will remain in Japan in GHQ reserve initially; (d) R.O.K. Army forces only will conduct operation north of the line Chungjo-Yongwon-Hungnam; (e) tentative date for the attack of the Eighth Army will be not earlier than 15 October and not later than 30 October.

Who was to point fingers at the thousands of North Korean soldiers who had escaped the Eighth Army trap and made their way into the mountains to set up guerrilla operations?

From the standpoint of military strategy, the MacArthur plan was based on the premise that neither the Soviets nor the Red Chinese would enter the war. Otherwise no commander would have separated his forces, having them operate on opposite sides of the Korean peninsula with a fifty-mile gap between. That gap—much of it the Taebaek Mountains—was alive with North Korean and local guerrillas. So each army's flank would be left open. No danger, one could say, because the North Korean army was virtually on the ropes. But what if another half million troops were to enter the war on the side of the enemy? MacArthur's plan did not envisage the danger that had occupied Washington's thinking for the past two months. The Soviets had been very quiet in the UN these past three months. MacArthur believed they and the Peking government would not interfere.

When the Joint Chiefs of Staff studied the MacArthur plan, at least General Collins, the new chairman of the Joint Chiefs, had some personal reservations. But Collins was also certain that this was no time to air such suspicions. MacArthur was a popular hero riding a wave of success. Who could quarrel with the brilliant effect of the Inchon landing, which MacArthur had carried out despite the worst fears of the Joint Chiefs of Staff? It had worked like a charm, had it not? Also, MacArthur was the darling of the public and particularly of the Republicans. The congressional elections were just over a month away. A presidential election was coming up in 1952.

So the Joint Chiefs of Staff made no challenges. They were cautious enough to ask General Marshall to get the plan approved at the highest level, and it was. Two days later Marshall sent MacArthur an encouraging message: "We want you to feel unhampered tactically and strategically to proceed north of the 38th parallel."

Nearly all of America was reacting positively, although all these orders and messages were unknown to them, held in the secrecy of the military establishment. On September 30 *The New York Times* editorialized in favor of crossing the parallel. Dozens of other newspapers were doing the same.

The negative criticism at home was conditional and highly speculative: lest President Truman "subvert our military victory by calling a halt at the 38th parallel," as Republican Senator Hugh Scott of Pennsylvania put it. "The scheme [of the State Department] is to cringe behind this line. . . ."

Wrongheaded as this accusation was, it did represent the general Republican distrust of the State Department, which was a development of the McCarthy excesses and must have been part of the reason that the State Department hawks were in the ascendance.

Even in the UN the reaction was generally in favor of ignoring the 38th parallel. The British labor government was in full support. So were the Australians. Trygve Lie, the secretary general, saw the unification of Korea under UN auspices as a logical solution.

With such backing it was no wonder that General MacArthur felt he had a green light to do as he wished. He called on President Kim Il Sung, commander of the North Korean military forces, to surrender. Kim Il Sung ignored the demand. MacArthur then said that unless the enemy capitulated, he regarded all Korea as open for his military operations.

Yet even as all this hawkish brew percolated in Washington, elsewhere signs of trouble were showing up. On September 27, the day the new policy directive was sent to MacArthur, the Indian foreign minister in New Delhi told U.S. Ambassador Loy Henderson his government had information that if the UN forces crossed the parallel the Chinese would intervene. That same day in Washington the British ambassador showed the State Department two messages to Indian Prime Minister Nehru from his Peking ambassador. The ambassador had been talking to Chou En-lai, foreign minister of the Peking government, and Chou had indicated that if the UN forces crossed the 38th parallel, China would intervene in the war on the side of North Korea. Also that day, O. Edmund Clubb, an old China hand who was director of the Office of Chinese Affairs in the State Department, sent a memorandum to Assistant Secretary Rusk, warning that the Chinese Communist 4th Field Army had just moved into Manchuria, and that there could be no reason for that but an intention to fight in Korea.

The CIA had been following the steady movement north of many Chinese divisions and had so informed MacArthur's intelligence officers. On July 8 there had been 116,000 Chinese troops in Manchuria. By September 21, the number had risen to 450,000 men.

From Moscow came a message from U.S. Ambassador Kirk that Chinese and Soviet sources had indicated to the British and Dutch that Peking's attitude was getting very hard; if MacArthur crossed the parallel, the Chinese were saying, the army of the People's Republic of China would intervene.

At the State Department, the hawks pooh-poohed these indications. On September 29 Chou En-lai warned publicly:

"The Chinese people absolutely will not tolerate foreign aggression, nor will they supinely tolerate seeing their neighbors being savagely invaded by the imperialists. . . ."

This, too, was passed off either as bluff or as a Chinese overreaction to an incident the Americans agreed had been unfortunate. A few days earlier two U.S. fighter planes had attacked a Chinese airstrip on the Manchurian side of the Yalu River. The Chinese were furious. The U.S. State Department had sent a message, by way of Britain through India for the Chinese, apologizing and offering to pay indemnity. It had been, said the message, an accident. The planes had strayed. Were the Chinese to believe this? In view of the state of

Sino-American relations, it seems ridiculously naive that the State Department would expect them to believe. In Peking the American air attack was regarded as a portent of things to come. In Washington's mood of righteousness, that view was ignored.

So, as of the end of September, the UN forces were driving hard toward the 38th parallel, and had no intention of stopping there. Each day the confidence of MacArthur and his generals increased. It was now just a matter of a speedy windup to the war, elimination of the last of the North Korean People's Army, the occupation of Pyongyang, and then the politicians could decide what was to be done with all Korea.

That is how it looked on September 30 in Tokyo and to the hawks in Washington.

18

The Chinese Warning

By the end of September the advancing U.S. Eighth Army had captured about 24,000 prisoners of war. This is a sizeable bag; but consider how many North Koreans got away of the total of nearly a hundred thousand who had been fighting below the 38th parallel. Then the total is not nearly so impressive.

Where did the rest of the North Koreans go? Thousands of them went into the South Korean mountains to organize as guerrillas. More thousands escaped up the middle corridor, particularly after General MacArthur began to align his forces toward attacks on east and west. Most of the key officers of the NK I Corps and II Corps escaped back north either overland or by boat. Considering the complete collapse of the North Korean military force in South Korea, the number of prisoners taken was disappointingly low.

On September 29 MacArthur's headquarters informed General Almond that the next move would probably be a new amphibious landing on the east coast of Korea, and X Corps informed its subordinate commands. For the moment, however, X Corps had plenty to do in consolidating its gains around Seoul. The marines were to form a semicircle around Seoul on three sides. On October 1 and October 2 there was some fighting in the Suyuhyon area as two small groups of North Koreans tried to break through toward North Korea. These efforts were repelled by the 5th Marines. The 1st Marines had only a few patrol actions.

The 7th Marines, however, were to move north toward Uijongbu, where enemy troops had concentrated after the battle for Seoul. They marched at six thirty in the morning of October 1, in column up the Uijongbu road. Intelligence studies indicated that if there was going to be a line of resistance on the route up, it would probably be established at a point halfway along the road where the highway ran through a deep valley between two steep ridges. Colonel Litzenberg ordered the 1st Battalion out on both sides of the road, while the 3rd Battalion moved into the potential trap with tank support. The 2nd Battalion was held back in reserve.

Lieutenant Colonel Raymond Davis sent his 1st Battalion troops out on both sides of the valley. But the 3rd Battalion was delayed in entering the valley because the North Koreans had laid a minefield on the road. The tanks had to stop and wait for the engineers. Meanwhile Davis' men had discovered that, as expected, the North Koreans had dug in along the ridges on both sides of the defile. What the marines did not then know was that they had come upon the new main line of resistance, manned by three battalions of the NK 31st Regiment plus odd lots of troops from the Seoul Division and the 17th Division. They had thirteen T-34 tanks. As the marines slowed, the North Koreans began firing mortars and artillery at them. The marines called for air strikes and the Corsairs of VMF-312 responded. As night fell it was a standoff, but when morning came the marines attacked again. Halfway through the little valley they were held up once more by mines. The North Koreans pelted the engineers with a steady hail of rifle fire as they worked. The U.S. tanks responded by firing on enemy concentrations and destroyed two huts that turned out to be enemy positions. The 1st Battalion crossed a stream east of the defile and captured the ridge beyond. But in the valley the going was rough. The marines advanced only about two city blocks that whole day.

This enemy position was defended with a vigor that belied the collapse of the Seoul front. The third day of the attack began with an air strike, and then another. The North Koreans were serious about this defense, pilots of VMF-312 found a convoy of eight trucks coming up with reinforcements for the enemy positions. They slashed in to attack and destroyed seven of the trucks. But the North Korean antiaircraft fire was very heavy, and two planes were hit so hard they crashed. Major Charles McLean managed to get his Corsair back over friendly territory and survived, but Lieutenant Robert O. Crocker was killed by a North Korean rifleman when trying to get back to the marine lines after crashing. Other planes continued all day to support the marines on the ground, buzzing around the hills like furious wasps. They plastered the enemy defense area with twenty thousand rounds of machine gun fire and nearly two hundred 90 mm cannon shells.

Under this air umbrella, the marines on the ground managed to advance.

The 1st Battalion cleared the east side of the road, and the 3rd Battalion cleared the west, and the 2nd Battalion came out of reserve to drive up the road. It soon became apparent that the air support had done a fine job. The 2nd Battalion began to encounter abandoned enemy artillery and vehicles. They came upon an intact supply dump, a sure sign that the enemy had moved out in a hurry. Late that afternoon they entered the ruins of Uijongbu and found that the enemy was gone.

It had been a furious battle and the 7th Marines had comported themselves in a manner most satisfying to General Smith. Together with the marine aircraft they had destroyed four T-34 tanks and captured two. The other seven had escaped in the general retreat on the third day. The marines had suffered 124 casualties, 13 of them killed, but they had cut the line of communications of the North Koreans east and west of Uijongbu.

That was virtually the end of marine operations in the Seoul–Inchon area. Then it was back to Inchon to board ships and prepare for a new landing at the east coast port of Wonsan.

General Smith was not enamored of the new assignment. It was true that General MacArthur's bold stroke at Inchon had also aroused the objections of marines, navy, and some of the planners in Washington. But it had succeeded so brilliantly that no one felt inclined to criticize MacArthur at this point, even if they were sure his plan violated all the sensible rules of warfare. Hadn't Inchon done the same? And wasn't Inchon now called MacArthur's brilliant stroke of strategy?

That Inchon landing and its success had retrieved America's respect for the American fighting man, in sad decline during the dreadful days of summer when nearly every report from Korea had been one of defeat and retreat.

The Inchon operation had liberated Seoul and reestablished the Republic of Korea in its capital.

And the Inchon landing had caused the North Korean vise around the Pusan Perimeter to collapse, hadn't it?

But there was a rub, raised a few weeks later by the U.S. Air Force in a strategic study of the collapse of the North Korean army in the south. The North Korean drive would have collapsed anyhow, said the air force, arguing that the real reason for the North Korean failure was the pressure put on the North Korean supply lines by the air force. For one thing, the constant daily air attacks forced the North Koreans to do most of their moving and fighting by night. As one NK division operations officer put it:

> Our experience in night combat up to now shows that we can operate only four to five hours in the dark, since we start night attacks between 2300 [11 P.M.] and 2400 [12 midnight]. Therefore if the battle

continues after the break of dawn, we are likely to suffer losses. From now on use daylight hours for full combat preparations and commence the attack soon after sunset. Concentrate your battle actions mostly at night and thereby capture enemy base positions. From midnight on engage the enemy in close combat by approaching to within 100 to 150 meters of him. Then even with the break of dawn, the enemy planes will not be able to distinguish friend from foe, which will enable you to prevent great losses.

Another indication of the enormous effect of the air activity on the North Koreans was found in an order to the NK 25th Rifle Regiment: ". . . When enemy planes appear, fifty percent of the infantry weapons will be diverted for anti-aircraft defense."

Interrogation of prisoners indicated that the most effective weapon in disorganizing North Korean combat units was the artillery, but the attack by aircraft was second. And as the fighting grew fiercer and the UN attacks stronger, morale of the North Koreans dropped. The first reason for this declining morale was the shortage of food, largely caused by air interdiction of supplies, and the second was the attacks by tactical aircraft.

Those aircraft destroyed the North Korean line of communications. By September there were few undamaged bridges in all South Korea. The North Koreans' lines of communication were kept open—barely—by constant repair, but the air attacks were constant, too. A bridge would be destroyed, rebuilt, then destroyed again. It was a constant struggle, and by September enemy communications were in shambles. The North Korean People's Army had so few truck drivers (because of air attack and desertion to avoid air attack) that the high command forced American prisoners to drive North Korean vehicles under guard. They used more animal-drawn transport and more Korean civilians to make up human supply trains.

The direct damage done by air attack to fighting units was another factor. For example, the NK 8th Division on August 5 lost to air attack ten 76 mm guns, three 122 mm howitzers, twenty tanks and fifty trucks loaded with ammunition and equipment. A prisoner reported that fewer than half the 16th Tank Brigade's tanks ever made it to combat, having been destroyed on the roads.

The U.S. Air Force, then, concluded that:

North Korean offensive power, so invincible at the start of the Korean operations, had been decimated by United Nations air and ground action well prior to the invasion at Inchon. Cut off from his source of supplies, his equipment being destroyed and his personnel slaughtered by air and ground action on the battlefield, the North Korean aggressor had been sustaining his offensives around the Pusan perimeter only by sheer desperation. Such North Korean power as remained was an encrustation around the 8th Army's lines. Viewed in the light of prisoner of war reports, it was evident that the North Korean People's Army was defeated by relentless air-ground action in South Korea—not by the opportune amphibious invasion at Inchon.

That study was in process during the early weeks of October and was not available either to the public or to the military planners. Would it have made a difference if anyone had known?

Probably not. General Matthew Ridgway, then a member of the staff of the Joint Chiefs of Staff, noted that MacArthur's ploy at Inchon had succeeded so far beyond anyone's expectations (save perhaps his own) that he was riding high. He was the man who could do no wrong. "Had he suggested that one battalion walk on water," said Ridgway ". . . there might have been somebody ready to give it a try."

The MacArthur plan for the next phase of the Korean War troubled many an officer. General Marshall was bothered, for reasons he could not quite put together at the moment. The victory had been too fast, it had all been too easy, and that disturbed him. There had been no time to examine consequences and results of past actions. And now here MacArthur was, rushing into a new unorthodox operation.

The orthodox manner would have been to put all the forces in Korea under a single command and fan them out northward to destroy the North Korean army. General Walker had hoped that a unified command would be achieved by X Corps under the Eighth army along with the two corps he had. But MacArthur had no such intention. He did not trust Walker, and he believed Walker had failed him in the early days (a view for which there seems to be no independent confirmation). Further, General Almond was one of "MacArthur's boys," his chief of staff even now, and MacArthur did not want to put him under Walker. (Of such stuff are major military decisions made.) So Walker was to march north to capture Pyongyang, and General Almond was to go around to the other side of North Korea and attack.

At the beginning of October, General Smith, in particular, suspected that at the rate the ROK Army was moving up the eastern side of the peninsula, the ROK troops would reach Wonsan long before the marines could be shipped over there. So why ship the marines, moving them off the west coast and depriving the command of their services in cutting off and capturing the remainder of the North Korean army?

But General MacArthur was in charge of the military operation in Korea and the Joint Chiefs at this moment did not feel inclined to challenge his plan. There had already been enough confusion.

As for subordinate officers, they knew only too well that when a senior officer questioned the judgment of a superior, he laid his career on the line. General Walker, for example, had some serious reservations about the MacArthur plan, quite apart from his own hurt feelings at being denied field command of all the forces in Korea. But the nearest he came to voicing these was toward the end of September when he radioed MacArthur asking for information about X Corps progress so that he could coordinate his own activity. MacArthur snubbed him cold. He would be informed in due time of X Corps' next operation, said the commanding general. So Walker shut up and said nothing more about his views. When some of his subordinates questioned the MacArthur plan, Walker replied that he had raised the issue once and that he did not propose to do so again.

There were some military commanders in history with whom subordinates could argue, at least to a point, with a chance of making their views felt. Unfortunately for the UN effort, Douglas MacArthur was not one of them.

So the furious pace of the UN march northward went on. Indeed everything was happening so quickly that the Eighth Army staff could scarcely keep up with the situation map. The Eighth Army had moved north and was in the area of X Corps operations, at Suwon.

There was a good deal of confusion in the last days of September. Various officers of the Eighth Army and of the Far Eastern Command offered various plans and modifications of plans. General Walker reached the 38th parallel and stopped, not quite sure what he should do. MacArthur did not like that. With his grand habit of rewriting history MacArthur claimed (later) that the stop at the 38th parallel had been caused by logistic problems. He also issued instructions to the UN Command:

> Under the provisions of the United Nations Security Council Resolution of 27 June, the field of our military operations is limited only by military exigencies and the international boundaries of Korea. The so-called 38th parallel, accordingly, is not a factor in the military employment of our forces. To accomplish the enemy's complete defeat, your troops may cross the border at any time, either in exploratory probing or exploiting local tactical conditions. If the enemy fails to accept

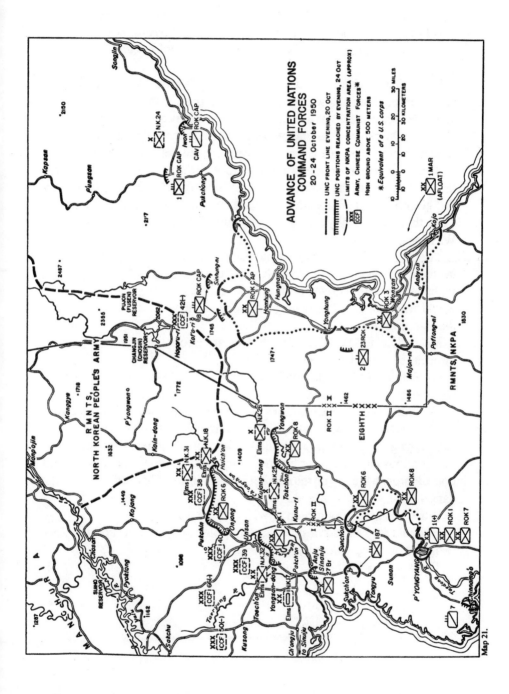

Map 21.

the terms of surrender set forth in my message to him of 1 October, our
forces, in due process of campaign will seek out and destroy the enemy's
armed forces in whatever part of Korea they may be located.

MacArthur paid no attention to Chou En-lai's warning of that day. Nor
did he see anything noteworthy in a Soviet proposal in the UN on October 2
that called for a cease-fire in Korea and the withdrawal of all foreign troops.
Nor did either he or Washington believe the report via the Indians that the
Chinese would intervene if the Americans crossed the 38th parallel.

Such a concern, of course, was more properly the province of Washington
than of Tokyo. But the politicians and the military strategists in Washington
had given up their prerogative to MacArthur without apparently realizing
what they were really doing. Indeed, the Tokyo tail was wagging the
Washington dog.

The best view that could be put on MacArthur's new plan was that it would
facilitate the encirclement of the North Korean capital at Pyongyang. The
Eighth Army would drive north, and the X Corps, landing on the east coast,
would drive along the Pyongyang corridor and fall on the enemy capital from
the rear. (See Map 21.)

Meanwhile thousands of North Korean troops were escaping north
through the Wonju–Chunchon corridor.

On October 9 MacArthur broadcast his final demand to the North Koreans
to surrender. He was ignored.

The difficulties of MacArthur's plan should have warned Washington
when on October 10 the ROK I Corps captured Wonsan. The marines were
still sitting aboard ship in Inchon harbor far from their newly resigned area.
Ten precious days had been wasted. Thousands more North Koreans had
poured through the gap up the middle of the peninsula. That "middle" was the
danger zone, a no-man's-land.

What was MacArthur to do now?

He could stop and reconsider the whole plan in light of the new development. Or he could ignore the unpleasant truth.

The latter is what he did.

19

Northward Ho!

On October 3 the Eighth Army prepared to begin the new assault on the North Koreans above the 38th parallel. The I Corps was to seize an area west of the Imjin River. The IX Corps was to come up to that area and relieve I Corps, and then I Corps was to attack again northward. The 1st Cavalry Division was to lead the attack, with the 24th Infantry Division and the ROK 1st Division on the flanks.

The IX Corps was also ordered to destroy the remaining North Korean forces in South Korea. That was a casual addition to the orders; in fact, the destruction of the far-flung North Korean forces inside South Korea was not going to be nearly so easy a task.

About 3,500 North Korean officials and troops had escaped into the Chiri mountains of southwest Korea. One concentration of guerrillas was located south of Kumchon and the other was north of Taejon. They were already proving to be troublesome: on the night of October 1, a small force established a roadblock across the highway from Kumchon to Seoul. They maintained the block for ten hours and in that time about two thousand North Korean troops of the NK 6th Division escaped through the lines. Other concentrations of guerrillas were located on the east in the Taebaek mountain range. They, too, would begin to give trouble.

While the United States Eighth Army's I Corps consolidated its forces just

Chosin
Reservoir

Fusen
Reservoir

Yudam-ni

Hagaru

Koto-ri

Huichon

Chinhung-ni

Sinhung

Sudong

Majon-dong

Huksu-ri

Oro-ri

Hamhung

Hungnam

Chigyong

Tokchon

Chongpyong

Yonpo AF

Yonghung

Kowon

Munchon

Munpyong-ni

Togwon

Yangdok

Wonsan

Majon-ni

Anbyon

N

Kojo

AREA OF OPERATIONS

1st Marine Division

October - December 1950

+++++ Railroads

Roads

0   10   20   30

MILES

Map 22.

below the 38th parallel, the ROK II Corps was ordered to move into the area between Chunchon and Uijongbu. The ROK I Corps, which included the experienced Capital and 3rd divisions, was to go to the area between Yongpo and Chumunju-up on the east coast prepared to attack northward. And then the U.S. X Corps was to land at Wonsan and drive westward toward Pyongyang. Meanwhile on the east coast, the ROK Army forces were moving ahead without any regard for what the others did. Advance patrols of the ROK 3rd Division crossed the 38th parallel on the last day of September. On October 2 the ROK Capital and 3rd divisions put their headquarters at Yangang, eight miles north of the parallel. Then the ROK 3rd Division began a race to reach Wonsan. (See Map 22.) They traveled day and night, bypassing concentrations of enemy troops, but moved on at about fifteen miles a day. Ahead of them was the remnant of the North Korean 5th Division, numbering about twenty-five hundred men. These troops fought a delaying action all the way with mortars, mines, and machine guns. They slowed, but in no way stopped the advance of the ROK Army.

From this activity it might have been deduced that the North Korean army was in such a state of dissolution that the South Koreans could finish the job of capturing Pyongyang. If there was a time to stop MacArthur, this was it. His plan was already in disarray, and Washington knew it. Further, developments on the political front had come very quickly. On October 3 Chinese Foreign Minister Chou En-lai called K. M. Panikkar, the Ambassador to India, to Peking, into his office to tell him that if UN forces crossed the 38th parallel, the Chinese would send troops across the border from Manchuria to participate in the defense of North Korea. But the Chinese would not intervene if only the South Koreans moved above the 38th parallel.

At this point, one must examine the concerns and motivation of the Chinese. The United States had a long history of friendship for China and the Chinese people. American missionaries had been very active in China from the nineteenth century. After the Boxer Rebellion only the United States among the powers involved did not try to bleed the Imperial Chinese government for territory or reparations. The reparations money was turned into scholarships so that Chinese students could study in America. In the 1920s American business did participate in the economic colonization of China, but never in the political. When war with Japan came in 1936 the United States supported the Chinese government, which by that time was led by Chiang Kai-shek. That support continued throughout the Pacific War. By the end of the Pacific War the Chinese Nationalist government was riddled with corruption, and it had lost the support of the peasantry in many areas through harsh measures of taxation and drafting of troops. The Communists gained peasant support by promising land and government reform. After some preliminary attempts in August and September 1945 to fabricate a coalition government, the effort collapsed. Neither side wanted a coalition, so neither side was willing to make the necessary compromises. They squared off against one another.

During the Pacific War years there had also been American contact with the Chinese Communists in Yenan and the northeast. American observers traveled with the Chinese Communist armies in the early days; one of the best known was a marine officer, Major Evans Carlson, who put what he had learned to use in the formation of a Marine Raider Battalion.

As the war ended, then, the American friendship for China was an accepted fact, accepted more completely, of course, in Chungking and then Nanking than in Yenan. But the Americans were not regarded by either side as enemies. During the first postwar months, the American navy moved troops of both sides around China ports, trying to alleviate tensions. Slowly the Americans began to get caught up in the tangle of the civil war. The navy did a good job of maintaining neutrality, but the same could not be said of the American army. Lieutenant General Albert C. Wedemeyer was a firm convert to the Nationalist cause, and the Communists knew it. They also saw the Americans supplying planes and guns to the Nationalists *after* the Japanese surrender.* Of course the Communists secured thousands of tons of arms—mostly Japanese arms— courtesy of the Soviets. But they did not equate these gifts. The Soviet presence in Manchuria was brief and consisted largely of guarding the Japanese factories that the Soviets were looting. This development did not sit very well with the Chinese Communists but was never properly exploited by the Americans. And as the Communists saw American support of the Nationalists and demands from the China lobby for more of it, up to and including direct intervention, the Communist resentment of United States policy grew.

From the beginning of President Truman's administration in 1945 he found himself in a box built by Franklin D. Roosevelt. Nationalist China had been treated as a "great power" all during the war, equal in the propaganda eye to the USSR, Britain, and the United States. All concerned knew that this Chinese position was fictional, but the fiction was retained to confound the Japanese and as a British-American buffer against the Soviets. China was party to many of the conferences of the Big Powers, and when the war ended China was made a member of the United Nations Security Council and as

---

*The rationale was that Chiang's was the "legitimate" government of China.

such held veto power over council decisions, along with the U.S., Britain, and the USSR.

This position, of claiming big power status for a country in a state of civil war, was the box in which President Truman found himself. It would have taken a man far more skilled in foreign affairs than he to have gotten himself out of it. For "legally" the Nationalist government was the "legitimate" government of China, despite the obvious fact that the Communists held a large and growing share of the country, including Manchuria, into which they had been eased by the Russians. The American reaction was a sincere attempt to mediate, and General Marshall had undertaken that task in the spring and summer of 1946. Despite his best efforts, the mediation had failed and the civil war had begun in earnest. The Communists won the war because the Nationalists lost the people; Chiang Kai-shek's generals failed him, they turned over whole armies and all their equipment to the Communists.

After Chiang Kai-shek fled the mainland ahead of the advancing Communist armies in 1949, he kept up a ceaseless barrage of propaganda, threatening to reorganize his forces and invade the China coast. He was protected constantly by the American fleet, which had created a cordon between mainland and the island.

Unfortunately, the Chinese civil war reached its height at a time when the unreasoning anti-Communist hysteria coursed across America like a plague. There was, obviously, a deep schism between the United States and the USSR. The distrust and fear of Communist expansionism and the American experience with espionage and the loyal subservience of the American Communist party to Moscow led most Americans to equate all communism with Soviet expansionism. Wild talk by American politicians, plus the evident fact that the Americans protected Chiang, added to the Peking government's feelings of irritation and distrust.

By 1950 the Americans should have learned something about the nature of exported communism. It turns out not to be the same as the Soviet variety. They had the example of Yugoslavia, a defector in 1948 from the Soviet camp. Some in the Defense and State departments obviously did believe it was possible to wean Peking from Moscow, and, as noted, that attitude showed in several of the draft memorandums of the two departments in the period. But the memorandums did not become policy.

A major problem was created when, in the 1948 presidential and congressional elections, the Republicans made an issue of the Truman China policy. They were goaded by an enormously wealthy China lobby, with powerful media support led by Henry Luce's Time Inc. organization. The China lobby accused the Democrats of having "lost" China. The Republicans, seeing in this area a Democratic weak spot, jumped on the bandwagon. The amount of evil wreaked thus on the American international stance was enormous but almost totally unrecognized at the time. The final blow to China was the refusal of the United States to recognize the political facts of Asia. Nationalist China had been defeated and its continued existence was dependent on the United States. Communist China, as the de facto government of the country, demanded the Chinese seat in the United Nations. Had the United States behaved sensibly, all else could have been forgiven and forgotten, but the U.S. government refused China that seat, dealing her a tremendous psychological blow and setting up a real feeling of enmity in Peking.

That is how matters stood in the summer and fall of 1950. President Truman would have liked to release himself from the clutch of Chiang Kai-shek, but he found it politically impossible. The Chinese, watching the American media and the political didoes of Washington, feared that the United States would try to extend the war and conquer the Chinese mainland and turn it back to Chiang Kai-shek. This was the first anniversary of the Chinese People's Republic in power, and they were still extremely nervous. Unfortunately, official Washington, having either weeded out or suppressed virtually every public servant who suggested that the Chinese Nationalists were a failed government, was almost completely ignorant of the Chinese political facts or the reasoning of Peking.

In this climate anything could happen. President Truman had taken one positive step toward China when he refused an offer of Chiang Kai-shek's to send three divisions to fight in South Korea. God knows what they would have done if they got up near the Manchurian border. But except for avoiding that outright provocation, Washington was paying no attention to the sensibilities of Peking, where Chairman Mao and his counselors were worrying about just how far the Americans intended to go. It was not that Peking cared for the North Koreans more, as the actions of the next few days would show, but that they cared for the actions of the Americans less. And they knew, as did Washington, that President Syngman Rhee was totally overwhelmed by a homespun jingoism that justified any means to wipe out the North Korean government.

On that October 3, the warning from Chou En-lai was transmitted to New Delhi, and from there very quickly to the British Foreign Office in London, and from there to the American charge d'affaires, who rifled off a coded cable to Washington. Because of the favorable time frame from east to west, the cable arrived at the State Department just after five thirty in the morning of October 3.

The early shift at the State Department then had time to digest the matter. Some believed. Some did not. Secretary Acheson was among the doubters, but he sent the message over to President Truman by noon. The President, unfortunately, was so much the creature of his personality that he refused to believe the message *because he did not like Ambassador Panikkar*. Truman said Panikkar played the Soviet game too often. He did not seem to consider the fact that in this matter Panikkar was simply the messenger boy. Besides that, the President said he thought Chou En-lai was playing games, trying to influence the UN not to take a strong stand on the coming matter of Korean unification by elections directed and overseen by the UN, which the United States expected to press, once the North Korean government was destroyed.

So—Truman's own warning of a week earlier that UN forces were not to be sent north of the 38th parallel if there seemed any threat of Soviet or Chinese intervention was ignored by the President himself. So was Chou En-lai's warning of October 3 ignored.

The 1st Cavalry Division moved out from Seoul on the morning of October 5. The 5th Cavalry Regiment's Company I crossed to the north side of the Imjin River at Munsan-ni. The 8th Cavalry fanned out to Kaesong and was followed by the 7th Cavalry. These units were soon joined by the British. As indication of the unanimity of thought of the western powers on the question of the Korean War, the Australian government had sent to Korea the 3rd Battalion of the Royal Australian Regiment, which had joined forces with the 27th British Brigade. The unit was then renamed the 27th British Commonwealth Brigade. It moved up to join the concentration of troops just south of the 38th parallel.

General Walker also moved up to Seoul, as did the ROK Army headquarters. The fighters and fighter bombers of the Fifth Air Force moved up to Kimpo airfield. Thus the UN forces prepared for the drive north to wipe out the North Korean People's Army. On October 7, the American patrols began crossing the 38th parallel. That day the UN General Assembly adopted one of those vague resolutions for which it is famous, this one encouraged and shaped by the United States, which sanctified the current military operations as "appropriate steps to be taken to ensure conditions of stability throughout Korea."

If you had been sitting in your parlor in Peking, and had read those words, even without any interlocutions from Tass, the basic source of Chinese Communist information from New York, what would you have thought?

Chou En-lai stated the official Chinese position on October 9:

"The American war of invasion in Korea has been a serious menace to the security of China from its very start. . . ."

It was growing very late. The 1st Cavalry Division, the 24th Infantry Division, the 27th British Commonwealth Brigade and the ROK 1st Division all moved across the 38th parallel in force. As the Chinese said, the only unit the Chinese would countenance there was the ROK 1st Division. The warning had been ignored. The provocation was complete.

Now what would happen?

On the eastern side of Korea, the ROK Capital Division followed the ROK 3rd Division, sending some of its units into the Diamond Mountains of the northeast. Up the center of the peninsula came the ROK II Corps, toward Hwachon. It encountered two regiments of the NK 9th Division. The battle lasted two days, but then the ROK 6th Division took Hwachon. The ROK 7th and 8th divisions also headed north. On October 10 the 8th Division had a fight with a large number of North Koreans but made its way into Chorwon. They had now entered the area that would be known as The Iron Triangle, in the mountains of east central North Korea. (See Map 15.) It is located about twenty miles above the 38th parallel, fifty air miles northeast of Seoul, bounded by the towns of Chorwon on the western base, Kumwha on the east, and Pyonggang on the north. This area was the communications center of North Korea, and the ROK troops were here converging on Kumwha and Pyonggang.

So by October 10 all the ROK divisions except the 1st Division were across the 38th parallel and moving along nicely. The Capital Division to the west of Wonsan captured an enormous amount of North Korean materiel, tanks, artillery pieces, mortars, machine guns, five thousand Soviet-made rifles, and two boxcars of supplies. At six o'clock the next morning the Capital Division and the ROK 3rd Division entered Wonsan. The town was defended by the NK 24th Mechanized Artillery Brigade and the 945th Regiment of naval amphibious troops (like marines).

The fighting was strenuous. The North Korean artillery put up a stubborn defense, but both ROK divisions fought their way inward. By ten o'clock that morning they had most of the town, but the North Koreans had moved the artillery back to the northwest corner and there continued to fire on the advancing South Koreans. In the afternoon the ROK troops captured the airfield on a peninsula east of the coastal city. As night fell they were still fighting in the streets of Wonsan. During the night an enemy armored column came back to the airport and shot it up, burning most of the hangars.

On the morning of October 11 the ROK forces secured Wonsan and occupied the airfield. That day General Walker came up to inspect and so did General Partridge of the Fifth Air Force. The field was in good condition and

Partridge sent in planes with supplies for the South Korean troops on October 12.

So by Columbus Day 1950, the South Koreans had captured Wonsan, even as the 1st Marine Division sat in ships in Inchon harbor. They might as well have been playing pinochle, for all the influence they were just then having on the war effort, courtesy of General MacArthur's master plan.

They set out, finally, for Wonsan, but what would happen next was all very muddy. General MacArthur's Tokyo headquarters was filled with euphoria and misinformation. No one seemed to realize or care that the plan was in shambles.

During the next week, the ROK Capital Division moved north and captured Hamhung and its port, Hungnam, against very slight resistance.

North Korea was on the ropes. There could be no question about it. President Kim Il Sung issued new orders: "Do not retreat one step further. Now we have no space in which to fall back."

The Americans and ROK forces were driving on Pyongyang; but the ides of October were nigh, the Chinese had issued their warning. Danger was in the air.

20

The Ides of October

There was some truth in General MacArthur's contention that the reason for the delay in the Eighth Army's crossing of the 38th parallel was logistical. General Walker expected to meet a fierce North Korean defense. His intelligence officers told him that the enemy had laid out defenses in three lines, each consisting of fortified pillboxes, barbed wire, and entrenchments.

The first of these lines was along the 38th parallel. It was about a third of a mile deep. The second was three miles back. The third line ran irregularly along the high ground that lay between the parallel and Pyongyang, facing south. To man these defenses, intelligence reported, the North Koreans would have some 60,000 men.

On October 7 and 8 General Gay's scouts were across the parallel and on October 9 the 1st Cavalry Division began to move across in force. This was, then, the provocation that Chou En-lai said the Chinese would never bear.

And what did China do on October 9? Absolutely nothing that MacArthur or his generals knew of. In fact the moment that the Chinese learned the Americans had crossed the parallel, the mobilization in Peking became furious. Chou En-Lai conferred with Chairman Mao, and they both conferred with their military leaders. Mao directed Chou to go to the Soviet Union and see Stalin. He did. He met Stalin at the latter's dacha at Sochi. They discussed the question of American troops moving right up to the Chinese and Soviet

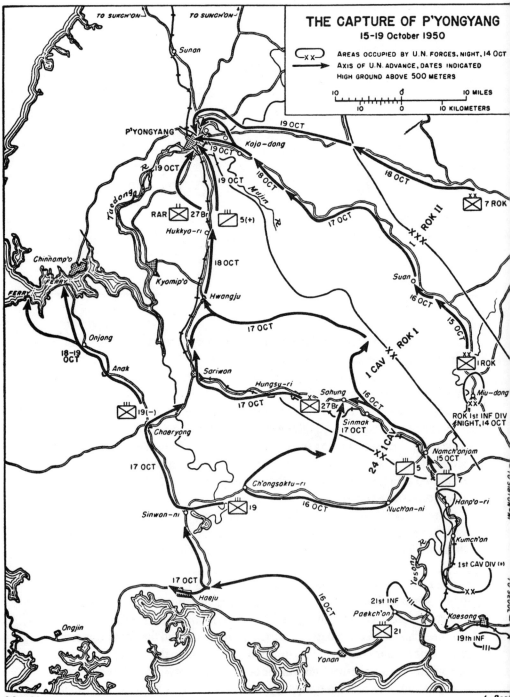

THE CAPTURE OF P'YONGYANG
15-19 October 1950

⊏x x⊐ AREAS OCCUPIED BY U.N. FORCES, NIGHT, 14 OCT
→ AXIS OF U.N. ADVANCE, DATES INDICATED
HIGH GROUND ABOVE 500 METERS

10   0   10 MILES
10   0   10 KILOMETERS

TO SUKCH'ON   TO SUNCH'ON

Sunan

P'YONGYANG
19 OCT
19 OCT   Koja-dong   19 OCT
19 OCT   18 OCT   18 OCT

Taedong R.   19 OCT

RAR ⊠ 27 Br   ⊠ 5(+)   Mulin R.
Hukkya-ri   17 OCT   17 OCT

18 OCT   7 ROK ⊠
ROK II

Chinnamp'o   Suan
FERRY   18 OCT   Kyomip'o   16 OCT   15 OCT
FERRY   Hwangju

Onjong   17 OCT   1 CAV ROK 1   1 ROK ⊠
18-19 OCT   Miu-dong

Anak   19(-) ⊠   Sariwon   Hungsu-ri   Sohung   ROK 1st INF DIV
NIGHT, 14 OCT
17 OCT   27 Br ⊠   16 OCT

Chaeryong   17 OCT   Sinmak   1 CAV
17 OCT   Namch'onjom
15 OCT

24   ⊠ 5 7 ⊠

Ch'ongsoktu-ri   Hanp'o-ri
17 OCT   Sinwon-ni   ⊠ 19   16 OCT   Nuch'on-ni
Kumch'on

17 OCT   1st CAV DIV (+)

Haeju   16 OCT   Yesong R.   Kaesong
Ongjin   21st INF
Paekch'on   19th INF
⊠ 21
Yonan

Map 23.   L. Boo

borders. Stalin at first indicated that there was little to be done; he was not ready for war. Chou indicated the Chinese insistence that the Americans stay out of North Korea. In the end Stalin refused to commit the USSR, but Chou had completed his mission. He had secured Stalin's benevolent regard for the military adventure on which the Chinese Communist leaders were determined. They could expect weapons and supplies from the USSR.

From Tokyo just then, the Korea situation looked so satisfactory that it seemed to be mute proof that the Chinese had been bluffing.

There was no mistake about the North Korean defenses at the parallel, however. The main road north, via Kumchon (see Map 23), was heavily mined, and the 8th Cavalry armored column inched along, stopping frequently so that the engineers could come up and clear the way.

On the right of the 8th Cavalry, the 5th Cavalry was also having problems against the ridge lines manned by troops of the NK 27th Infantry. The fighting was particularly bitter. On the morning of October 12, a particularly gloomy, foggy morning, Company C was ordered to take an enemy strong point called Hill 174. Lieutenant Samuel S. Coursen's 1st Platoon was on the left. They moved up with the 2nd Platoon on the right. They passed an emplacement that appeared to be unoccupied. One man jumped in to check it out and found himself overwhelmed by enemy soldiers. Coursen heard the racket and jumped in himself. The American soldier was wounded and down. Coursen attacked the enemy, firing, jabbing, and smashing with the butt of a rifle. The platoon had drawn enemy fire elsewhere and had to respond to that so it went on. Later, Lieutenant Lewis L. Zickel, commander of the 2nd Platoon came back looking for Coursen, his West Point classmate. He found him, dead in the trench, with seven dead North Koreans scattered around him. The wounded GI was still alive.

The hard fighting was enough, but to add to the troubles came false intelligence and defective air observation, a serious matter for units moving into strange territory. The maps showed a good road that moved around northwest of Kumchon. General Gay assigned the 27th British Commonwealth Brigade to take that road and flank Kumchon from the northwest as the 8th Cavalry came up straightaway north. An aerial observer blithely confirmed the excellent quality of the road. So the British and Australians set off with tanks of the U.S. 6th Medium Tank Battalion. At the end of the first day the road petered out. The column tried another. It was a cart track that ended in the mountains. Another track did the same. The column was completely bogged down and out of the fight, because of faulty intelligence.

Meanwhile on the far right of the Eighth Army front, the ROK 1st Division crossed the parallel on October 11 and took the road from Korongpo-ri that converged with the 5th Cavalry's route. They met up on October 12 at a crossroads and the traffic jam slowed them down.

Over on the far left the 7th Cavalry crossed the Yesong River, a neat trick, since they had no bridging equipment and the river was half a mile wide. They found a bridge on the Kaesong–Paekchon rail line. It was damaged but could support foot traffic. On October 9, after an artillery barrage, the Americans crossed over. They took casualties, the 1st Battalion alone had seventy-eight killed and wounded. On the other side, the enemy counterattacked and the 1st and 2nd battalions spent a hard night but fought off the counterattack. That night the engineers worked till the morning strengthening the bridge, and the reinforcements that came across the next morning moved forward and took Paekchon that afternoon. On October 10, the entire 7th Cavalry was deep inside North Korean territory.

Their supply line depended on thirteen LCVs they secured from Inchon. These came up to the Yesong River crossing, and the engineers built a pontoon ferry across the river. That was how the tanks and the trucks got across to support the infantry.

Two days later they captured the bridges at Hanpo-ri north of Kumchon and thus closed off the escape route to the west for the North Korean troops.

On the night of October 12 at the roadblock, the 7th Cavalry ambushed a whole convoy of North Korean trucks moving northwest with their lights on. Among the casualties was a mortally wounded North Korean officer who had in his possession orders indicating that the NK 19th and NK 27th divisions would try to break out of Kumchon on the night of October 14.

On October 13, the 1st Cavalry Division moved to close the Kumchon pocket. The 5th Cavalry had been moving slowly on the right, bogged down by minefield after minefield. The 8th Cavalry was coming up the road from Kaesong and faced constant opposition from the best the North Koreans had to throw against it. It was a great help to have an almost constant air umbrella with fighters striking the enemy lines in close proximity to the U.S. troops. That still did not make the going easy. The North Koreans were fighting as hard as they had in the early days of the war when their morale was superior.

In one NK counterattack on October 13, the U.S. tanks engaged a number of T-34s. Sergeant Marshall D. Drewery's tank attacked the lead T-34 at a range of fifty yards and split the muzzle of its 88 mm gun. The tank came on. A second round of 90 mm hit the enemy tank when it was only twenty yards away. The tank came on and rammed the U.S. tank. Drewery's driver reversed and backed off. At point-blank range they put another shell into the

T-34, which was now ablaze. It came forward again and rammed Drewery's tank a second time. It took a fourth shell to knock the tank out. The tanks and the recoilless rifles and the bazookas destroyed seven more tanks that day.

Pressed by the 8th Cavalry on the main road, the North Koreans began to move out of Kumchon. A long column was ambushed at the Hanpo-ri bridge by the 7th Cavalry, and the orderly retreat routed. Five hundred North Koreans were killed and two hundred captured. But most of the thousand soldiers escaped into the mountains on foot.

At this time, the Americans began to feel the effects of the failure to close off the escape routes of the North Koreans from South Korea and to mop up earlier.

Part of the NK 43rd Division had been stranded below Paekchon, and on the night of October 12 several hundred of these troops moved into old North Korean defensive positions that had been captured by the Americans and then bypassed. On October 13 this group ambushed the last of the 7th Cavalry, some engineers and some artillery. A few Americans escaped and one hurried into Paekchon to find help. He found the commander of the 3rd Battalion of the 21st infantry, Lieutenant Colonel John A. McConnell. The colonel sent a company rushing to the scene and they engaged the enemy and drove them off. They captured thirty-six North Koreans. But the North Koreans had killed twenty-nine American soldiers and eight South Koreans and wounded thirty more Americans and four South Koreans. They had also destroyed four vehicles and damaged fourteen—just one result of rushing the war and leaving pockets of resistance behind the lines.

On October 14, the UN forces captured Kumchon and routed the troops remaining there, many of whom tried to escape along the road northwest. The 7th Cavalry roadblock at Hanpo-ri stopped the organized retreat, but most of the twenty-five hundred troops involved escaped into the mountains.

With the fall of Kumchon, the North Korean defense of Pyongyang broke down. President Kim Il Sung indicated as much in his orders against further retreat. He announced that deserters would be shot on sight. To carry out this discipline, he organized a "supervising army" of trusted political loyalty. But everywhere the defenses crumbled.

As the Eighth Army moved toward Pyongyang, and the ROK Army on the right moved up the east side of the Korean peninsula, General Almond's X Corps men sat in their ships, still doing nothing. One officer observed that the whole corps could have marched overland and been in Wonsan by this time. But General MacArthur was determined to stage another amphibious operation, and no one even yet was willing to argue with him.

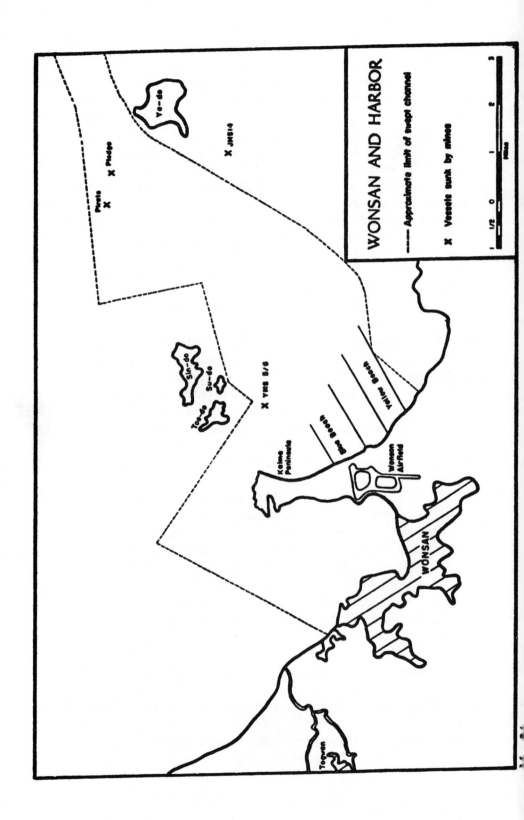

WONSAN AND HARBOR

----- Approximate limit of swept channel

X   Vessels sunk by mines

Yo—do

X Jwste

X Pirate
X   X Pledge

Sin—do

Su—do

To—do

X vms B/s

Kalma
Peninsula

Green Beach

Yellow Beach

Wonsan
Airfield

WONSAN

Tugon

The 1st Marine Division went into its ships at Inchon. The 7th Division was sent down to board ships at Pusan. On the way south the division ran into new ambushes by the North Korean remnants left behind, in the Mungyong mountain area. The last elements of the 7th Division did not arrive at Pusan until October 12, the day after the ROK Army entered Wonsan. (See Map 24.)

Another reason not to stage the new amphibious landing soon appeared. The North Koreans had mined their northern waters, and very effectively too. Late in September the U.S. Destroyer *Brush* struck a mine off Tanchon. Thirteen men were killed, thirty-four wounded, and the ship was badly damaged. Two days later the ROK YMS *509* was mined off Yongdok, with thirty-one casualties. On October 1 the destroyer *Mansfield* nosed into the harbor of Changjon to pick up a downed airman. She struck a mine which blew off her bow and injured twenty-eight men. That day while sweeping for mines along the northeast coast, the minesweeper *Magpie* hit one, blew up and sank, with twenty-one members of her crew. On October 2, the ROK YMS *504* hit a mine at Mokpo. So seriously did the UN naval command regard the situation that ships were instructed not to operate within the 100-fathom curve. In Tokyo Admiral Struble tore up the plans for the initial phases of the new amphibious landing and made minesweeping the first order of business. He would send twenty-one minesweepers to Wonsan harbor.

They began arriving on October 10 and soon discovered that indeed the area was heavily mined inside the 30-fathom curve. One channel had to be abandoned altogether. So difficult was the sweeping job that bombers were brought in to drop 1,000-pound bombs to explode the mines.

It seemed a good idea at the time, but it was not that good. After the bombing, the sweepers *Pirate, Pledge,* and *Incredible* entered the area full of confidence. Northwest of Yodo Island the *Pirate* hit a mine at noon on October 12 and sank. Six minutes later the *Pledge* hit one and sank. The *Incredible* spent most of the afternoon in rescue work.

The heavy casualties at sea continued. On October 18, two ROK ships struck mines near Wonsan, one sank, the other was disabled. The next day another minesweeper struck another mine and sank.

By this time the ROK Army forces were well past Wonsan traveling north. So why send X Corps into these dangerous waters at all? Because General MacArthur wanted to; that is the only reasonable answer.

Then, in the middle of the operation to clear out North Korea and finish the war, President Truman decided it was necessary for him to have a face-to-face meeting with General MacArthur, whom he had never met.

On the basis of what he and MacArthur knew of each other, they did not like each other. Truman considered MacArthur to be an arrogant grand-stander. MacArthur looked upon Truman as a dolt, boor, and small town shopkeeper whose proper place was Independence, Missouri, not the White House.

Nevertheless, they were meeting for the first time on October 15, at Wake Island. It was to be a conference of war.

Why President Truman wanted to go to Wake to meet with MacArthur is a mystery still not properly unraveled. MacArthur said snidely that it was a political ploy. Were not the congressional elections just three weeks away?

Certainly the Korean War had become a political football, and certainly Harry Truman was primarily a political creature, trained in the hard school of boss politics. But that could not have been Truman's only motivation, for no man had dedicated himself more completely to the good of the nation than Truman did when he fell into the presidency from the vice-president's chair. His personal political victory over the Republicans in 1948 had not made him arrogant. In this fall of 1950 Truman was deeply concerned about events in Asia, and he wanted all the information he could get.

Also, there had been two troublesome incidents in recent days: the attack on that Chinese airfield in Manchuria, and a similar attack on a Soviet airfield across the Tamen River in Siberia. The United States had apologized in both cases, but Truman was well aware of the sort of emotion such incidents could arouse. They certainly emphasized the nearness of American fighting forces to the Chinese and Soviet borders.

Furthermore, Truman wanted to get "a feel" for this troublesome com-mander, on whose judgment so much depended. He had already considered firing MacArthur for the obvious insubordination of the VFW message. He had refrained partially from respect for MacArthur's previous accomplish-ments, and partly for political reasons. William Manchester, MacArthur's biographer, says that Truman's statement in his memoirs that he wanted to have a personal talk with the general is "inadequate." That judgment indicates how little the biographer of the general knew about the President, or how concerned he was about the conflicting signals he was getting from advisors in Washington about the crossing of the 38th parallel. But the President was not coming with any idea that this meeting would be a lovefest.

It began badly enough. The Truman plane landed at Wake early on the morning of October 15. The general had come in earlier and had driven to the airfield in a jeep. Truman looked out the open door of the plane. Instead of getting down and approaching the plane as a subordinate was supposed to do, MacArthur sat in lordly splendor in his vehicle, waiting for the President of the United States to come to him. Truman had been half-expecting this. He saw it as a serious breach of protocol and felt that MacArthur knew it. The President was furious and refused to get down from the plane. MacArthur then realized he could not upstage the President, and he "materialized," as the Truman aides said, at the foot of the gangway.

MacArthur was annoyed, an indication that his ego had once more overwhelmed his judgment. As Biographer Manchester put it, the general recalled only too well how he had been ordered to meet with President Franklin Roosevelt in Honolulu, in the summer of 1944, and MacArthur had decided then that the reason for the meeting was to get votes for Roosevelt in the elections of that year.

That opinion had been a long way from the truth. At that moment, the Marianas campaign had just been completed, and the burning question in Washington was whether the next step in the Pacific war should be in the hands of the army or the navy. The navy had made a good case for a landing on Formosa or the China coast. MacArthur had been operating the Southwest Pacific Campaign, really a sideshow after Guadalcanal, for two years while the navy carried the war in the Central Pacific. He wanted his place in the sun. At the Honolulu conference Roosevelt gave it to him: out of that meeting came the presidential decision that the next invasion would be the Philippines and that MacArthur would run the whole show. So for MacArthur to later bite the hand of his benefactor was less than generous although completely typical. Now, it was like him to put the worst face on the motivations of President Truman and to show his feelings with such a gesture. When he saw that it was not going to work, he rushed to make amends.

When they did meet, MacArthur was at his most charming. He apologized for any embarrassment the VFW incident may have caused the President. Truman liked that. But Truman wanted to get down to cases, and he did, even on the short ride to the quonset hut where they would hold their talks.

Did the general think the Chinese would enter the Korean War? the President asked.

Intelligence reports indicated that they would not, said the general. Even if they did, he, MacArthur, would defeat them, he said.

The President expressed relief. He had been much concerned about that problem, he said. And indeed he had. Just before leaving for Wake Island, Truman had asked the CIA for a new assessment of the possibility of China's entering the war. What he got was a weaseled, or tail-protecting, statement:

"While full scale Chinese Communist intervention . . . must be regarded as a continuing possibility, a consideration of all known factors leads to the conclusion that barring a Soviet decision for global war, such action is not probable in 1950. During this period intervention will probably be confined to continued covert assistance to the North Koreans." That last referred to arms shipments and some indication that Sinicized Koreans who had fought with the Chinese were now coming back to Korea to fight.

So the CIA, the President's bastion of worldwide intelligence, said the Chinese would not come in (although Chou En-lai said they would). Now General MacArthur said the same. President Truman seemed comforted.

During the more formal conference several other advisors sat in: General Bradley, Dean Rusk, Ambassador Muccio, Secretary of the Army Frank Pace, Jr., Averell Harriman, Admiral Radford, and several members of Truman's and MacArthur's staffs. Several times in several ways, various members again brought up the issue of Chinese intervention. MacArthur was supremely confident. He told Dean Rusk that he expected to get the troops back to Japan for Christmas. The war was now won. Hostilities would end completely by Thanksgiving. He would be able to send a division to Europe in January. He said again, when the matter came up, the Chinese would not enter the war. They had only about three hundred thousand troops in all Manchuria and only about a hundred and twenty-five thousand along the Yalu River. Since they did not have air power they could not expect that more than fifty or sixty thousand of these could cross the river into North Korea. Also, if either the USSR or China had been going to intervene, would they not have done so initially when their efforts would have been decisive, and the Americans would have been pushed out of Korea? It was an impressive argument.

Also once again MacArthur showed how the end would come, with the two forces in west and east entrapping the enemy. No one in the room, including the two high military professionals, General Bradley and Admiral Radford, argued. As the meeting ended, President Truman awarded MacArthur his fourth Distinguished Service Medal: ". . . his vision, his judgment, his indomitable will and his unshakable faith . . . have set a shining example of galantry and tenacity in defense and of audacity in attack matched by few operations in military history," said the citation.

No matter who wrote it, Truman said it, and there is no indication that anyone at the conference disagreed with the sentiments. MacArthur had Washington in thrall.

21

The Plan in Shambles

The two elements of the UN army were strung out along the length of Korea like two great snakes, one on the left side of the peninsula and the other on the right. The supply officers were distressed because the logistical problems were growing more serious every day. As the Eighth Army surged north toward Pyongyang, the supply line grew longer. Worse than that, the supplies were just not coming up from Inchon. General Frank W. Milburn, commander of I Corps, was concerned. He felt that he should have at least three thousand tons of supplies no farther south than Kaesong, to continue his advance. He did not have them. The reason was that for the first seventeen days of October the Inchon port facilities were strained to handle the debarkation of the 1st Marine Division for the abortive Wonsan operation.

This meant that the units in the line never had more than a day or two of supply. The tanks set out each morning not knowing if they would have the fuel the next day to continue.

The result of this supply shortage was that IX Corps remained behind the 38th parallel while I Corps forged north. That was not the way MacArthur had planned it, but there was nothing to be done, until the 1st Marines sailed away and Inchon port could get down to work supplying the Eighth Army. Before the war, South Korea's rail facilities from Seoul to Pusan had been excellent, but now they were in shambles. At the first of October rail communications from Pusan did not extend north farther than the Naktong River. Meanwhile the Eighth Army was two hundred miles north, so emergency transport—air, road, sea—had to be the answer. This factor was just another of those virtually ignored by General MacArthur in his rush toward the Yalu River.

Beginning in late September, Eighth Army engineers strained to rebuild the bridges and the rail lines, along with the South Korean government. But the rail traffic to Seoul would be another month in getting going again.

Meanwhile, the Eighth Army had reached Kumchon and was ready to set out on the second phase of the drive toward Pyongyang.

On October 15, as General MacArthur was meeting with President Truman at Wake Island, the 7th Cavalry marched toward Namchonjom. (See Map 23.) The attack was preceded by artillery barrage and supported by air strikes. After fierce fighting the Americans reached Namchonjom at noon.

Now came a new difficulty: the autumn rains. The rain came down in sheets and soon the roads were muddy tracks. Maneuvering off the roads was virtually impossible for vehicles, so an attempt by the 5th Cavalry to flank the retreating North Koreans failed.

But the Americans still pressed on quickly. On October 16 they secured Sohung, seventeen miles to the north. They prepared to move on Hwangju.

On the right flank the ROK 1st Division was moving even faster. On October 15 they reached Miu-dong and the next day entered Suan. They were only forty air miles south of Pyongyang.

The U.S. 24th Division was supposed to go up the left. It bogged down, moving from Paekchon to Haeju. Part of the problem was a North Korean roadblock. Part of it was a traffic jam on the bad road. General Milburn was in a hurry to get to Pyongyang, and he told the commanders of the 1st Cavalry and the 24th Division that the first to reach Sariwon would win the honor of leading the corps in to Pyongyang. Within the divisions the regiments competed to be first. Competition is a great spur, and this competition led to the following:

On the night of October 16 the 7th Cavalry reached Sohung. The 27th British Commonwealth Brigade was to pass through early the next morning to attack along the main highway to Sariwon. South of Sohung was a 7th Cavalry roadblock, and the orders were to shoot at anything that moved.

The men at the roadblock did not know that the 5th Cavalry was moving up that night in its hurry to get to Sariwon. Up it came, into the teeth of the 7th Cavalry and a firefight soon developed between the American units. Before it could be stopped seven men were wounded by "friendly fire."

On October 17 the 7th Cavalry was again on the move, with the British up ahead this time. They were on the main highway to Sariwon, which was thirty miles up the road, due west from Sohung. Here was the key to Pyongyang. The road and railroad came down out of the mountains and turned north through the coastal plain to Pyongyang, which was only thirty-five miles away. The advance from that point was going to be easy, the land was almost flat with just a few low hills. Sariwon, then, was the logical place for the North Koreans to make their last ditch defense of Pyongyang.

This day the Argylls led the attack, with Major David Wilson's company at the point, riding on American tanks. Brigadier General Frank A. Allen, Jr., the assistant division commander of the 1st Cavalry Division, was along with them, apparently to maintain the American presence.

It all seemed so easy. They passed dozens of enemy vehicles, abandoned along the road. They passed knots of North Koreans, standing on the roadside waiting to surrender. Then they came to an apple orchard about four miles from Sariwon. As they moved up, rifle fire suddenly erupted from the orchard. General Allen grew quite excited and jumped out of his jeep waving a map. His aide climbed up on a tank and began to give fire directions. A spotter plane overhead dipped its wings to show that the orchard was full of enemy troops. And it was. The Americans saw them, for as the tanks began firing a horde of North Koreans burst out of the orchard and ran up the ridge behind it and disappeared. The Argylls moved in and swept through the orchard, killing forty of the North Koreans who had chosen to fight and capturing a number of others. So the defense of Sariwon had come to nought. The British troops captured ten heavy machine guns in the orchard, and outside, near Sariwon, a battery of antitank guns. The Argylls were the first into Sariwon.

Late that afternoon the Australians came up through the Argylls and moved north about five miles, towards Hwangju. Before them was a line of hills that ought to be heavily defended by the North Koreans. The Australians stopped and lined up their perimeter, prepared to attack next morning.

That night North Korean and UN forces mixed it up. One North Korean unit came up in trucks toward Sariwon, ran into the British, fought their way through, found the northern road closed and fought their way back south again, losing about half their number. Lieutenant Colonel Leslie Nielson, commander of the Argyll 1st Battalion, was driving through Sariwon a little later, when he ran straight into a column of North Korean troops coming the other way. His driver jammed down the accelerator, they sped four miles through the column, North Koreans giving way on both sides, and they escaped, shots still ringing after them. The confusion was as bad inside the town. Several parties of North Koreans came into Sariwon that night and mistook the British uniforms for Russian. The Argylls fired on them, and

killed a number. This sort of incident did not occur just once, but several
times. Also, north of the town the Australians kept capturing North Koreans
who came up to its roadblock. Lieutenant Colonel Nielson's long column
finally appeared. Major I. B. Ferguson of the Australians got up on a tank and
called on them to surrender. They were surrounded, he yelled. They believed
it, and most of them laid down their arms. By morning the Australians had
captured 1,982 North Koreans.

As the British and the Australians carried the point on the highway, the 1st
Battalion of the 7th Cavalry moved onto secondary roads to the north. Late in
the afternoon a liaison plane dropped a message telling Lieutenant Colonel
Clainos that the roads out of Sariwon were jammed by hundreds of North
Korean troops retreating. So the 1st Battalion turned south to meet the British,
who were on the other side of the hill, and entrap some more of these North
Koreans. They reached the hills and came under fire. Their South Korean
interpreter managed to worm his way up to the enemy forward position and
announced that the North Koreans were surrounded and were firing on
Russian troops. They believed him. A platoon came down to meet the
"Russians" and was captured. Thereupon hundreds of North Koreans
poured down from their position and surrendered. Some, who did not, fought
valiantly for several hours. Finally most of them were persuaded to give up.
Altogether, then, the battalion captured 1,700 North Korean soldiers and
thirteen nurses that day.

Up on the east coast, the U.S. Navy was still preparing the Wonsan area for
the X Corps landings that were no longer necessary. The ROK forces had
moved out from Wonsan, north toward the Soviet and Manchurian borders
and west toward Pyongyang.

Finally on October 16, the restless marines sailed from Inchon, and the
Eighth Army could then begin to get its supply lines in order. It was about 850
miles from Inchon, around the southern tip of Korea, past Pusan, and up to
Wonsan. They arrived on October 19, but they did not land. Admiral Struble
was still worried about mines, so the ships steamed back and forth outside
Wonsan harbor in what the marines came to call Operation Yo-Yo. The most
effective fighting men of the American expeditionary force were at sea, and, as
yet, were doing nothing useful in this phase of the war. Fortunately they were
not needed at the moment, since the Republic of Korea Army was doing just
fine. Three divisions were driving north and approaching Pyongyang, racing
each other to be first. And also toward Pyongyang from the south came the
U.S. 1st Cavalry Division, the British and Australians, the U.S. 24th Division
and the ROK 1st Division, all hurrying to be first into the North Korean

capital. On the evening of October 17 they were only fifteen miles southeast of the city. (See Map 23.)

After the fall of Sariwon it was apparent to the Eighth Army intelligence officers that the North Koreans had "shot their wad." The defense of the city was to be carried out by the NK 17th and 32nd divisions. But those divisions totaled only about eight thousand men, against the seven divisions of the UN forces. The South Koreans alone were moving about forty thousand men north.

Since the 27th British Commonwealth Brigade had been first into Sariwon, and it was attached to the 1st Cavalry Division, General Milburn announced that the 1st Cavalry would lead the way into Pyongyang. The 7th Cavalry was farthest north, so it was ordered to move out at dawn on October 18. As ordered, the tired troops of the 3rd Battalion (they had been up all night moving into town) crossed the ford at Hwangju and advanced. Everything went swiftly until they reached a ridge south of Hukkyo-ri, about halfway from Sariwon to Pyongyang. There they encountered a reinforced battalion of North Koreans equipped with artillery and 120 mm mortars, half a dozen T-34 tanks, and a minefield. The Americans called for an air strike and one came in. The North Koreans shot down one of the P-51s. The resistance was strong, and General Gay, who had come up to watch, decided to commit the rest of the regiment. Captain Webel suggested that the enemy position was all but taken so why risk more lives? General Gay insisted, and the other two battalions spent the night of October 17 moving to outflank the enemy position. When morning came they rushed in to discover that the enemy had moved out during the night.

Having exhausted the 7th Cavalry in that unnecessary "full regimental attack," General Gay then had to move the 5th Cavalry up through the 7th to take the lead. The 5th Cavalry was strung out along the road behind the 7th Cavalry, so it took Colonel Marcel B. Crombez most of the night to bring his forces up to the attack point.

The "honor" of taking the lead in the race now went to Lieutenant James H. Bell and Company F. Five tanks, a platoon of engineers, and a section of heavy machine guns went with them. Up ahead of them a forward bazooka team of the 7th Cavalry had just finished knocking out three North Korean tanks when Company F appeared to march through. A U.S. fighter pilot coming by saw the tanks, swooped down and rocketed one of them, very nearly knocking out the forward element of Company F.

Everyone was in a rush. Colonel Crombez was right behind Company F, pushing. At eleven o'clock the men reached the Mujin-chon River, at the southern edge of Pyongyang. They encountered enemy troops behind a twenty-foot embankment on the north side of the river. They had three antitank guns trained on the highway bridge. Company F had to stop for half an hour while the mortar men lobbed shells into the concentration and finally caused the North Koreans to abandon their guns and retreat. So Company F was the first unit into Pyongyang. Colonel Crombez had to be proud.

He had beaten the ROK 1st Division into Pyongyang by a few minutes. General Paik's ROK 1st Division had a much harder time of it. Only eight miles from Pyongyang on the night of October 18, they had attacked only to find that they faced strong defenses protected by a minefield. It was an hour after daybreak, following all night fighting, that they broke through and moved toward the city. Again at Kojo-dong, six miles from the city, they were stopped. Tanks of Company C of the U.S. 6th Tank Battalion fought on the flanks, and the ROK 12th Regiment's 2nd Battalion kept moving. Just before 11 A.M. they were on the edge of Pyongyang, just a few hundred yards from the U.S. 5th Cavalry.

The 5th Cavalry then spread out through the town, fighting for various objectives. The North Koreans fought, but they did not put up a heroic defense here. It was too late. They did blow up the Taedong River highway bridge just a few minutes before the soldiers reached that part of town.

The South Koreans, who knew Pyongyang, moved through the city much more quickly and by nightfall most of the ROK 1st Division was inside the city. Also, coming down from the north the 8th Regiment of the ROK 7th Division was also in the city, capturing Kim Il Sung University on the north before 5 P.M.

On October 20, the ROK 1st Division took over the center of the city, including the government buildings. The enemy was totally demoralized and did not fight at all.

A special U.S. task force concentrated on the capture of several buildings that they thought would yield valuable intelligence material. Most of these buildings were taken on October 20, and the intelligence matter was sent to General MacArthur's command in Tokyo.

In Tokyo General MacArthur's intelligence officer, Major General Charles Willoughby, declared tentatively that the war was over:

> Organized resistance on any large scale has ceased to be an enemy capability. Indications are that the North Korean military and political headquarters may have fled to Manchuria.

What was still puzzling, however, was the refusal of the North Korean high command to surrender. As Willoughby noted, the enemy still had the capability of fighting small-scale delaying actions—and, although Willoughby did not mention them, also of harrying the troops in the south by guerrilla activity.

General Walker established Eighth Army headquarters in the offices that had been the seat of Kim Il Sung's government. General Gay established his headquarters in the North Korean Military Academy a few miles southwest of Pyongyang. A civil affairs office was immediately set up with Colonel Crombez in charge. Troops of the 7th Cavalry rushed to Chinnampo, the port for Pyongyang and captured it without real trouble. The North Korean government seemed to have collapsed completely, although Kim Il Sung and his troops and government officials had moved north, taking many American prisoners of war with them.

General MacArthur flew to Pyongyang to help celebrate the victory. Exercising that public relations genius for which he was famous, he presided over a touching ceremony. With the press as audience, he reviewed Company F of the 5th Cavalry, which had beaten the ROK 1st Division in the race to get into Pyongyang. On July 19, the 5th Cavalry had landed at Pohang-dong, a fishing town sixty miles east of Pusan. It had been sent immediately to the defense of Taejon.

They had come in green as grass, two hundred of them, fresh from their pleasant occupation duties in Japan. They had suffered for the U.S. high command's five-year inattention to battle training, and they had died.

The men of Company F had fought in the battle for Yongdong, to be overwhelmed by the North Koreans. They had fought along the Naktong. They had fought for Hill 303 at Waegwan. They had fought their way out of the Pusan Perimeter. And now they had fought their way north to MacArthur's triumph. When General MacArthur, with his shrewd showman's instinct, asked that all the men who had landed with Company F at Pohang-dong just ninety-six days earlier take one step forward, he knew what would happen next. They stepped out, one . . . two . . . three . . . four . . . five. That was all.

22

Rescue Attempt

General MacArthur's original request for airborne units had been based on the precept that they would be useful in spearheading an assault on the enemy. Finally he got his paratroops, the 187th Airborne Regimental Combat Team, or Rakkasan (named for the Japanese word for parachute). But since the request was made in the summer the war had turned around, and there was no real need for these parachute troops. They were to participate in the X Corps operations at Inchon. The task was to be to drop on Kimpo airfield and seize the field. The drop was scheduled for September 24. But by the time the aircraft arrived over Kimpo they had word that the marines had gotten there first and cleared the field. So nobody jumped. The planes landed and taxied to a stop. Aboard one C-119, the last man on the left side opened the big door. He was promptly shot between the eyes by a North Korean sniper. Sergeant J. H. Alexander of Company A led a small expedition that hunted down and killed the sniper. The high command had assumed that the paratroops would drop and fight, and so there were no trucks to take them anywhere. They were ordered to Suwon, five miles south. They marched. They bivouacked. They were then given the very secondary job of clearing the Kimpo Peninsula between the Han River and the sea. But secondary or not, it involved hunting down and eradicating the threat posed by some three thousand enemy troops cut off by the marine assault inland. The Rakkasans lost some men, but they

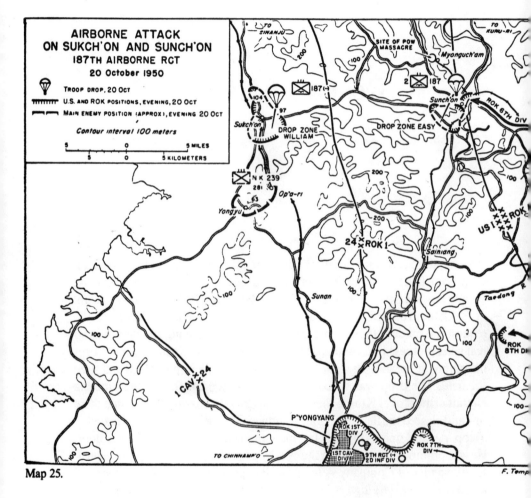

**AIRBORNE ATTACK
ON SUKCH'ON AND SUNCH'ON**
187TH AIRBORNE RCT
20 October 1950

Troop drop, 20 Oct

U.S. and ROK positions, evening, 20 Oct

Main enemy position (approx), evening 20 Oct

Contour interval 100 meters

5   0   5 MILES
5   0   5 KILOMETERS

TO
SINANJU

TO
KUNU-RI

SITE OF POW
MASSACRE

Myonguch'am

104

97

2   187

187(−)

Sukch'on

DROP ZONE
WILLIAM

DROP ZONE EASY

Sunch'on

ROK 8TH DIV

N K 239

281

63

Op'a-ri

200

Yongyu

200

US I   ROK

24   ROK I

Sainiang

Sunan

Taedong

ROK
8TH DIV

1 CAV   24

P'YONGYANG

ROK 1ST
DIV

9TH RGT (−)
2D INF DIV

ROK 7TH
DIV

TO CHINNAMP'O

1ST CAV
DIV

Map 25.

F. Temp

did their job well and captured or killed all but ten percent of those three thousand North Koreans.

The 187th then sat down again to play the old army game: hurry up and wait. So the Rakkasans guarded Kimpo airfield during the Eighth Army drive north. Two more plans were made for use of the airborne troops, but each time the ground forces took the objective before they could get into action. It seemed that the war had ended before they could get into it.

In Tokyo, however, General MacArthur was still planning grandly. Guided by his intelligence officers he estimated that some 30,000 North Korean troops were located between the Sukchon–Sunchon area and Pyongyang. The Rakkasans, said he, would be dropped there and would smash this force, about half of the known remaining enemy units, against the anvil of the 1st Cavalry and the ROK 1st Division at Pyongyang. Also, someone had the idea that they might effect the rescue of hundreds of American prisoners of war being taken north by the North Koreans.

By the time this idea became operational Pyongyang had been captured. Just before the fall of the city, came a report to intelligence that a trainload of American POWs was to be taken north. But by which of the two major rail routes to the Yalu no one knew for sure. They thought it would be the Sunchon route. The date for the air drop was then set for October 20, and the drop was to be made in two zones about thirty miles north of Pyongyang. (See Map 24.) The 1st Battalion was to drop just south of Sukchon, along the road and coastal railroad. The 2nd Battalion was to drop south of Sunchon, located on a second north-south artery and rail line farther inland.

The paratroopers were up at two o'clock in the morning. It was raining hard. After a meal they were trucked to the plane parking area of Kimpo airfield. There they waited and watched the rain come down. The pilots of the 21st and 314th Troop Carrier squadrons waited with them. The high command was waiting for some indication of improvement in the weather over the drop zone.

Dawn broke, gray and rainy. Midmorning came, and the rain still pelted down. But at about eleven o'clock the rain let up and in half an hour the sky showed signs of clearing. The men began boarding the transports, the familiar C-47 left over from World War II and the new big C-119 which could carry forty-six paratroops and nineteen bundles of supplies. Colonel Frank S. Bowen, Jr., commander of the 187th Airborne, was aboard the plane that took off first. It circled and waited, and the others came up one by one. Then they formed up and headed north.

The formation was preceded by a group of fighter planes that strafed the ground around the drop zones with machine guns and rockets. Just before two o'clock that afternoon the lead planes began dropping their paratroops in the Sukchon drop zone. Colonel Bowen stood in the doorway of his C-119 and watched for landmarks. The twenty-minute warning light went on and the men fidgeted in their seats. At 1:50 the green light went on. The men got up and moved to the door and the first one clipped his automatic ripcord to the wire. Colonel Bowen yelled, "Go," and the first man was out the door. Soon 1,470 paratroops and seventy-four tons of equipment were floating in the air. It was a good drop, generally speaking.

General MacArthur, General Stratemeyer of the Air Force, General Wright, and General Whitney all came to watch the show from MacArthur's plane. He was very pleased, and when he landed at Pyongyang that day he told the press in his grandiloquent manner that "This closes the trap on the enemy," and that the war was just about wound up.

The drop zone was paddy field, and the paratroops did, as General MacArthur said, catch the enemy by surprise. The only trouble was that there weren't anywhere near 30,000 of them. The only firing was a scattering of rifle fire from the north. They captured many North Korean soldiers just struggling into civilian clothes, the approved NK method of escape. One stick (twenty-three men) dropped outside the drop zone and had a bad time getting to the main group. One man was killed. Twenty-five men were injured in landing.

The 1st Battalion's task was to clear Sukchon and hold the high ground north of the city. The North Koreans delayed them but by late afternoon the command post was established at Chang-ni.

The North Korean enemy might be on the ropes, but he was still to be reckoned with. The paratroops of one platoon saw an air force fighter hit by ground fire. The plane crash-landed in a paddy field. The pilot was wounded but he dragged himself out of the plane and began to crawl across the paddy, toward the American line. North Korean troops on the right side of the paddy field opened fire on him. He stopped crawling and lay still. The Americans kept the North Koreans off by firing every time they saw an enemy move, but the paratroops could not reach the pilot either. The impasse continued until dark, when both sides sent out patrols. The North Koreans got to the pilot first and killed him. The Americans chased the North Korean patrol but lost them in the hills. On the way back to their line, they encountered three North Korean soldiers. Two tried to run and the paratroops shot them with great relish, remembering the fate of the American pilot. The other North Korean tried to surrender, but they shot him, too, for the same reason. The only good "Gook" was a dead Gook. That's the sort of war it was, and any sensitive souls who believed otherwise were soon to have their minds changed.

The second objective of the 187th that day was Sunchon. The town was taken easily enough by the 2nd Battalion. They were also directed to prepare the railroad bridge across the Kimchon River at Sinhung-ni for demolition, to stop the POW train. There was some delay occasioned by North Korean resistance, but by the end of the day Colonel Bowen could report that all objectives had been taken. There was only one problem. The POW train had not shown up.

In fact, it had. The train had gone through Sunchon early in the morning as the paratroops sat soggily in the rain of Kimpo airfield waiting for the weather to lift.

That day on the ground, General Gay authorized the formation of a new task force based on the 1st Battalion of the 8th Cavalry, with tanks and engineers. Task Force Rodgers it was called, after Lieutenant Colonel William M. Rodgers of the 70th Tank Battalion, who was in command. Task Force Rodgers was to go north and link up with the airborne troops to smash the anvil. The armored unit set out on the Sunchon road that night. Along the way they picked up five American POWs, who had managed to escape their captors. They ran into some North Korean resistance, but it was really guerrilla resistance: for example, the paratroops were working on that bridge south of Sunchon when Task Force Rodgers came up. Without warning someone opened fire and killed two men of the task force. The infantry scurried down below the bridge and routed out a dozen North Koreans who had dug into deep holes in the bank. They had been waiting to make this gesture of defiance. The Americans killed them. The nutcracker effect of the meeting of ground forces and airborne had crushed a dozen North Koreans.

That afternoon of October 21, Brigadier General Frank Allen, Jr., drove up to Sunchon in his jeep. At the airborne command post, he heard an excited Korean civilian telling of the murder the night before of two hundred American POWs in a railroad tunnel northwest of Sunchon. Allen set out immediately, joined by several ROK officers and soldiers, and two American correspondents, Don Whitehead of the Associated Press and Richard Tucker of the *Baltimore Sun.* Five air miles northwest of Sunchon they reached the village of Myongucham, and a railroad tunnel just north of it. An ROK officer went into the tunnel and emerged to report finding seven dead Americans. Allen went down. He found the seven dead POWs lying on straw mats beside the railroad track. Apparently they had starved to death. The ROK officer went on through the tunnel. At the far end he saw five Americans on the ridge line. Allen came up. He saw Private First Class Valdor John staggering down the hillside. He wrapped the shaking soldier in his jacket. The soldier pointed toward the brush.

"They're over there," he said.

Allen and correspondent Whitehead crossed over and found the bodies of seventeen American POWs, all shot down. John said he had escaped by falling as the others were murdered and pretending to be dead until the North Koreans went away.

Correspondent Whitehead felt sick. He walked away from the scene to a cornfield on the other side of the railroad track. There he stumbled on fifteen more American bodies. The prisoners had been shot as they sat on the ground, with their rice bowls at hand, having been promised a meal. As the Americans looked around, more escapees came up, nine in all. They told the story of the train.

Actually it was two trains, not one. Each had been loaded with about 150 American prisoners. They were riding in boxcars and open steel coal gondolas. They had no heat and few clothes and they were fed when their captors felt like it. The trains had set out from Pyongyang on the night of October 17. These men were all from the second train. Their group had originally numbered 350 when they had left Seoul by train a month earlier.

The pace was very slow. The American bombers had destroyed so much of the track that the train crew had to carry repair crews who went ahead repairing track as the trains inched along.

Every day men died from starvation, dysentery, or exposure. A handful escaped. The first train reached Sunchon and went on. As the Rakkasans were dropping from the air on October 20, the second train was in the tunnel, hiding from the fighter planes that had been strafing ahead of the airdrop. That evening as the paratroops consolidated their position only a few miles away, the guards took the prisoners from the train and into the field in three groups, promising them a meal. Then they shot them down with burp guns. They had begun by burying the first group of the dead in a common grave. But then the commander must have realized what would happen to him and his men if the Americans caught them, so they left the second and third groups where they had been killed and sped away in their train. Only the fact that the North Koreans had been in such an enormous rush that they did not check the dead allowed the few lucky survivors to escape death. And not all of them were so lucky. Two died that night.

The final search revealed the first murdered group, thirty-four bodies in a common grave. Altogether there were sixty-eight dead and twenty-one survivors of the massacre.

And there would be more victims: North Koreans who wanted to surrender to American soldiers who had heard of the Myongucham massacre.

Through no fault of their own the Rakkasans had failed to rescue the

American prisoners of war. Through no fault of their own, their main mission, of containing 30,000 enemy troops, was also a failure. They did not cut off any sizeable force of North Koreans. The last of the important enemy units was a full day ahead, having withdrawn from Sukchon and Sunchon, north of the Chongchon River. Actually Kim Il Sung and his government had fled Pyongyang on October 12. Had MacArthur's intelligence been better, the Rakkasans might really have put a crimp in that retreat, but the intelligence was ten days to two weeks behind. No important army or government officials were captured or killed. They were all safely in Manpojin up on the Yalu River.

The most important action was that of the 3rd Battalion of the Rakkasans, which had been assigned the sector of Opa-ri, eight miles south of Sukchon, to set up a roadblock, and then work back to link up with the U.S. and ROK troops coming up from Pyongyang.

On the morning of October 21 the Rakkasans moved out, Company I following the railroad tracks south, and Company K moving along the highway. At one o'clock in the afternoon Company I reached Opa-ri and ran into a reinforced battalion of North Koreans. This was a battalion of the NK 239th Regiment, the last large unit to leave Pyongyang, whose mission was to fight a rearguard action north and hold up the Americans and South Koreans. The fight was bitter; Company I took the town but was driven out again by the North Koreans with their 120 mm mortars and 40 mm antitank guns. Two platoons of Company I were overrun, and the company had to fall back. When noses were counted it was found that ninety men were missing. The North Koreans had raised hell with Company I. But they did not exploit their advantage. Their task was to hold this high ground and they moved back to it, leaving the Americans to get away. At the same time Company K, moving along the highway, ran into another North Korean battalion a mile north of Yongyu. Once again after a sharp fight, the North Koreans withdrew to high ground southeast of the town. The Americans marched through into Yongyu and took Hill 163. They were three miles from Company I at Opa-ri.

The Rakkasans had suffered heavily in the day's engagement, but the NK 239th position had suddenly become completely untenable, with American forces on both sides of them. At midnight on October 21 the North Koreans tried to break through the Rakkasan lines and escape north. A small group of North Koreans invaded the Company K command post. The Americans fought them hand to hand. Captain Claude K. Josey, the company commander, was wounded twice by a North Korean's burp gun, but he wrestled the gun out of the enemy's hands. In a few minutes it was all over and the North Koreans were killed or driven away. No prisoners were taken.

The North Koreans also attacked the roadblock near Hill 163 and forced the Americans back. They attacked along the American perimeters in several places, and at five forty-five that next morning they made a major attack against the Company L perimeter. The Rakkasans were waiting for them, and they fought hard. The trouble was that three companies were facing an entire regiment. They needed help and they called for it. The help came up from the south.

General Milburn's I Corps had been ordered to move up to what was called the MacArthur line drawn along the north about thirty-five miles from the Yalu River. The 24th Division, now with the 27th British Commonwealth Brigade attached, crossed the Taedong River at Pyongyang early that morning of October 21, and they headed north. By nightfall they had reached Yongyu. They could hear the sounds of battle north of them. At dawn on October 22, the Australian 3rd Battalion took the lead and moved north. Captain A. P. Denness and his Company C were riding American tanks. They knew that the 187th Airborne was up there somewhere so they moved cautiously to avoid the problem of "friendly fire." Just north of Yongyu they ran into some definitely unfriendly fire. It began with enemy rifle shots coming from an orchard on both sides of the road. The Australians jumped off the tanks and charged with fixed bayonets into the orchard. It was the first bayonet charge of the Korean War. What the North Koreans thought about it has not been reported, but what the Americans thought has. They were thunderstruck. One American reported how he saw a big red-haired Australian jump into an enemy trench. He heard lots of noise, then the Australian came out, bleeding like a stuck pig, but still on his feet. Down in the trench were eight dead North Koreans.

That sort of fighting routed the North Koreans from this position. A second company moved up to seize high ground on the right side of the road. A third company followed the second when it came under attack. The fourth company then moved to the left side of the road through the orchard. Having committed all his troops, Lieutenant Colonel Charles Green, the commander, moved into the orchard with his headquarters staff. They were attacked by a large number of North Koreans and in the battle that followed they killed thirty-four of them. Those British were not fooling around. One Australian platoon crossed a paddy field, kicking over stacks of straw and shooting down the North Koreans who came out. The vigor of the British attack was enormous, and effective. *De l'audace, encore de l'audace, et tourjours de l'audace!** The old master had been proved right again. The brigade accounted for about five hundred enemy troops, killed and captured, with

*Danton, to the French legislative assembly, 1792.

casualties of their own of seven wounded, including that big red-haired Australian. The enemy survivors fled to the west as the Middlesex 1st Battalion moved on through and made contact with the beleaguered Rakkasans at eleven o'clock that morning. The British and Americans compared notes, and the Rakkasans said they had counted about eight hundred enemy dead in their sector and had nearly seven hundred prisoners. So the North Korean 239th Infantry Regiment was just about shot to pieces in twenty-four hours of fighting.

The Rakkasan 3rd Battalion returned to Sukchon that afternoon and the British came up and relieved the 187th Airborne from its positions. The Rakkasans then went back to Pyongyang. They had suffered something over a hundred casualties in the past three days of battle and had captured 3,800 prisoners, to say nothing of the 2,000 or 3,000 North Koreans killed. Given this sort of intelligence, and not paying too much attention to what was happening elsewhere, General MacArthur's command had to believe that the Korean War was just about over.

23

To the Yalu

In the United Nations, Secretary Trygve Lie was promoting a compromise measure that had the virtue of saving face for the North Koreans. The Lie proposal would have allowed the Kim Il Sung government to continue as de facto rulers of North Korea pending UN-sponsored national elections which would truly unify the country.

Secretary Lie was a dreamer. By this time, Kim Il Sung already had the assurances of the Chinese that they would not allow his government to fall without a fight. So he retreated to Sinuiju, on the Korean side of the Yalu, just across from the Manchurian industrial center of Antung, and shouted curses over the radio waves at the United Nations, President Syngman Rhee, and the United States.

Meanwhile, in Tokyo General MacArthur continued to muddle along. General Almond's X Corps was to continue to operate separately from General Walker's Eighth Army.

At Eighth Army headquarters the strategy of late October 1950 was based on the belief that the North Koreans were on their last legs and the Chinese would not enter the war. General Walker's intelligence officers informed him that the North Koreans would be incapable of mounting a major defensive effort at the last apparent point possible: the Chongchon River barrier forty-five miles north of Pyongyang. The enemy would continue to withdraw

247

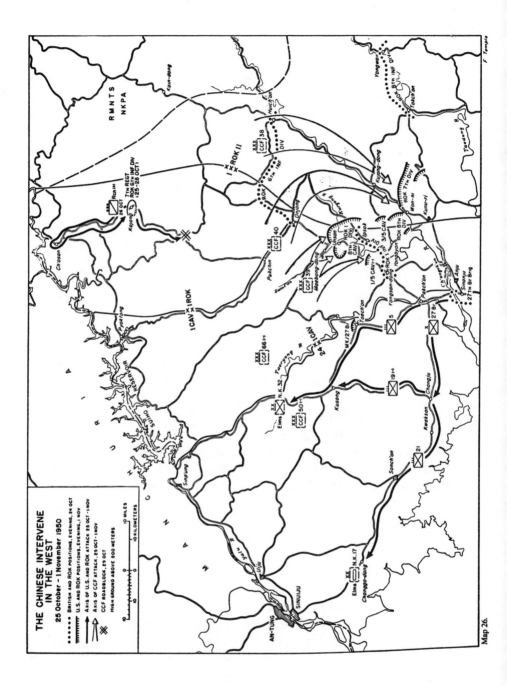

THE CHINESE INTERVENE
IN THE WEST
25 October – 1 November 1950

• • • • • BRITISH AND ROK POSITIONS, EVENING, 24 OCT
⌄⌄⌄⌄⌄ U.S. AND ROK POSITIONS, EVENING, 1 NOV
⇈⇈ AXIS OF CCF ATTACK, 25 OCT–1 NOV
✕ AXIS OF U.S. AND ROK ATTACK 25 OCT–1 NOV
⊠ CCF ROADBLOCK, 29 OCT
HIGH GROUND ABOVE 500 METERS

0   10 MILES
0   10 KILOMETERS

Map 26.

northward along the two major rail and road lines, running north from Sinanju and Anju up into the mountain country of the north. That belief was given credence when Kim Il Sung moved his government to the mountain town of Kanggye. This area had been the center of Korean resistance against the Japanese during the old days. It seemed logical that a defeated but defiant North Korean government would move there to continue guerrilla resistance.

On October 22 Task Force Elephant set out to the north to put up a roadblock at Kujang-dong. The force was led by Company C of the 6th Medium Tank Battalion. Behind came the ROK 1st Division. The force reached its objective and then turned west into the valley of the Chongchon River. Along the way they picked up several escaped American prisoners who were returned to Pyongyang. On the afternoon of October 23 they found the bodies of twenty-eight American prisoners along the railroad tracks. Three who had escaped death came out of the brush. It was the same old story.

General Paik's ROK 1st Division forged on. They knocked out two T-34 tanks and two self-propelled guns. It seemed a long time since June, when the ROK troops had been frightened to death of tanks they did not know how to fight. Now with bazookas and artillery they were capable of handling them very well. The tanks moved fast enough to take a damaged bridge across the Chongchon northeast of Anju before the North Koreans could destroy it. That was the only one, the enemy had blown up all the others in the area. (See Map 26.)

The repair of the Anju bridge began immediately. All night long the engineers worked, and on the following morning, October 24, the bridge could take 2½ ton trucks. Three miles east of the bridge scouts found a tank ford and the tanks crossed there. The task force and all three regiments of the ROK 1st Division were north of the Chongchon on October 24, and attacking toward Unsan.

Meanwhile, the U.S. 24th Division and the 27th British Commonwealth Brigade moved up to Sunan and Sinanju. The British crossed the Chongchon there, their infantry moving over in assault boats, while the vehicles went around to use the Anju bridge. The engineers worked on the highway to Sinanju, preparing it to carry the traffic that would be needed for the forward elements to drive to the Manchurian border.

On the right, the ROK 6th and 8th divisions moved forward into the Kanggye mountain area. Near Kunui-ri the ROK 6th Division captured two entire trains, one of them carrying eight tanks. They also captured fifty boxcars full of ammunition. After a fight with a full regiment of North Koreans south of Huichon, the division took Huichon on October 23 and there captured another twenty T-34 tanks. At Huichan the ROK 6th Division turned northwest, toward Chosan on the Yalu River. It was way out in front of the UN forces.

By the end of October, the Republic of Korea Army was in the best shape it had ever been. New divisions were being activated from troops trained by the Americans and attached to the American divisions in the last few weeks. And on the way or newly arrived in South Korea were military forces from Turkey, Thailand, the Netherlands, Canada, and another brigade from Britain.

The problem of the UN forces—and it did not seem very important at the moment—was logistical. General MacArthur's insistence on splitting his forces had created that bottleneck at Inchon from which the Eighth Army had not recovered. The railhead from Pusan had been brought up to Yongdungpo through the herculean efforts of South Korean and American engineers. But that still meant a long truck haul north, to Pyongyang and beyond. The trucks were wearing out, and if there were replacement parts, they were on the high seas, not in Korea. Most of the existing trucks were operating on a 24-hour basis. In other words, the Eighth Army on the western side of the Korean Peninsula was strung out and in constant danger of outrunning its supply train.

But who cared? The men of the 1st Cavalry Division were handed flyers from the Post Exchange Service, listing some Christmas presents they could order. They threw them away; they would be back in Japan, they said, in plenty of time to shop for Christmas.

Over on the eastern side of the peninsula, the X Corps wrestled with confusion. During Operation Yo-Yo the marines had never figured out why their transports went north, then south, then north again. For a while they thought the war was over. Ashore at Wonsan they received several sets of conflicting orders within a week. After the landings on October 26, the marines began repairing the port facilities of Wonsan. It was going to take weeks for all of X Corps to get assembled in this northeastern area. The minesweeping of the inner harbor was not finished until November 2. By this time all the American commands were sure the war was just about over. The Pentagon and MacArthur were exchanging messages about redeployment of troops that were either in the Far East or on their way. On October 25 the Department of the Army told MacArthur they were cancelling the shipment of enlisted reserve troops scheduled for shipment to Japan. General Walker began diverting ammunition ships from Korea to Japan. He had all the ammunition he could use, he said. MacArthur went further, he had half a dozen ammunition ships carrying artillery shells sent back to Hawaii and the West Coast.

Early in October, General MacArthur had been careful to refrain from provoking the Chinese and Soviets any more than necessary, at least as he saw it. He had drawn a line about forty miles from the Manchurian and Siberian borders. The UN forces would remain below that line, except the South Koreans, who could go anywhere within the limits of Korea.

But on October 24 MacArthur once more indicated his supreme arrogance: *without orders,* he removed all the restrictions on the use of UN forces and instructed the commanders to press forward to the borders. When the Joint Chiefs learned of this, they sent a rocket demanding an explanation. His action went beyond his orders of September 27. MacArthur replied airily that it was "a military necessity," the ROK troops could not handle the occupation themselves. He felt he had the latitude to do what he wished, and, besides, all these problems had been settled at the Wake Island conference. So the UN troops forged ahead towards the Yalu.

The ROK 6th Division raced on along the valley of the Chongchon. On the night of October 24 the 7th Regiment passed through Onjong. (See Map 26.) Chosan and the Yalu were only fifty miles away. Late on the afternoon of October 25 the South Koreans reached Kojang, just eighteen air miles south of Chosan. There they stopped to bivouac for the night.

On October 25 the ROK 1st Division was strung out along the road from the Chonchon River to Unsan. Its 15th Regiment passed through Unsan. The 6th Medium Tank Battalion led the way. A mile and a half out of town on the northeast side they came to a bridge, and, as the tanks rolled up to it, the bridge was suddenly splashed with mortar fire. The ROK infantry deployed along the sides of the road and began to fight. Half an hour later they reported there were three hundred enemy troops in the hills just north of Unsan—Chinese troops. A little later they captured the first Chinese soldier to be taken prisoner. He said there were ten thousand Chinese troops in the hills north of Unsan and another ten thousand troops east toward Huichon.

By late afternoon a liaison plane pilot had brought the alarming news to Eighth Army headquarters. Just about then, General Milburn put out an order in reaction to General MacArthur's instructions. He said I Corps was to go all the way to the Yalu.

Before nightfall the Chinese prisoner was brought down to Pyongyang. Later more Chinese prisoners were brought in. At first the Eighth Army intelligence officers doubted that the prisoner could be Chinese, but, as the others came, they had to be convinced. They looked Chinese, they spoke Chinese, and they did not understand Korean.

The impossible had occurred. General MacArthur had been proved dead wrong.

If there was lingering hope in the line that it was all a fluke, that only a handful of Chinese had crossed the Yalu, the hope quickly died.

The 3rd Battalion of the 2nd Regiment of the ROK 6th Division started north from the village of Onjong, northeast of Unsan. They were headed for Pukchin. Eight miles west of Onjong, they came under fire from a roadblock ahead. The column stopped and the infantry dismounted to fight what seemed to be a small force of North Koreans. But it was a trap. The enemy came down on them from three sides and in the action that followed they killed or captured more than half the battalion. Among those captured was Lieutenant Glen C. Jones, an American advisor to the ROK troops.

The war had been going so well for so many days that this defeat came as a shock. Back at Onjong, the 2nd Battalion of the ROK 2nd Regiment heard of the debacle and saw troops moving in the hills. Patrols went out. One came back with a prisoner. The shock intensified.

The prisoner was Chinese.

So much for General MacArthur's assurances that the Chinese would never enter the struggle. The prisoner reported that Chinese units had been across the river from Manchuria for more than a week, waiting. And now the UN troops had come up. If the Chinese needed any proof that the South Korean troops were not alone, they had Lieutenant Jones.

Besides, they had the fulminations of President Rhee of the Republic of South Korea, who was now demanding on the international radio waves that the UN go all the way, not stop at the Yalu, but clear out a defensive zone well inside Manchuria. Rhee's demands were echoed by several bombasts in the American congress. How could that have sat in Peking? It had to fortify the worst fears of the Chinese Communist government.

That night of October 26, the Chinese attacked Onjong. The South Koreans panicked and fled. By the end of the night's fighting not a single unit of the ROK 2nd Regiment remained intact. The problem was that the excellence of the ROK Army was only surface deep. Some units, such as the 1st Division and the 3rd Division, had indeed been toughened remarkably. But other units, such as the relatively new 2nd Regiment, were just beginning to look like combat troops. Their morale was not sufficient to sustain a defeat.

On the morning of October 26, the ROK 7th Regiment's Reconnaissance

Platoon forged ahead into Chosan. They encountered North Koreans fleeing across the Yalu into Manchuria on a foot bridge. They opened fire on them.

This unit was the only bit of the Eighth Army that ever reached the Yalu.

For everywhere the Chinese were now on the advance. On October 26 the ROK 15th Regiment got hit, so did the 11th. By day's end the ROK senior officers realized that they faced an entire division or more.

The intelligence officers at Eighth Army headquarters still had a logical explanation. Sure, these were Chinese soldiers. They were individuals who had been enlisted to reinforce the North Koreans. Nothing to worry about, really, just a temporary setback.

"There are no indications of open intervention on the part of Chinese Communist Forces in Korea," said the Eighth Army intelligence estimate of the day. The great Mikado back in Tokyo could not be wrong.

General Paik, the ROK 1st Division commander, had been off duty at a party on October 25 when his troops first encountered the new enemy north of Unsan. The next day he came up to the line to look over the enemy dead. They were all Chinese, he said. He ought to know. He had fought with the Japanese Kwantung Army in Manchuria against the Chinese during the Pacific War and he knew the Chinese well. He estimated that his men faced at least a division of 10,000 Chinese.

Back at Pyongyang, General Walker and his staff shook their heads numbly. It was impossible. MacArthur had said the Chinese would not enter the war. They stuck to their belief that the Chinese prisoners were basically a hallucination.

But in two days the march of the Eighth Army north was stopped dead. The ROK II Corps had been engulfed in the Onjong and Huichon areas. On the morning of October 28, General Walker ordered all the elements of the 1st Cavalry into action, to attack to the Yalu. On the morning of the 29th the ROK forces were ordered to attack again. They did. In spite of artillery and air support they made no progress.

The elements of the 1st Cavalry Division pushed north. The collapse of the ROK II Corps left a hole in the UN line and the ROK 1st Division was stuck out as a northern salient. On its left was a gap of fifteen miles, then the U.S. 24th Division. The 8th Cavalry came up to support the ROK forces. On October 31 they had a tough fight with the enemy and lost ground. The defense line was still just north of Unsan. But the ROK forces, so confident just days ago, were now growing ragged. The fighting of November 1 did not go well for them. The enemy had plenty of artillery and was using it. At four o'clock in the afternoon a battalion commander of the ROK 12th regiment announced that if he was not relieved he would quit the position anyhow. He did. The ROK troops fell back through the 8th Cavalry.

So that was the way it went. All day on November 1 in this sector the ROK forces retreated, and in the end the retreat became a panic. The knowledge that the Chinese had entered the war might still be a great mystery to the Eighth Army and Tokyo commands, but in the field both North and South Koreans felt it immediately; the North Koreans, dispirited a few hours earlier, began again to fight like tigers. The South Koreans lost that veneer of competence they had just begun to acquire. One 5th Cavalry officer came upon the retreating ROK II Corps:

"They were a solid mass of soldiers on the road—indifferent to vehicles moving, indifferent to all that was around them. They were a thoroughly defeated outfit at this particular time."

And that afternoon the men of the 8th Cavalry discovered that the troops they were fighting were Chinese.

On the road to Chongju the 27th British Commonwealth Brigade also felt the renewed strength of the enemy. They drove along, knocking out tanks and self-propelled guns but they had to fight fiercely for them, and they had to knuckle down into a tight formation. The days of the wild joyride north were definitely over. On October 30 the Australians had a busy day, destroying more tanks, and fighting off a counterattack before Chongju. That night they lost their commander, Lieutenant Colonel Charles H. Green, who was mortally wounded by a freak shell that bounced off a tree and exploded just outside his tent.

Next morning the U.S. 24th Division moved up through the British brigade, and on through Chongju in heavy fighting that left the town burning. At noon on November 1, the forward elements of the division were on the outskirts of Chonggodong, eighteen air miles from Sinuiju and the Yalu River.

There they fought a tank battle and defeated the enemy. This enemy was North Korean, but the UN troops did find a few Chinese in the ranks, stragglers from their own units not far away.

Still, Eighth Army headquarters puzzled over the strange turn of events.

The 24th Division was still operating under MacArthur's orders to drive on, drive on, when just before midnight on November 1, they had word from Eighth Army headquarters that they were to stop and withdraw toward Chongchon. Finally, General Walker believed. He was consolidating his position to await events.

The remarkable matter in this whole confused situation is that General MacArthur knew and had known from October 16 that Chinese units had crossed the Yalu River into Korea. When he returned from the Wake Island conference, there was a report waiting for him about the Chinese units that had marched across to the Chosen and Fusen dams. He chose to ignore its significance.

In Washington, during that last week of October, officialdom was also upset. Secretary of State Acheson was seriously concerned about MacArthur's exceeding of his instructions. It was suggested that MacArthur be forced to withdraw to the Pyongyang–Wonsan line, and hold there. Acheson, seeing the dangers, now agreed. Later he wrote:

"If General Marshall and the Chiefs had proposed withdrawal to the Pyongyang–Wonsan line and a continuous defensive position under a united command across it—and if the President had backed them, as he undoubtedly would have . . ."

Indeed such a course might have solved the problem, even at this late hour. For, as noted, the Chinese crossed the Yalu, and then just south of it, they waited in the hills. If the UN forces had not come up, they would not have come down. They had much here to protect of their own, not just the North Korean pride. Those big reservoirs along the Yalu served not only the North Korean electrical system but also the Manchurian. All this was a heritage from the old days of Japanese rule when both Korea and Manchuria were a part of the Japanese empire and there need be no differentiation about borders.

One important installation the Chinese moved to protect was the Sui Ho electric plant. Without such facilities, Manchurian industrial potential would be dealt a serious blow.

The CIA said as much in a report to the President, which he approved. But he did nothing to stop MacArthur, even after MacArthur had made the statement that all had been settled at Wake Island.

Harry Truman knew it had not been settled. It was his understanding that MacArthur had agreed to send none but South Korean troops north. But his Chiefs of Staff argued on military tradition (established by Lincoln during the Civil War) that "once a field commander is assigned a mission there must be no interference with his method of carrying it out."

Even if his method was so wrongheaded as to invite disaster? Here the West Point protective association was at work, and President Truman allowed himself to be buffaloed. He forgot another Lincolnian adage: "War is much too important a matter to be left in the hands of the generals."

If only Truman had remained true to himself.

If. The trouble was that to withdraw to the Pyongyang–Wosan line and create a unified command, the Joint Chiefs would have had to fight MacArthur. And that they were afraid to do. Better to fight the Chinese.

In a search for the facts of this matter for his biography of MacArthur, William Manchester made contact with many people, including the British traitor Kim Philby, who with Guy Burgess and Donald Maclean pirated a whole stream of American defense secrets for the Soviets, some of them pertinent to this period. MacArthur later claimed that the enemy was reading his mail, that he was being betrayed each day by spies somewhere in the American establishment. But the fact is that he did not have to be betrayed. He had betrayed himself first of all by splitting his forces, putting the Eighth Army on the west and the X Corps on the east, with no contact, no unified command, and a huge mountain range between them. MacArthur had in effect two half-armies in Korea, not a single army. And just now his enormous ego caused him to disbelieve the facts that appeared before his face.

The first Chinese captive appeared in UN hands on October 25. That day Colonel Percy W. Thompson, intelligence officer of I Corps, interrogated him at Pyongyang. Five days later they had ten prisoners. They were interrogated intensively, even by lie detector. The intelligence men learned from the prisoners of the presence of Chinese armies in Korea. But they did not believe. And one reason is they had no understanding of the Chinese philosophy or of General Chu Teh's method of confusing the enemy.

For the fact was that in North Korea at the time were six Chinese armies. Because of the international situation they were masquerading as "volunteer" units. The Chinese story was that these irrepressible patriots had vowed to help their fellow Communist soldiers drive out the imperialists. In line with that story, the true natures of the armies were concealed, and American intelligence fell into the trap. Here is the claim, and the substance:

A prisoner said he came from the 54th Unit. Read 38th Chinese Army.

Another prisoner said he came from the 55th Unit. Read 39th Chinese Army.

The intelligence trap was sprung. The Americans decided these were small units, probably battalion size. For had not one of the prisoners said he came from the 1st Battalion of the 55th Unit? What the code meant was that he came from the 115th Division of the 39th Army. So in the last week of October the facts were there, but the American intelligence officers did not read them. Hundreds of thousands of Chinese troops were in the Korean mountains, waiting.

Volunteers, said the prisoners. Volunteers, said the Chinese government. Volunteers, said the Communist press. And the Americans believed.

These Chinese units, they said, were "token units" and they were in Korea only to protect the southern border of Manchuria.

24

"Only Limited Objectives. . . ."
–MacArthur

In the marine 1st Division area on the east coast of Korea, the day before the Chinese entered the war was marked by a feeling of euphoria. General Smith was told of the future: General Almond was about to be appointed commander of the occupation force for North Korea. The occupation would be carried out by a single army division, and the rest of X Corps and the Eighth Army would return to Japan. His division was still on the Yo-Yo train, the ships moving up and down in front of Wonsan.

So when the orders came to relieve the ROK I Corps in the Wonsan area, it seemed almost like temporary occupation duty. Then came the anticlimactic landing at Wonsan. General Smith moved from the command ship *Mount McKinley* to the division command post, an old Soviet barracks a mile north of Wonsan. He knew nothing about the entry of the Chinese into the war.

On the morning of October 26 the 1st Battalion of the 1st Marines boarded trains at Wonsan to travel to Kojo, thirty-nine miles south, to protect the supply dump of the ROK I Corps. This was hardly the sort of duty for which the marines had trained, but if the war was really over, who could complain?

It was a pleasant trip, the weather was bright and sunny and the riflemen rode the thirty-nine miles in open gondola cars. They tensed as they went through several tunnels—fine spots for ambush—but there was no opposition at all. And when they reached Kojo, they found it to be a small seaport, with a white sand beach and pleasant bay, and almost totally undamaged by the war.

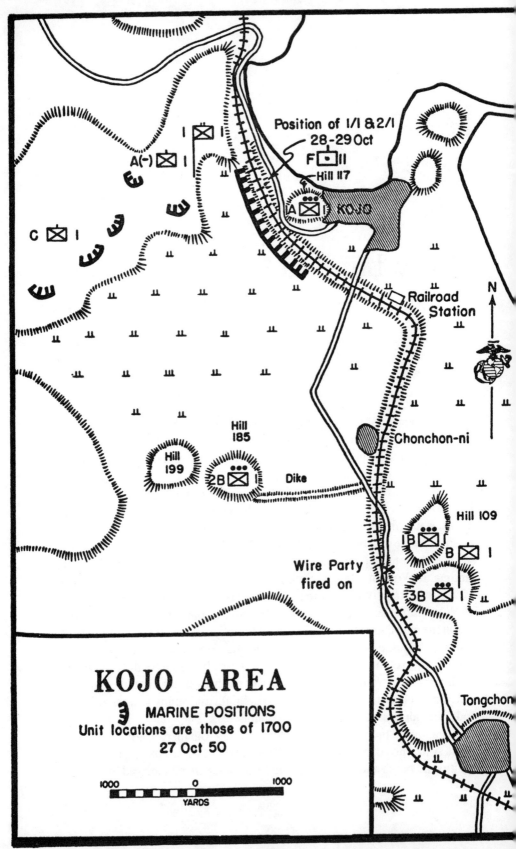

Position of 1/1 & 2/1
28-29 Oct

F · II
Hill 117

A KOJO

I I

A(-) I

C I

Railroad
Station

N

Hill
185

Hill
199

2B I

Dike

Chonchon-ni

Hill 109

IB I

B I

Wire Party
fired on

3B I

Tongchon

KOJO AREA

MARINE POSITIONS
Unit locations are those of 1700
27 Oct 50

1000   0   1000
YARDS

Map 27.

The marine task was to protect the coastal plain. The ROK officers they relieved told them nothing was happening here. Once in a while they would catch a small band of North Koreans trying to steal food, but that was all.

The marines disposed themselves on a perimeter that ran from the 160-foot hills north of the town along the coastal plain. (See Map 27.) Their assignment evaporated with the departure of the 7th ROK I Corps troops—they took the last of the supplies north to Wonsan with them. So the assignment turned out to be of a piece with all that had happened to X Corps since Seoul: total confusion, totally unnecessary.

The morning of October 27 was marked by quiet. The only activity was provided by a long stream of Korean refugees moving north toward Wonsan. By afternoon about three thousand had appeared. Lieutenant Colonel Hawkins had them sequestered on the peninsula northeast of Kojo for the night, since he could not examine them. The pose of refugees was a favorite of the escaping North Korean troops. Two days after the emergence of the Chinese on the scene, and the revitalization of the North Korean army, the marines on the east coast of Korea still knew nothing of the change in the war scene.

The first hint of trouble came at four o'clock on the afternoon of October 27. A wire team in the vicinity of Hill 185 was fired on. Two hours later a truck and jeep were fired on; the truck broke down and was abandoned. An hour later a patrol went out to retrieve the truck and it was also fired on.

Lieutenant Colonel Hawkins was not overly concerned. There were North Korean guerrillas about, and he suspected that these irregulars had been responsible.

He was wrong. The troops who had attacked his were regulars, a battalion of the NK 10th Regiment of the NK 5th Division. The officers and many of the noncoms were veterans of the Chinese civil war and, despite the collapse of the North Korean People's Army organization, and the lack of supply, the 5th Division had maintained its organization. Besides the 5th Division in this general Wonsan area, there were the NK 2nd and NK 10th divisions.

Darkness came and the marines settled down. Because there had been no previous trouble the marines were on normal security, with a 50 percent watch. In the two-man foxholes one man was on watch and the other was in his sleeping bag.

At about ten o'clock that night Company B was hit at both ends of its perimeter by North Koreans who infiltrated inside grenade range. Before the alarm could go up seven marines were killed in their sleeping bags. But marine discipline stood up. The mortars had all been zeroed in before nightfall. The 60 mm mortars fired to within fifty yards of the lines and the 81 mm mortars fired directly in front of the position. The attack was repulsed.

A few minutes later another attack was made on the 3rd Platoon of Company B. The platoon was forced out of position. Then came a report that the 1st Platoon had been forced off its hill and that thirty men were missing.

The fighting continued all night long around Kojo. As morning came, the marines were still fighting. Lieutenant Colonel Hawkins called for reinforcements or orders to evacuate the area, since at least three thousand troops were in the hills around the town. The marines had suffered nine men killed, thirty-nine wounded, and thirty-four missing in action. Because of poor communications the message did not get through until midmorning. Then, because no one had told General Smith that the ROK supply dump was nonexistent, he decided the position should be held. Colonel Puller and a battalion were ordered to Kojo. Later that day Hawkins learned that there were about seven thousand North Korean troops of the NK 5th Division at Tongchon, down south.

When division and corps began to act, they really acted. Marine fighter bombers came in to smash Tongchon until there was virtually nothing left of the place. The U.S. destroyers *Hank* and *English* came in close to bombard Kojo. The transport *Wantuck* came in with a navy surgical team to tend to the wounded. Helicopters were sent to evacuate the wounded. Colonel Puller arrived on the scene at about ten thirty that night of October 28. The expected night attack had not materialized. Seventeen of the marines listed as missing had made their separate ways back to their units. On the morning of October 29 General Craig arrived at Kojo. He found the crisis was over. The situation was well in hand. In the next few days more marines were rescued in the vicinity of Hill 109, where the ambush had been accomplished. A dozen bodies were also found and brought back to the marine lines. The final casualty count was 23 men killed, 47 wounded and 4 missing. The enemy lost about 250 men killed and 83 prisoners of war.

It was not until October 31 that the marines learned that Chinese troops had been encountered in the area north of Hamhung. Lieutenant General Lemuel C. Shepherd, Jr., commander of the fleet marine force in the Pacific, came over from Tokyo and told them. But the word from Tokyo was still that the Chinese entry into the war was minute and virtually meaningless.

By this time General Almond was pulling his staff together to make some plans that would employ the marines other than as guards of nonexistent supply dumps. The 7th Marines were to move up into the Hamhung area and take over from the ROK forces that had driven all the way up the east coast from Yongdok. Cold weather clothing was issued since ice was already forming on the paddy fields. The regiment moved up to Hamhung by motor convoy between October 29 and October 31. The X Corps drive to the Yalu was shifting into gear; the 7th Infantry landed at Iwon on October 29 with orders to push north as rapidly as possible.

But now a new problem began to trouble the marines. As the 2nd Battalion of the 1st Marines moved back from Kojo to Wonsan, they discovered that the railroad tracks had been blown in two places. The effort had been made by guerrillas. Now and in the future the guerrillas would trouble the UN forces. These guerrillas were left over from the campaign in the south because General MacArthur had been in such a rush that thousands of North Koreans were bypassed or allowed to escape into the hills. This element added a new problem.

The 3rd Battalion of the 1st Marines arrived at Majon-ni on October 28. The town was important because it stands at the headwaters of the Imjin River and the junction of roads leading to Wonsan, Seoul, and Pyongyang. These roads were being used by thousands of North Koreans in civilian clothes escaping northward. The marine mission was to protect the road that led to Wonsan and set up a defensive position to cover the area. How difficult that would be was soon to be seen.

One of the new duties of the marines was to search transient travelers for weapons, a task necessary because of the large number of North Korean soldiers encountered.

How were the marines to tell the soldiers from the civilians, when all stoutly claimed that they were refugees? There were ways. The civilians did not wear their hair closely cropped in the North Korean People's Army fashion. Their necks did not show tanned V lines left by North Korean uniforms. Their feet did not have the callouses left by soldiers' boots. Those who failed the tests were sent to the stockade—prisoners of war. And some admitted readily that they were soldiers and were ready to give up. Altogether, in the next three weeks, the marines would average eighty-two prisoners a day picked out of the ranks of "refugees."

Every day the marines sent out patrols along the various roads. For the first four days the patrols found virtually nothing of interest. Then, on the fourth day civilians warned the marines that a large force of North Koreans was massing for an attack on Majon-ni. The unit was identified as the NK 15th Division commanded by Major General Pak Sun Chol. Because of the failure of the high command to clear out South Korea, this division had made its way steadily northward, maintaining discipline, after it left the Pusan Perimeter. Its new mission was to be the conquest and occupation of the northern Imjin valley as a base for guerrilla activity. The Majon-ni position was the chief objective. The villagers said the total number of North Koreans was 11,000 men.

On the morning of November 2 a platoon from Company H was ambushed in a deep gorge five miles south of Majon-ni. Lieutenant Kenneth Bott drove a jeep at breakneck speed back along the road to Majon-ni to get help. It came, if a little tardily. The other two platoons of the company came up, and an air strike arrived. The North Koreans faded off into the hills. That day another convoy was ambushed on the road to Wonsan. Again help came up and extricated the convoy, but not before three vehicles had been lost and several casualties sustained.

Almost every day there was such an incident. The guerrillas were all around the marines, and they were fighting to eat. The area became known to the marines as Ambush Alley. On November 4 Captain Barrow tried a new technique. He sent his infantry ahead of the vehicles by a thousand yards. He figured the enemy's method was to listen for the approach of the vehicles and then get ready for the ambush. By putting the infantry half a mile ahead he hoped to surprise them. He did. Lieutenant Donald Jones' platoon rounded a bend on the road and surprised seventy guerrillas as they were eating. The marines fired all their weapons as fast as they could, killed fifty-one of the enemy, and took three prisoners.

On the night of November 6, Colonel Puller had word of an impending attack by the NK 15th Division. Lieutenant Colonel Ridge prepared. The attack came at one thirty in the morning. The marines knew of it when enemy soldiers stumbled into trip wires which sent up flares, and they could hear the sound of explosions as others fell afoul of booby traps laid by the engineers around the perimeter. When the enemy saw that the marines were ready, they backed off. The night was filled with the popping of rifles. When fog settled in over the area, the North Koreans did isolate one unit, but when dawn came and the Corsairs came over, the enemy withdrew. The marines had suffered two men wounded during the whole engagement.

But the guerrillas continued to harry the marines. On November 7 Lieutenant Colonel Sutter's 2nd Battalion was ordered to move to Munchon-ni and undertake the same sort of mission that the other marines were carrying out at Majon-ni. Company E led the way in a motorized column. Four miles short of Munchon-ni they were ambushed in a horseshoe bend where the left side of the road was a sheer drop, and on the right was a cliff two hundred feet high. The last vehicle had just entered the horseshoe when the first was stopped by a landslide roadblock. The enemy began firing from camouflaged positions on the high ground at the far end of the roadblock. The marines scrambled out of the trucks and launched an attack. They drove off the enemy, but they sustained forty-six casualties: eight killed and thirty-eight wounded. They counted sixty-one dead North Koreans, and figured that as many had been wounded. They captured fifty cases of 120 mm mortar ammunition and three hundred cases of small arms cartridges.

There were more attacks. But friendly civilians kept warning the marines, and they responded. Finally General Pak tried to terrorize the natives, but they reported again to the marines, and suddenly the general moved out, taking his NK 125th Division south to harry an easier area. On November 13, the marines were relieved by troops of the U.S. Army 3rd Division. They were scheduled to fight to the north, to carry out General MacArthur's plan of driving to the Yalu.

By November 1, General Walker's intelligence officers had begun to sing a different tune. They now believed that the Chinese must have at least two regiments in North Korea. Three days later they decided it was two divisions. The day after that they decided it was three divisional task forces—maybe 27,000 men. In fact there were just then well over 100,000 Chinese across the Yalu.

General Walker had a well-established sense of self-preservation and he sensed that something was very, very wrong. From above, however, the bumbling continued. General MacArthur was furious that the Eighth Army had restrained the 24th Division advance. General Hickey telephoned General Allen to demand the reason. On November 6 General Walker had to explain to General MacArthur.

General Walker said he intended to attack again as soon as conditions permitted. He called attention to his dreadful logistical situation. He mentioned the Chinese Communists and the fact that they were still an unknown factor. By this time General Walker believed there were possibly 60,000 Chinese inside North Korea. Actually there were about 200,000 Chinese soldiers of five armies. Walker also mentioned the need to secure his right flank, which was protected by the faltering ROK forces up against the mountain mass. Somewhere over there on the east was General Almond's X Corps, but MacArthur's blunder had denied General Walker contact or control.

In Tokyo, General MacArthur was behaving like a wild man. On November 1 he said he did not know if any Chinese Communist units had actually been committed to the Korean War, and if they had he did not know if they represented the Chinese government. On November 2 Major General Charles Willoughby, MacArthur's intelligence officer, announced that there were almost 600,000 Chinese troops and security forces in Manchuria. On

November 2 General MacArthur said the Chinese constituted a serious threat. On November 4 he announced that the Chinese were in Korea in such numbers as to threaten his whole command. The next day he told the Joint Chiefs of Staff he still did not believe the Chinese would enter the war. That day the Chinese moved troops into North Korea across all six of the Yalu River bridges and they were spotted by American pilots, a steady stream of men, coming south.

On November 6 MacArthur appealed to the UN and world opinion to censure Communist China. On the night of November 6, MacArthur ordered General Stratemeyer to launch an attack with ninety B-29s on the Yalu River bridges at Sinuiju. He sent a copy of the message to the Joint Chiefs of Staff, over a routine channel, and went to bed. He also issued a statement to the effect that he had already won the war with the capture of Pyongyang. The Chinese Communists, he said, had committed one of the most dastardly acts in history by sending troops into North Korea, after the war was won by the Americans. They had tried to lay a trap for him at the Yalu, he said. But he had skillfully maneuvered out of the trap.

Indeed, at this point, General MacArthur sounded very much like a mental case. And that is precisely the impression he gave the Joint Chiefs of Staff in Washington. For weeks, MacArthur had been violating the instructions given him in September about holding back his troops from the Chinese and Communist border areas. On the basis of his brilliant Inchon stroke, he had bullied the Joint Chiefs and the Truman Administration into letting him have his way.

But in recent days, chilling news had been coming into Washington from other sources. On November 2 the American Consul General in Hong Kong radioed a message to Washington that had the dreadful ring of truth. The consul reported that in August, a meeting of Sino-Soviet leaders had discussed the possible need for the Chinese to enter the war. The final decision had been made on October 24 at a meeting over which Chairman Mao presided. That day the wheels were put in motion to move twenty Chinese armies into Manchuria. All these reports suddenly began to come together in the Washington situation rooms. Maybe the Chinese were not kidding.

On receipt and digestion of that message, the Joint Chiefs had demanded an evaluation of the situation from MacArthur. He had replied in gobbledygook, giving every alternative the Chinese might follow and indicating none.

"I recommend against hasty conclusions," he had said, "which might be premature and believe that a final appraisement should await a more complete accumulation of military facts."

The Joint Chiefs had felt relieved. MacArthur was sounding very sage, very careful.

Now, suddenly, the Joint Chiefs learned that MacArthur was planning to attack the Chinese on the border. Worst of all, they did not learn it from MacArthur. The channel he had used to Washington meant that the mission would have been accomplished before the Joint Chiefs ever learned of it. General Stratemeyer spilled the beans. When he received those orders from MacArthur he recognized their drastic nature, and instead of going ahead straightaway, he sent a hot message to air force headquarters in Washington, describing MacArthur's orders to him. Within minutes after the receipt at the Pentagon, Under Secretary of Defense Robert Lovett had been informed, and then the telephones in Washington began ringing.

Lovett went to see Dean Acheson, the Secretary of State, and Assistant Secretary Rusk. The latter pointed out that the United States had promised the British government not to take any action attacking Manchuria without British consultation. The Chinese, after all, had a mutual defense treaty with the USSR.

They spoke to Defense Secretary Marshall. He agreed that unless MacArthur's forces were in dire threat, they should hold up. They called President Truman who was off in Missouri. He agreed that MacArthur should be restrained unless there was dire threat. What confused them was MacArthur's volte-face. His last message had counseled patience. Now he was acting like a wild man. What had occasioned the change? Would MacArthur please explain?

When MacArthur received the order to desist from bombing the Yalu bridges, he erupted. "The most indefensible, the most ill-conceived decision ever forced on a field commander in our nation's history," he called it.

The real question then was posed at last: who was running the war, General MacArthur or the United States government? That question was going to have to be resolved, and in its resolution lay the future of the war.

Notes

Generally speaking, I have returned to original source material for my books on various aspects of military operations, particularly those on the Pacific War. But in the case of the Korean War the official U.S. Army and U.S. Marine Corps histories are so complete that only rarely have I felt impelled to consult the records.

There is another reason for this approach to this particular war. Unlike previous American wars (the Civil War excepted) there was serious confusion within the government as to the best method of prosecuting the war. Also it is the first American war in which the objectives were clouded from the beginning and never did become clear, until General Eisenhower recognized the American exhaustion with the unwelcome effort and moved to extricate the nation, without regard to pride or profit. So throughout, the politics of the war was far more important a matter than had ever been true before. The personalities of President Truman and General MacArthur were vital factors, so were the shifting defenses and foreign policies of an America that did not know quite where it stood in the world, what it wanted and wanted to be, or how to manage its relations with other nations now that it had become a self-proclaimed "superpower." Writing from the vantage point of 1984, it seems that these confusions still exist.

1
Surprise Attack!

"That's it," he said. "Let's get a cup of coffee," is from Montross and Canzona, p. 90. The best discussion of the planning difficulties for the Inchon operation is to be found in Schnabel, chapter 8.

2
Inchon

The story of Typhoon Jane is from Field, chapter 7. The mention of Lieutenant Eugene F. Clark's intelligence mission to the Inchon area does not do justice to his audacity. For a complete story see the CIA Far East Division's report, "Operation Trudy Jackson," and Field's history of U.S. naval operations. The account of the Wolmi-do landings is from Montross and Canzona, and from Field.
"Captured 45 prisoners . . ." is from Montross and Canzona, p. 91.
"The Navy and the Marines . . ." is from the same work, p. 92.

3
The Landings

"In midafternoon Colonel Taplett on Wolmi-do . . ." (p. 37.) This discussion is based on the account in Montross and Canzona, and in Field. It seems apparent that if Lieutenant Colonel Taplett's suggestion of sending tanks across the causeway had been followed it would have hastened the operation and saved some American lives. One of the obvious deficiencies of the Inchon operation was the failure to secure more intelligence cooperation from the ROK forces, who knew the area and could infiltrate the port area for intelligence purposes. They would have learned how lightly the Inchon area was held by the North Koreans. Probably this failure to ask the ROK Navy for that sort of help was a hangover from the early days of the war, when betrayal followed betrayal—such as the story of the capture of General William Dean, commander of the 24th Division, who was betrayed by South Koreans. Nonetheless this operation and later ones were marred by many intelligence failures.
Again, speaking of intelligence, it seems remarkable that in three years of occupation of South Korea, the Americans would have failed to map the land

and chart the ocean areas. But they had not done so, and because of it, as noted in *The Pusan Perimeter* and this volume, innumerable difficulties were encountered, such as coming up against the little cove at Blue Beach (p. 41) without knowing the terrain. The matter was further confounded because the Japanese had been almost equally careless in their thirty-five years of occupation, and when the Koreans regained control of their own country they so despised the Japanese that they changed the names of geographical and hydrographic features back to the ancient ones. Moreover, having changed the names, they did not take the next logical step and rectify their maps and charts.

The confusion attendant to the landings on Blue Beach is an indication of the value of constant military training for military men. Whenever a writer criticizes anything the navy has done in the past, the criticism triggers the navy defensive mechanism. "Chairborne admirals" and "hindsight" are the usual pejoratives the critic must endure. But the fact remains that in recent times each generation of military men seems somehow loath to profit from the study of the errors of the past. This comes readily to mind because at this writing the United States is suffering from the shock of the unwarranted deaths of more than two hundred marines at Beirut, a direct result of incompetent security management of the marine position. (They were put in an exposed position against known terrorists and denied permission to keep their guns loaded.) Lord knows the marines and the navy had enough experience with suicide operations in the war against Japan.

But the lessons hard learned are soon forgotten. The Inchon landings were sloppy because the navy had not kept up on the amphibious techniques learned at high cost at places like the Solomons, Tarawa, and Iwo Jima.

4
Breakout

Probably before the Inchon landings, General MacArthur would have done well to replace General Walker as commander of the Eighth Army, not because Walker was inept, but because MacArthur, who had his favorites, did not like Walker or have any confidence in him. "We have been bastard children lately," Walker told MacArthur's General Hickey on September 21, "and as far as our engineering equipment is concerned we are in pretty bad shape." What he was concerned about was bridging the Naktong, since for two months the Americans had been concentrating on knocking out the bridges to keep the North Koreans from coming across. MacArthur showed no apparent sympathy for Walker's problems. What he wanted was a nice clean drive north immediately, based on the principle that the Inchon landing would frighten the North Korean army commanders in the south into panic and they would break off the Pusan Perimeter fighting and retreat immediately. That did not happen. As noted, for the first few days the North Koreans around the perimeter fought even more fiercely, as Walker's staff had suggested they would. The fact was that, except for the top levels, the commanders did not know anything about the Inchon landing for about a week.

5
Kimpo

"A good sight for my old eyes..." When General MacArthur came up to visit the front and pin medals on commanders, he was accompanied, as usual, by a raft of war correspondents, pencils at the ready to record the general's words of wisdom. This quotation comes from a number of sources, all published in the U.S. press, and theatricalized by the reporters as well as by the general. He was the willing victim of celebrity fever, and the old expert at using the press for his own purposes. I did not deal with one ridiculous aspect of the campaign to seize Kimpo airfield since the plan was never put into execution. General Almond was so eager to secure some of the glory of the landings for his army troops that he proposed that on D-Day a special commando-type company move in to shore from a South Korean picket boat, paddle three miles up the Han in rubber boats, land, and make a surprise attack on Kimpo at dawn. General Smith, the marine commander, pointed out that the troops would be rowing up stream against a strong tidal current and would then have to struggle across an enormous mud flat. Almond's reply was to demand a hundred marines to help. General Smith and General Shepherd both objected, and finally Almond withdrew the plan. It was fortunate, because as it turned out the company would have walked right into the main strength of the North Korean force. What the incident does illustrate is the questionable nature of General MacArthur's appointment of his chief staff officer to a vital post of command. There is a lot of difference between administrative excellence and command judgment.

6
The Road to Yongdungpo

The account of General MacArthur's expressed dissatisfaction with General Walker and the alternative plan to secure the "anvil effect" by a new amphibious landing at Kunsan comes from Heinl, pp. 147–148. He got the story from General Shepherd's papers and from General Wright. Field puts the date of the MacArthur idea at September 17. No one but the general seemed to care much for the plan, since it meant nothing but trouble and further fragmentation of forces, and he was talked out of it. Kunsan never was invaded from the sea, although that special operations company headed by Colonel Louis B. Ely made a raid on the place after the cancellation of the Kimpo special operation. They had to be used somehow, didn't they?

The Houghton swimmers' assault on the north bank of the Han does not seem to have been the most brilliantly conceived operation of the war. Again it was hampered by a paucity of realistic intelligence. "The Marines have landed . . ." is from Montross and Canzone, p. 191.

7
The Fight for Yongdungpo

The story of Captain Barrow's company and their one-company assault through the middle of Yongdungpo is from Montross and Canzone. It is a tale that celebrates the greatest qualities of the marines as fighting men: their ability to fight in small units, even when surrounded or virtually so, as though they had the entire resources of the division at their back. Captain Barrow's company that day carried out one of the most successful operations of the Korean War and saved the 1st Division the hundreds of casualties that would have ensued had Company A not captured and held that traffic circle in the middle of Yongdungpo.

8
On to Seoul

Perhaps there is some way that marine and army troops can operate together successfully under a single command, but neither World War II nor the Korean War proved it. In World War II during the central Pacific campaign, Lieutenant General Holland M. Smith had army troops under his command, and the result was three unsatisfactory invasions: the Gilberts, the Marshalls, and the Marianas. In the end, the general removed the army general under him and created an interservice incident of magnificent proportions. The same sort of thing happened in Korea, notably in the late stages of the drive on Seoul. General Barr's army 7th Division did not keep in touch with the marines on their left, which cost them the marines' trust. Again this was a problem of command, not of the fighting men. The 7th Division troops performed very well, against stiffening opposition. They were, remember, just fresh from the United States and no better trained than the rest of the American army of the period.

Another command difficulty in the Korean War was that between the Americans and the ROK forces. In the beginning most of the ROK Army performed badly because of inexperience. There were big exceptions, such as the ROK 1st Division, which fought well by anyone's definition. There were also the Korean marines, who also fought well. But at this stage the KMC was an unknown quantity. That's why Colonel Murray of the 5th Marines assumed (wrongly) that the reason the KMC troops in the middle of his front failed to move was because of inexperience. He replaced them with American marines, who did not do one whit better.

The story of Task Force Lynch comes from Appleman. So does the sorry tale of the P-51 napalm attack on Argyll Highlanders. The North Koreans, as noted, were quick to learn, and they had captured some of those white recognition panels ground troops were to use to identify themselves as friends of the UN aircraft. On September 23 they certainly put them to good use, to the detriment of the British.

General Almond's pressure on the marines to capture Seoul by September 25 is certainly an indication of his loyalty to his boss, General MacArthur. But it also reminds one of a remark made by President Truman months afterward, when discussing the relief of General MacArthur from command. "I should have fired the s.o.b. in the beginning," said the President. Should he? MacArthur did perform adequately in the first months of the war. He jogged a somnolent Washington out of its torpor. But it seems likely that any general in that position would have done the same. He did also execute the brilliant stroke at Inchon. But that victory also had its demerits. One of them was that it indicated General Almond was much more proficient in command than was actually the case. The pandering to MacArthur's whimsical demand for Seoul by September 25 was an indication of the opposite.

9
A Ridge Named Smith

The story of the assault on Smith's Ridge is from the U.S. Marine Corps files and from Montross and Canzona. Here again is one of those moving tales of bravery and death that have so marked the history of the U.S. Marine Corps in war.

10
Seoul and the Nutcracker

General Almond's breach of military courtesy in discussing his change in plans for marine-army operations with General Smith's regimental commanders before he talked to Smith had the sad effect of again decreasing the marine trust for the army. It also indicates General Almond's ineptitude for the task he had been given. It seems doubtful if his employment of the 7th Division did a thing to hasten the capture of Seoul.

The unseemly haste forced on General Walker by General MacArthur and by Walker on his divisions also had its negative side effects. Most important of these was the failure to seal off South Korea at the Seoul neck, to prevent the escape of the entrapped North Korean forces that had so lately vacated the Pusan Perimeter. This ranks with the British failure at the Falaise gap as one of war's lost opportunities. The gain to the UN forces was virtually nonexistent, except for public relations purposes; the ROK Army was rushing up the east coast, and the X Corps surrounding Seoul. The bypassed North Korean troops in South Korea either went into the hills to become guerrillas who would harry the UN forces for months, or straggled north to safety to reorganize and fight again. All this takes nothing from the efforts of the troops; Task Force Lynch's brave dash northward is a marvelous story of military diligence. What it accomplished is something else.

11
Seoul

The poignant story of Koo Chul-hoe and his friends is from Riley and Schramm's *The Reds Take A City.* They devote an entire chapter to the Koo case under the title "The Treatment of Reactionaries." The remainder of the Riley and Schramm work deals with many other aspects of the North Korean occupation, virtually all of them brutal. The book ought to be required reading for Americans who seem to favor a policy of preemptive surrender to Soviet expansionism, but most of it really was not germane to this work.

The 7th Division's 32nd Infantry was a little slow in getting going on the attack against Seoul, but they did serve a useful purpose by getting up on top of South Mountain and there engaging the attention of the North Korean defenders.

The stories of the 5th and 1st marines' adventures in this drive against Seoul is told in chapter 13, Montross and Canzona, vol. 2.

12
"Enemy fleeing. . . . You will attack NOW"

The story of General Almond's orders to the marines to make a night attack is told in Montross and Canzona, volume 2, in some detail. Appleman's army history has the story in less detail, as might be expected. Of course, the attack never came off, because, as the marines knew very well, the North Koreans were not fleeing Seoul but were determined to make a street-by-street stand. As the marines got ready to move out that night, the North Koreans began a counterattack that lasted all night long. Almond's zeal to secure Seoul for MacArthur to meet that three-month mark so dear to the general's heart certainly did nothing to increase his credibility with the marines or with the press. His communiqués that night and the next morning were misleading to say the least, and so were those that came out of Tokyo. It has become popular to place the breakdown of press-military relationships as beginning with the Vietnam War. In fact, right here was the beginning, for the press correspondents were not blind, and their faith in the veracity of the communiqués of MacArthur and his lieitenants had to be shaken. During World War II the military made a point of dealing honestly with the press, although they felt betrayed several times. Once, a *Chicago Tribune* reporter wrote of the American breach of the Japanese naval code, which could have compromised that intelligence weapon. After the assassination of Admiral Yamamoto, an Australian correspondent sneaked the news of the ambush out through censorship and against orders. That again threatened the radio intelligence value of the naval code breach. Luckily the Japanese high command refused to believe either story. Another breach came when the Associated Press violated the confidence of SHAEF and put out news of the German surrender prematurely. Despite such breaches of faith, the military was generally honest; Admiral Nimitz prided himself on this, and only when the Kamikaze threat at Okinawa worried the navy more than any other event of the war, did they fudge on truth. Even MacArthur's press promotion machine confined itself to exaggeration and stopped short of deliberate misstatement. The Almond statements of September 25 and September 26 were something else again.

The relationship between press and military would never again be quite the same.

13
The Long, Long Day

The story of the movement of the various elements of the Eighth Army, as delineated in this chapter, is gleaned from several sources, including Appleman and the unit records. Appleman is also the basic source for the accounts of North Korean atrocities. The difficulties of General Gay in operating under I Corps can again be laid to the fact that the war was moving too fast. The I Corps was a brand new military entity, and its staff was not experienced enough to know when to give a divisional commander his head. As noted in the account of the 7th Marines, the North Koreans around Seoul, General Wol's rear guard, still had plenty of fight in them.

"Seoul, the capital of the Republic . . ." is from MacArthur's communiqué of September 26. Again it was premature, another strike against MacArthur with the press.

14
Linkup

The story of Task Force Lynch's dash north is told in Appleman. The exploits of Captain Webel that day make material for a TV movie.

15
Scouring the South

It seems remarkable that General Gay's offer of tactical assistance to the 31st Infantry would be denied on the basis of protocol, but it was. The only logical explanation is once again the battle immaturity of the 31st Infantry. The net effect was to deny General MacArthur any immediate value from the linkup of Eighth Army and X Corps troops.

Seoul was captured this day—September 27. Three decades later the fuss about the importance of the 25th as the date of capture still seems as ridiculous as it did in 1950. It certainly was not worth the promotional value if that meant shattering the confidence of fighting troops and the media in the veracity of the high command. Unfortunately that is a lesson the military still did not seem to have learned by 1984. Granted the growing venality of the media in the years after 1950, the military still owes a running report of warfare to the American people.

16
Clearing the Rubble

The story of Sergeant Reifers' lone adventure in Namwon is told in Appleman. The tales of North Korean brutality and atrocities ought to be required reading for those strange souls who consistently sympathize with enemy causes against those of the United States. It is true that in the heat of battle, particularly after coming across an atrocity, the American troops were not eager to take prisoners, and some North Koreans were shot down brutally. Anyone who has ever seen napalm in action must also realize the horror of that weapon, whether fired from a flamethrower into a cave or dropped from an aircraft onto a troop concentration. It makes a hellish death. But there is a major difference between the brutality of battle and the considered policy of an army that murders its prisoners, often torturing them or using them for bayonet practice beforehand. Prisoners are hors de combat, and under guard are of very little danger to anyone. Even worse than the mistreatment of the soldiers was the North Korean brutality against their own kind, including women and children, thousands of them murdered in cold blood as the North Korean People's Army retreated from its zone of conquest.

"But General MacArthur had other ideas. . . ." It is remarkable how General MacArthur had his own way in these early stages of the war. At home in Washington, the Truman Administration's civilian advisors had strong reservations about restoring President Syngman Rhee to power. Had they stuck with their guns and persuaded President Truman to set up a provisional government, that factor might have prevented the Chinese from entering the war. For Dr. Rhee was anything but an asset to the UN forces; his constant fulminations against the enemy, and his demand that the drive be carried to the Yalu River and beyond, sent a series of messages to Peking and Moscow. MacArthur's embrace of Rhee and Washington's failure to stop it were certainly part of the reason for what was soon to happen.

". . . The prestige of the western world . . ." is quoted in various accounts of the meetings between MacArthur and the Joint Chiefs of Staff representatives. It bears consideration, for MacArthur suggested that if the United States lost the war against communism in Asia the future of Europe would be jeopardized. Obviously he was not talking just about driving the North Koreans back to the 38th parallel. It seemed very much as if he wanted to carry the war against China, too. And, of course, that was precisely true. If one understood that, in the words of another generation, one knew where MacArthur was coming from. But somehow the full impact of the general's rhetoric failed to cross the Pacific and the American continent to reach Washington.

I have dealt with MacArthur's "royal visit" to Seoul, to reinstall President Rhee as head of the South Korean government in some detail because the whole trip shows a great deal about MacArthur and the personage he now felt himself to be. His remark to the marines when they told him they had no bridge for his triumphal crossing ("Then build one") was the statement of an egomaniac. His carefully staged humility in Seoul ("... my officers and I ...") fooled no one on the scene. All were indicative of a personality crisis in an advanced stage of development.

17
Crossing the Parallel

In this chapter I have tried to suggest the depth of the debate that raged in Washington over Korean War policy, as well as the narrowness and shallowness of the consideration given. Somehow the hawks among the advisors failed to give any consideration to China's possible reactions and options. Knowing as they did that their hearts were pure, it was impossible for them to believe that anyone else might suspect their motives. And if the hawks had considered their motives objectively they would have had to admit that they would not have opposed war with Red China, as long as they were sure they could win it. But thinking objectively for a moment, could the United States possibly win a war in China, which then had a population of over half a billion, and an army of more than 100 million? Perhaps such a war could have been won, but the cost to the United States would have been enormous and our commitment would have been total. Probably the atomic bomb would have been used again.

The fact was that as this debate raged in Washington, President Truman was opposed to becoming involved in a war that would tie the United States down in Asia. The question examined by military and political advisors was whether or not the extermination of the North Korean People's Republic would bring China into the war. And at this point in history American understanding of the ruling Chinese government was so slight that the advisors had little to go on but hunches. They refused to believe the stream of warnings emanating from Peking.

18
The Chinese Warning

"... North Korean offensive power ..." is from Futrell, p. 166.
"... Had he suggested that one battalion ..." is from Goulden, p. 232.
"... Under the provisions ..." is from MacArthur's October 2 order to General Walker to proceed to the Yalu River with all dispatch.

19
Northward Ho

General MacArthur's order to General Walker to move north of the 38th parallel with American troops was a clear violation of the spirit of the orders he had received from Secretary of Defense Marshall. How did he get away with it? For one thing, it is a long way from Tokyo to Washington, and MacArthur was past master at using the defense communication system to delay responses and obfuscate his activity. He had already done this several times during the Korean War. But there was another factor involved: most of the professional army officers agreed with MacArthur's contention that once a war was begun it should be carried to the logical conclusion of victory. Thus the whole of Korea should be the battlefield if necessary. All that need be done was assure China and the USSR that their territory would not be violated, and then try to live up to the promise. What they did not consider was the Chinese attitude, based on a well-earned distrust of the Americans, and the character of the reservoirs along the Yalu, built by the Japanese for hydroelectric purposes, and used by both Chinese and North Koreans. The reservoirs spanned the border. The Chinese vowed to defend them against any incursions by outsiders.

Also, in this chapter I have delved back into memory and old personal records to recreate the tensions of the times, and the attitudes involved.

20
The Ides of October

The army, the navy, the marine histories and the biographies of President Truman and General MacArthur all testify to the confusion that existed within the U.S. government and high military commands after the fall of

Seoul in September 1950. There is a warning here for the future: the problem of the United States was the lack of a considered war policy and specific war aim. It seems apparent in 1984 that the aim should have been confined to the restoration of the 38th parallel boundary between North and South Korea. It was not so apparent then in Washington, largely because the United States had no cogent policy toward the Peking government of China. The Truman Administration shied away from further confrontation with the Republicans, who still shrilled that Truman had "lost" China. The events of 1948–50 are certainly the greatest possible argument for a standard policy of recognition of de facto governments without regard to the American philosophical differences with those governments. Had the United States and China been in diplomatic contact in 1950, it seems almost certain that the Chinese would not have entered the war. By the same token, had the United States earlier accepted the transfer of the seat in the United Nations from the Chiang government to the Peking government, China would have vetoed UN participation, and that, too, would have militated for a limited U.S. war aim. What I have tried to show in this chapter is the bankruptcy of the American political-military establishment in dealing with fast-moving events, and the real national danger of remaining aloof from any major political and military force such as China, anywhere in the world. There was nothing modern about China's army, but its immense size still made it formidable. As for the MacArthur plan for a new amphibious landing, it is obvious from the facts that the Joint Chiefs of Staff should have dumped it at the beginning. The Truman–MacArthur meeting at Wake Island seemed to be a lovefeast, but was actually completely inconclusive and, as far as Truman and his advisors were concerned, most misleading. For MacArthur communicated to the White House group his own enormous confidence, when that confidence was completely misplaced.

21
The Plan in Shambles

With the Chinese making military noises in Peking, and the American forces separated into two separate commands, one would have expected the Joint Chiefs of Staff to have grown extremely nervous in the middle of October and forced MacArthur into a basic change of strategy. But they did nothing of the sort. It all seemed so easy, with the North Koreans on the run. The fall of Pyongyang came with little effort, creating still another illusion.

". . . Organized resistance on any large scale has ceased to be an enemy capability . . ." was the assessment of General MacArthur's intelligence officer. And of course he was right if one considered only the North Koreans.

22
Rescue Attempt

The employment of the 187th Airborne Regimental Combat Team was another indication of the confused state of MacArthur's strategy in the Korean War. Early on he had demanded airborne troops. But by the time they reached Korea it seemed they were no longer needed. So this mission of cutting off the retreating North Koreans was invented on the plausible but inaccurate premise that some 30,000 North Koreans could thus be taken out of the war. As far as the attempt to rescue the trainload of American prisoners of war was concerned, again it failed because of faulty intelligence.

"De laudace, encore. . ." is from Danton's speeches to the French legislative assembly, 1792.

23
To the Yalu

As of the last week of October 1950, the Chinese decision to enter the war had been made and so nothing that might earlier have been done in the diplomatic sphere could now work. The Americans and the British and Australians were far north of the 38th parallel and driving onward. The Chinese in army force were already in the mountains of North Korea, waiting to strike. Nothing in Korea was actually as it appeared to be. The euphoria of the American troops who expected to be back in Japan within a few weeks was totally misplaced, but how were they to know? This was what everyone in the world expected except the men in Moscow, Peking, and the North Korean provisional capital. When the first signs of the Chinese appeared, as prisoners, the Americans simply refused to accept what they saw. This, too, was understandable, because General MacArthur had geared everyone into the belief that the Chinese would not enter the war. So this October 25 proof of the Chou En-lai warning of September was ignored, and the UN forces marched on toward the Yalu. November 1 came, and MacArthur still did not believe. Nor did the Joint Chiefs of Staff, who by this time were mesmerized by the MacArthur concept of victory.

24
Only Limited Objectives. . . ."—MacArthur

By November 1, the war had become mad. The marines on the east coast were fighting what seemed to be the last-ditch efforts of organized units that had been cut off by the march of events. General MacArthur at one moment was certain the Chinese movement was a feint or a fake, and at the next moment he predicted disaster. The movers and shakers in Washington did not know what to think, given MacArthur's wide swings of opinion from day to day and the chilling messages that were coming in from other sources. A phase of the war ended on that November 6, when MacArthur ordered the bombing of the Yalu bridges. Here was reality, announced at last, be it left-handedly. The Chinese were in the war. And now, what was to be done?

Bibliography

Appleman, Roy E. *U.S. Army in the Korean War, South to the Naktong, North to the Yalu.* Washington, D.C.: Office of the Chief of Military History, Department of the Army, 1961.

Army Times Editors. *American Heroes of Asian Wars.* New York: Dodd, Mead, and Company, 1968.

Cagle, Malcolm W. *The Sea War in Korea.* New York: Arno Press, 1980.

Comparative Strategy, Vol. 2. Chicago: Crane, Russak and Co., 1980.

Davis, Larry. *MIG Alley.* Warren, Mich.: Squadron/Signal Publications, 1978.

Donovan, Robert J. *Tumultuous Years, The Presidency of Harry S. Truman, 1949–1953.* New York: W. W. Norton and Co., 1982.

Ferrell, Robert H., ed. *Off the Record, The Private Papers of Harry S. Truman.* New York: Harper and Row, 1980.

Field, James A., Jr. *History of United States Naval Operations–Korea.* Washington, D.C.: U.S. Government Printing Office, 1962.

Futrell, Robert Frank, Lawson S. Mosely, and Albert F. Simpson. *The United States Air Force In Korea, 1950–1953.* New York: Duell Sloan and Pearce, 1961.

Goulden, Joseph C. *Korea, The Untold Story of the War.* New York: Times Books, 1982.

Gugeler, Russell A. *Combat Actions in Korea.* Washington, D.C.: Combat Forces Press, 1954.

Heinl, Robert Debs. *Victory at High Tide, The Inchon–Seoul Campaign.* New York and Philadelphia: J. B. Lippincott, 1968.

Jackson, Robert. *Air War Over Korea.* New York: Charles Scribner's Sons, 1973.

Jacobs, Bruce. *Korea's Heroes, The Medal of Honor Story.* New York: Berkley Publishing Co., 1961.

James, D. Clayton. *The Years of MacArthur.* Vol. 2, *1941–1945.* Boston: Houghton Mifflin Co., 1975.

Kim Chum-Kon. *The Korean War.* Seoul: Kwangmyong Publishing Co., 1973.

Langley, Michael. *Inchon Landing, MacArthur's Last Triumph.* New York: Times Books, 1979.

MacArthur, Douglas. *Reminiscences.* New York: McGraw-Hill Book Company, 1964.

Manchester, William. *American Caesar, Douglas MacArthur, 1880–1964.* Boston: Little, Brown and Co., 1968.

Miller, Merle. *Plain Speaking, an Oral Biography of Harry Truman.* New York: Berkley Publishing Co., 1973.

Ministry of National Defense. *The History of the United Nations Forces in the Korean War.* Seoul: Ministry of National Defense, 1981.

Mosely, Leonard. *Marshall, Hero for Our Times.* New York: Hearst Books, 1982.

Montross, Lynn, and Nicholas A. Canzona. *U.S. Marine Operations in Korea, 1950–1953.* Vol. 2, *The Inchon-Seoul Operation (1955);* Vol. 3, *The Chosin Reservoir Campaign (1957).* Washington, D.C.: Historical Branch, G-3, Headquarters, U.S. Marine Corps, 1965, 1967.

Pogue, Forrest C. *George C. Marshall.* New York: Viking Press, 1963.

Riley, John W., Jr., and Wilbur Schramm. *The Reds Take a City.* New Brunswick, N.J.: Rutgers University Press, 1951.

Schnabel, James F. *U.S. Army in the Korean War, Policy and Direction: The First Year.* Washington, D.C.: Office of the Chief of Military History, United States Army, 1972.

Stone, R.I. *The Hidden Story of the Korean War.* New York: Monthly Review Press, 1952.

Sullivan, Jim. *F4U Corsair in Action.* Warren, Mich.: Squadron/Signal Publications, 1979.

Sung, Kim Il. *Yesterday-Today, U.S. Imperialism; Mastermind of Aggression on Korea.* Pyongyang: North Korean People's Republic Publishing House, undated.

Index

KMC: KOREAN MARINE CORPS

LVT: MARINE AMPHIBIOUS TRACTOR Pg 81